T0374732

DUMBARTON OAKS
MEDIEVAL LIBRARY

Jan M. Ziolkowski, General Editor

OLD ENGLISH POEMS OF

CHRIST AND HIS SAINTS

DOML 27

Old English Poems
of Christ and
His Saints

Edited and Translated by

MARY CLAYTON

DUMBARTON OAKS
MEDIEVAL LIBRARY

HARVARD UNIVERSITY PRESS
CAMBRIDGE, MASSACHUSETTS
LONDON, ENGLAND
2013

Library of Congress Cataloging-in-Publication Data
Old English poems of Christ and his saints / edited and translated by
Mary Clayton.
  pages cm. — (Dumbarton Oaks Medieval Library ; 27)
  Includes bibliographical references and index.
  ISBN 978-0-674-05318-2 (alk. paper)
  1. English poetry—Old English, ca. 450–1100—Modernized
versions.   2. Christian poetry, English (Old)   I. Clayton, Mary, 1954–
  PR1508.O546 2013
  829'.1—dc23   2013007292

Contents

Introduction

The ten anonymous Old English poems in this book were composed in England between the eighth century and the eleventh century. Eight are preserved in manuscripts; one is found on a stone cross and another on a lavishly decorated ornate cross, probably used in religious ceremonies. It is unlikely that any two are by the same author. Despite this diversity in provenance, they share a focus on Christ and the saints. Most take up traditional themes of salvation and redemption, and they offer different, sometimes highly imaginative, interpretations of scenes fundamental to Christian history: the fall of the angels, the coming of Christ, Satan's temptation of Christ, the Crucifixion, the harrowing of hell, and the Last Judgment. Two long poems focus on individual saints: the first deals with the apostle Andrew and his mission to rescue his fellow-apostle Matthew, in the process converting the cannibalistic Mermedonians, and the second with the Anglo-Saxon hermit-saint, Guthlac. The final selection is a two-line poem about an Anglo-Saxon royal saint, Kenelm.

The paucity of saints' lives in Old English poetry is striking. Apart from the two lines on Kenelm, Guthlac is the only Anglo-Saxon saint to feature in Old English poetry, and Andrew is the only individual apostle. The works of Cynewulf add poems on Elene (Helena), Juliana, a second poem on Guthlac, and a short poem called *The Fates of the Apostles*. It is a strikingly small body of work next to the large number of saints' lives in Old English prose, the majority of which were written by Ælfric (who worked between ca. 990 and ca. 1010). Other lives in verse have probably been lost, but we have a reference to only one: Ælfric, writing in the 990s, mentions a life of the apostle Thomas, which, he says, was translated long ago from Latin into English *on leoðwison,* "in poetry."[1]

The poems are presented here in the order in which they appear in the manuscripts, going from the manuscript with the largest number, the Exeter Book, to those with the smallest, the Junius manuscript and Cambridge, Pembroke 82, which has the Kenelm text. The Ruthwell Crucifixion poem and the Brussels Cross inscription follow the poem to which they are closely related, *The Vision of the Cross*. The titles of the poems are all editorial, the majority of them already well established, but some less so.

The Exeter Book

Exeter Cathedral Library 3501 has been preserved in Exeter Cathedral Library since the eleventh century, when it was donated to the library by Leofric, bishop of Exeter, who died in 1072. It was written by a single hand in the second half of the tenth century (probably in the middle of that half-century) somewhere in the south of England and is accurately described in an inventory of Leofric's donations as *.i. micel englisc boc be gehwilcum þingum on leoðwisan ge-*

worht, "one large English book about various things made in verse."[2] The contents of the manuscript were very deliberately ordered, beginning with three poems on Christ, then two poems on Guthlac, followed by the Old Testament poem *Azarias, The Phoenix,* Cynewulf's *Juliana,* a sequence of short poems (including some of the best-known Old English poems, such as *The Wanderer, The Seafarer,* and *The Wife's Lament*), two collections of riddles, the Old English *Physiologus,* and more religious texts, including *The Descent into Hell.* The first folio of the manuscript and some other folios have been lost, so *Christ I* lacks its beginning. The second of the three *Christ* poems and *Juliana,* each bearing the runic signature of Cynewulf, along with the second of the two Guthlac poems, have been edited separately in the Dumbarton Oaks Medieval Library, volume 23, *The Old English Poems of Cynewulf,* translated by Robert E. Bjork. Still other poems in the Exeter Book miscellany not concerning Christ and his saints appear in other DOML volumes.[3] All of the poems edited here from the Exeter Book are likely to be monastic both in origin and in intended audience.

ADVENT

Advent, also known as *Christ I* or the *Advent Lyrics,* is a poem based on Latin *O* antiphons (so called because they all begin with "O") sung as part of the Advent and Christmas liturgy in the Office, the daily round of prayers which those in religious life were obliged to recite. The beginning of the poem has been lost, but what we have consists of a series of expansions of antiphons sung at Vespers. Twelve antiphons were

INTRODUCTION

used as sources for the poem; the first folio of the manu-
script is missing, however, and this would have contained
approximately seventy lines of text, perhaps based on three
more antiphons. The first ten antiphons used as sources be-
long to the Advent liturgy, the eleventh is most likely an an-
tiphon to the Trinity, and the final one is part of the liturgy
for the Octave of Christmas.

Each of the twelve parts of the Old English poem begins
with *Eala,* corresponding to the opening word of a Latin *O*
antiphon, but the text is also organized into five manuscript
sections; we do not know how section one began, but the
second, third, and fourth begin with the Virgin Mary and
Christ's human parentage, before moving into Christ's di-
vinity and the incomprehensibility of this for human under-
standing. The five-part division may well go back to the
poet. *Advent* is a poem of meditation and of urgent entreaty,
the authorial voice repeatedly breaking into prayer and peti-
tion. It grows out of a profound understanding of the liturgy
for the season, with its mixture of expectant joy and intense
need, its Old Testament prophecies fulfilled in Christ, its
imagery of light and darkness, of imprisonment and libera-
tion, its architectural metaphors, and its focus on the Vir-
gin Mary; for the poet, as for the congregation of which he
imagines himself a part, Christ's advent is repeated annually,
and in this poem their longing for his coming merges with
that of the souls in hell waiting for Christ to rescue them
after the crucifixion. The "sons and daughters of Salem"
(Jerusalem) and Joseph function as the uncomprehending
voices of humanity, expressing bafflement in the face of the
mystery of the Incarnation. As the poem progresses, we
move toward the accomplished Advent, with the final two

parts (ll. 378–429) drawing on Christmas themes and being full of exultation and joy.

There seems to be a growing consensus that *Advent* may have been composed during the Benedictine Reform period, i.e., the second half of the tenth century, very close to the date of the Exeter Book itself;[4] this dating, however, raises problems concerning the antiphonal sources, as the repertory of *O* antiphons available to the poet is not matched in Benedictine Reform manuscripts. *Advent* is almost certainly the work of a monk who saw the Bible through the lens of the liturgy and of patristic exegesis and who had deep experience of the liturgy.

CHRIST IN JUDGMENT

Christ in Judgment gives a striking and vivid account of the second coming of Christ on Judgment Day. While *Advent* stands in intimate relationship to the liturgical use of the Bible, *Christ in Judgment* relies more directly on the Bible and on sermon literature. Its extensive description includes the sudden approach of Christ from the East; the rising of the dead; the dual appearance of Christ, benign to the good and frightening to the wicked; the signs of Judgment Day; the wailing and lamenting; Christ's judgment, when everything about people's thoughts, words, and deeds will be revealed; the cross standing before the multitudes; Christ's wounds; how all creation apart from mankind acknowledged Christ's divinity at the Creation; how the chosen will be on Christ's right, and the damned on his left; the signs of glory for the just, and of damnation for the unjust; how it would have been better for the damned to have suffered the shame of confessing their sins to a single man on earth than having to endure eternal shame; the necessity for everyone to examine their conscience now to ensure salvation; Christ's address to the multitude with his praise of the good and accusations to the evil; his account of his suffering and his demand that he be repaid for the lives of sinners which he had purchased with his own life; his judgment of the evil and their fall into hell and the joys of heaven, which the good will enjoy for all eternity. The poem is full of uncompromising moral didacticism, with admonitions to readers to ensure their own eternal salvation, and is clearly designed to produce strong emotions of repentance and fear.

Christ in Judgment draws on an impressive range of sources, from the biblical accounts of judgment to church fathers, such as Caesarius of Arles, Gregory the Great, and Augustine, to the apocryphal 4 Ezra 5:5, which is the ultimate source of the detail of the trees' sap turning to blood. The poet also seems to have been familiar with vernacular sermons. The language is noteworthy especially for its striking visual images, such as that of fire like a seething warrior or the mountains and cliffs melting away, its imagery of light and dark, the vision of cosmic upheaval that it presents, and its relentless hammering home of the message to repent while there is still time. The ultimate source of much of its description is probably Ephraem Syrus, whose work was very influential for medieval eschatology. Parts of this poem, in particular lines 219–64a, are similar to parts of *The Vision of the Cross,* a poem also concerned with judgment.

As is often the case, we do not know when this poem was written. Its similarities to Old English prose sermons may suggest a date rather late in the Anglo-Saxon period; the motif of confessing to one man rather than being shamed at the Last Judgment occurs in manuscripts from ca. 975 onward. However, it has also been argued that this is an early poem.

GUTHLAC A

Immediately following *Christ in Judgment* in the Exeter Book are two Guthlac poems; recent critical opinion attributes the second, *Guthlac B,* to Cynewulf, and so it has been edited in the Cynewulf volume in this series. Guthlac, who lived ca. 674 to 714, was an Anglo-Saxon warrior of royal descent who spent nine years fighting in Mercia before becoming a monk in Repton at the age of twenty-four and then, two years later, a hermit in the fens at Croyland (Lincolnshire). A Latin life was written in the first half of the eighth century by the monk Felix, but it is not clear whether Felix's life was known to the author of *Guthlac A* (although Felix served as the source for *Guthlac B*); there is also an Old English prose life of Guthlac. Important aspects of the narrative of *Guthlac A* are also in Felix's *Life:* Guthlac's youth as a time when, as stated in Felix and implied in the poem, he was a member of a band of fighting outcasts, his turning to God, his dwelling in the wilderness and temptations by fiends, his journey to the entrance of hell and Bartholomew's rescue of him. *Guthlac A* is the only Old English poem on a saint to have no known direct source, though the poet must have been familiar with Latin hagiography and with texts dealing with the soul leaving the body to journey to an otherworld destination. The poem begins with a kind of prologue on the death of the good soul, greeted by an angel as it arrives in heaven, and describes the heavenly joys awaiting the good, before briefly discussing the different ranks of the saints, the deteriorating condition of the world, the necessity of rejecting earthly wealth, and the dangers endured by those who worship God in the wilderness; this kind of didactic emphasis continues throughout the poem. It then turns to Guthlac, but the poem's interest is not in the telling of the story of his life so much as in the psychology of eremitic and monastic lives and in spiritual warfare for the soul. Guthlac is constantly tempted by the demons whom he has ousted from his dwelling place and who try both terror and temptation in their attempts to conquer his will; at the end of the poem, his wilderness dwelling is converted into an earthly paradise, and he is conducted to heaven by Bartholomew, sent to protect him. One of the most interesting aspects of the poem is its stark opposition between traditional values such as wealth and kinship and those of devotion to God.

Guthlac A appears to date itself to an early period by saying that Guthlac was tested within the time of people who remember (l. 154) and that "All these things happened in the age of our times" (753–54). However, there has been no agreement about how literally to take these lines, and Jane Roberts concludes only that the evidence indicates "an earlier rather than later time of composition within the Anglo-Saxon period," while Patrick Conner argues that *Guthlac A* was composed in the Benedictine Reform period, the second half of the tenth century.[5] It is highly probable that the author was a monk, writing for a monastic audience.

The Descent into Hell

The final poem from the Exeter Book, *The Descent into Hell,*
comes from much later in the manuscript; because the text
of *The Descent* is badly damaged in parts, some readings have
had to be reconstructed. This poem deals with the apocry-
phal theme of the harrowing of hell, Christ's rescue of the
patriarchs and the righteous from hell, where they had been
confined until Christ's death opened heaven to mankind.
Opening with the visit of the two Marys to the tomb, it
shifts suddenly to Christ's resurrection and his heroic and
powerful entry to hell, where he is greeted by John the Bap-
tist. A series of invocations to Gabriel, Mary, Jerusalem, and
the River Jordan follows, and the poem concludes with a
litany-like entreaty to Christ for baptism. The poem deals
with the multiple comings of Christ, at the annunciation
and nativity, in the harrowing, to the individual soul through
baptism. It is very reminiscent of *Advent,* in its use of *Eala,*
its evocations of the birth of Christ, and its wide-ranging al-
lusiveness, typological thinking, and the way in which the
plea of the patriarchs in hell, voiced by John the Baptist, be-
comes one with the pleas of the poet and his audience, the
Church at large. While no direct source is known, the poem
seems to be clearly inspired by the liturgy of Holy Week and
especially Easter Saturday. To quote Jackson Campbell, the
poet "certainly knew the exegetical tradition which drew a
theology of salvation from the events of the Descent story,
and he presented it in a unique, rhapsodical way which
clothes theology in emotional responses."[6] No parallel has
been found in other texts for the juxtaposition of the visit of
the Marys to the sepulcher with the harrowing, and it has

been suggested that it may be a feature that the poet derived from pictorial rather than literary sources.[7]

We have no evidence for the date.

THE VERCELLI BOOK

Vercelli Cathedral Library CXVII is another manuscript from the second half of the tenth century from the south of England, very possibly from St. Augustine's Abbey, Canterbury;[8] it contains a mixture of prose and poetry and is the earliest extant collection of Old English homilies. It was probably written by a single scribe over a period of time, drawing on a number of earlier manuscripts. It begins with five homilies, followed by *Andreas* and Cynewulf's *Fates of the Apostles,* then come thirteen further homilies, followed by three short poems, the third of which is *The Vision of the Cross,* four more homilies, followed by Cynewulf's *Elene* and a prose life of Saint Guthlac.[9] As a collection it was probably compiled for private reading, because the homilies are not arranged in the order of the liturgical year, and the compiler seems to have selected texts for their devotional benefit to his spiritual life.

ANDREAS

Andreas is a long poem based closely on the apocryphal *Acts of Andrew and Matthias,* first written in Greek at the turn of the fifth century, at the latest, and translated into Latin. Of the Latin versions extant, none is the direct source of *Andreas,* but the Old English text most closely resembles the

Greek along with some details most closely paralleled in a Latin version known as the *Casanatensis*.[10] The apocryphal acts deal with the apostle Matthew, captured and blinded by the cannibalistic Mermedonians, and with God's command to Andrew to rescue him; a very reluctant Andrew is compelled by God to set out, in a boat steered by Christ in disguise, and then, having rescued Matthew, he undergoes a series of tortures before he overcomes the Mermedonians, killing the most evil and converting the rest. Much of the poem is taken up with a long conversation in the boat between Christ and Andrew, in which Christ, whom Andrew has not recognized, gets the apostle to narrate Christ's own doings to him, an exchange characterized by comedy as well as didacticism. There is also an Old English prose version of the Acts of Matthias and Andrew.

The setting of *Andreas* is different from the Mermedonia of the source texts. It is described as an island and a borderland, and there has been much interesting work recently on the resonances of this setting for an Anglo-Saxon audience. Mermedonia is even given a climate like that of England, with a vivid description of a snowstorm on a winter night that has no parallel in the sources. The poet heightens the horror of cannibalism and the monstrosity of the Mermedonians, drawing attention to parallels between them and the Jews and to their cannibalism as a parody of the Eucharist. The suffering of Andrew, as in the source, is likened to the passion of Christ.

The *Andreas* poet draws freely on the heroic ethos of poems such as *Beowulf,* and Andrew's disciples express their undying loyalty to him in terms that would be appropriate for a poem of secular heroism but in this context conveys the sense of their being soldiers of Christ, *milites Christi,* with Andrew as their leader against the forces of the devil represented by the Mermedonians. Andrew's courage is manifested in his unwavering faith when he is tortured for days. But heroic diction is also used with comic incongruity, as when a large group of armed Mermedonians gathers to attack a single young man or when Satan, whose subordinate devils have been unable to overcome Andrew, is told by them to attack Andrew himself and advised that words are a better tactic than direct assault. As well as this general similarity, the *Andreas* poet seems to have known *Beowulf* and may have drawn inspiration from it for the opening of his own poem and perhaps for such features as the sea voyage or the description of the flood overcoming the Mermedonians as *meoduscerwan* in line 1526.

Andreas was almost certainly composed after *Beowulf,* the dating of which has been disputed. Some dates have been suggested for *Andreas* but they are conjectural. Brooks suggests a date between the middle of the ninth century and the date of the manuscript, while Boenig suggests the mid- to late-ninth century; however, we have at present no means of verifying such dates.[11]

The Vision of the Cross

The other poem from the Vercelli Book edited here, *The Vision of the Cross,* also makes use of heroic diction, this time to describe Christ's crucifixion. Commonly known as *The Dream of the Rood,* it is deservedly the best known Old English poem after *Beowulf.* It is also the first dream-vision poem in English, in which the first-person speaker recounts a vision at midnight in which a puzzling object appears towering in the sky. The poet draws on the strong riddle tradition in Old English to give a variety of descriptions of this object, which is itself in a state of flux; the speaker sees a jeweled, gold-covered "tree" or symbol, at times surrounded by light, at others times drenched in blood. In *Christ in Judgment* the cross appears in the sky as a sign of the Last Judgment; the virtuous see Christ in glory, and the damned see the wounded Christ on the cross. The fluctuating vision which the dreamer sees and to which he reacts with anxiety, consciousness of his own sins, and fear, along with the midnight setting, associated with the Last Judgment, suggest that the context of *The Vision of the Cross* is eschatological. The cross takes Christ's place, and the dreamer's eternal fate, symbolized by what aspect of the cross he sees, evidently hangs in the balance. By the end of the poem, when we return to the dreamer, we realize that this is not the Last Judgment itself, but a vision that allows the dreamer to prepare for it; he has now been given a means of salvation through the cross, and his eternal fate, imagined as a feast in heaven, is assured. The central part of the poem is spoken by the cross itself and it narrates its own life story, which began as an ordinary tree, and gives a highly distinctive account of the Crucifixion; while loyal to Christ, obedience to him meant that the cross had to stand firm and function as his slayer, a most desperate dilemma. Christ himself is depicted as a hero, mounting the cross rather than being nailed to it, and only through the cross's account of having nails driven through it can one infer the torment of the crucifixion.

THE RUTHWELL CROSS CRUCIFIXION POEM

Parts of the crucifixion narrative in *The Vision of the Cross* were carved in runes on the Ruthwell Cross. We do not know whether these passages already existed in a form similar to that in the Vercelli Book in the eighth century or whether only the central passion narrative was available then, with the dream-vision frame being a later addition. At any rate, the speech of the cross is the part of the poem clearly most suited to the large, carved stone cross, which, in effect, speaks its own story. The Ruthwell Cross, erected probably around the middle of the eighth century on the northern shore of the Solway Firth, now part of Scotland, was broken and torn down in the seventeenth century. Most of the parts were subsequently found, and it has been re-erected inside the church at Ruthwell. It is the only Anglo-Saxon stone cross with a vernacular poem. The front and back panels of the cross are covered with carved scenes, accompanied by Latin inscriptions, of the life of Christ, as well as one of John the Baptist and one of Saints Paul and Anthony, while the narrow side panels are covered with inhabited vine scroll. The runic inscriptions, giving the vernacular poem in an early Northumbrian dialect, fill the margins of the side panels. The cross has been damaged both by being broken up and by erosion, so many of the runes can no longer be deciphered; only those words of which at least a letter remains have been included in the text here.

THE BRUSSELS CROSS INSCRIPTION

The Brussels Cross, now exhibited in the treasury of the Cathedral of Saints Michel and Gudule in Brussels, is a reliquary designed to hold a relic of the true cross and to serve as a processional cross. The oak at its core was covered in gilded silver and jewels and was made in the south of England in the eleventh century. The front cover of the cross, originally gilded silver like the back, had twenty-four rubies and fourteen diamonds, but it was looted in 1793 and has been missing since; only the wooden core and the back cover, with an image of the *Agnus Dei* surrounded by symbols of the four evangelists, survives. The inscriptions, like those on the Ruthwell Cross, give us the speech of the cross itself. In addition, *Drahmal me worhte*, "Drahmal made me," is engraved on the crossbeam at either side of the *Agnus Dei*. The narrow sides of the cross are covered in ten narrow strips of silver; five of these contain the verse distich and the prose sentence recording the names of the two brothers who commissioned the cross and that of the third brother in whose memory they had it made. The distich is not a quotation from *The Vision of the Cross,* but a new piece evidently inspired by the earlier poem.

The Junius Manuscript

The Junius manuscript, Oxford Bodleian Library Junius 11, also from the second half of the tenth century, is largely devoted to Old Testament poems, *Genesis, Exodus, Daniel,* followed by one New Testament text, *Christ and Satan.*[12] The four poems seem to be by different authors, but, even more than the Exeter Book, there is a very clear arrangement, following the order of the Old Testament in the first three works. Junius 11 was planned as an illustrated manuscript, but this plan was never fully executed. *Christ and Satan,* in any case, does not seem to have been part of the original plan, as no blanks were left in its text. While a single scribe copied out the first three poems, *Christ and Satan* was copied by another three scribes, and it may have circulated originally as an independent, folded booklet. If so, then it was added to the other texts in the Anglo-Saxon period, indeed at the stage when the manuscript was sewn and bound, and intended at that stage to be an integral part of the manuscript. *Christ and Satan* concludes with the words *Finit Liber II,* suggesting that the Old Testament narratives may have been regarded as *Liber I.* Whereas in *Genesis,* the first text, Satan was able to deceive Adam and Eve, in this final text the consequences of that deception are reversed and mankind rescued with the comprehensive defeat of Satan.

CHRIST AND SATAN

Christ and Satan opens with the creation of the universe, an account indebted to patristic cosmology, and then describes the fall of the angels, the harrowing of hell, Christ's resurrection, ascension, and his coming in judgment; it concludes with the temptation of Christ by Satan. There has been debate about whether the text is a unified poem at all, rather than at least three separate texts (fall, harrowing, and temptation). Its unity is now generally accepted for linguistic and metrical reasons. The account of the temptation even begins in the middle of a manuscript section, which suggests that the scribe considered the temptation to be continuous with the previous part. Unlike the Old Testament texts in the Junius manuscript, *Christ and Satan* is not interested in a straightforward or chronological narrative (and its chronology at several points seems to be incompatible with the traditional time frames); the fall of the angels is told through the laments of the angels, and the temptation of Christ by Satan closes the narrative, after the account of the harrowing of hell and the Last Judgment. *Christ and Satan* has some affinities with wisdom literature, and it dwells on right understanding and knowledge in contrast to Satan's inability to know the truth. The conflict between Christ and Satan runs right through the poem and unifies it thematically. Christ is responsible for the Creation; it is against him that Lucifer rebels, and it is he who expels Lucifer from heaven; he harrows hell to rescue mankind from Satan; and he resists Satan's temptation and sentences him to terrible punishment. The first two parts are homiletic, pointing out the moral of the events for mankind and exhorting the reader to ensure eternal salvation by right thinking and actions. The laments of the fallen angels emphasize their exile from the joys of heaven in language reminiscent of the Old English elegies.

There is no single source for the poem; it draws on the Bible, apocrypha, and homiletic texts, probably both Latin and Old English. No source has been found for some of the most striking details, such as Satan placing Christ on his shoulders at the temptation or his offering Christ power over heaven as part of the same scene.

A wide range of dates has been proposed for *Christ and Satan,* from the seventh to the tenth centuries, with the majority favoring the ninth century.

DISTICH ON KENELM

The last poem is a couplet taken from Cambridge, Pembroke College 82, where it is transcribed along with other short items on an originally blank page in a manuscript containing a life of Saint Alexis, a copy of Bede's *Historia Ecclesi-astica,* and other texts. This is the earliest known copy of the distich, which is found also inserted in the Latin *Vita et Mi-racula Sancti Kenelmi* and in histories that draw on it. The manuscript is from the turn of the twelfth and thirteenth centuries and almost certainly belonged to a cell of the Ab-bey of Saint Alban's at Tynemouth.

Kenelm was the son and heir of Coenwulf of Mercia (d. 821), who was supposedly murdered by his tutor Æscberht after Kenelm succeeded to his father's throne at the age of seven; Æscberht acted at the request of Kenelm's sister, who hoped to gain the throne. According to the eleventh-century life, which is unlikely to have any basis in historical events, the body was hidden but its whereabouts were miraculously revealed to the pope as he was saying mass in Rome, when a dove (Kenelm's soul) dropped a scroll with these two verses at the pope's feet. The cult seems al-ready to have been in existence in the late tenth century, and it is possible that the verses were in circulation in the early eleventh century.[13]

Ideally, the works in this volume should be read in conjunc-tion with Bjork's edition of *The Old English Poems of Cynewulf* (DOML 23), because the poems in it, *Christ II, Juliana, Elene, The Fates of the Apostles,* and *Guthlac B,* fit under the larger rubric of Old English poems of Christ and his saints.

INTRODUCTION

Notes

1 *Ælfric's Catholic Homilies: The Second Series, Text,* ed. M. Godden, EETS SS 5 (Oxford, 1979), 298.

2 Quoted from Lapidge, "Surviving Booklists from Anglo-Saxon England," 65.

3 Some, for example, appear in DOML 15, *Old English Shorter Poems: Religious and Didactic,* trans. Christopher A. Jones (Cambridge, Mass., 2012), and in *Old English Shorter Poems: Wisdom and Lyric,* trans. Robert E. Bjork (forthcoming). Others will appear in a volume containing Anglo-Saxon riddles.

4 See, for example, Salvador, "Architectural Metaphors and Christological Imagery in the Advent Lyrics," and the further references there.

5 Roberts, *The Guthlac Poems,* 70; Conner, "Source Studies, the Old English *Guthlac A* and the English Benedictine Reformation."

6 Campbell, "To Hell and Back," 150.

7 Brantley, "The Iconography of the Utrecht Psalter and the Old English *Descent into Hell.*"

8 *The Vercelli Homilies and Related Texts,* ed. D. Scragg, EETS OS 300 (Oxford, 1992), lxxix.

9 See Cynewulf's *Fates of the Apostles* and *Elene* edited in R. Bjork's *Cynewulf: Old English Poems* (DOML 23, 2013).

10 Allen and Calder, *Sources and Analogues,* 15. The *Casanatensis* is translated on pp. 15–34.

11 Brooks, *Andreas and the Fates of the Apostles,* xviii–xxii, and R. Boenig, *Saint and Hero: Andreas and Medieval Doctrine* (Bucknell University Press: Lewisburg, Pa., 1991), 23.

12 *Genesis, Exodus,* and *Daniel* are translated in the DOML series by Daniel Anlezark, *Old Testament Narratives* (DOML 7, 2011).

13 *Three Eleventh-Century Anglo-Latin Saints' Lives: Vita S. Birini, Vita et Miracula S. Kenelmi, and Vita S. Rumwoldi,* ed. and trans. R. Love (Oxford, 1996), cxviii.

ADVENT

cyninge.
Ðu eart se weall-stan   þe ða wyrhtan iu
wiðwurpon to weorce.   Wel þe geriseð
þæt þu heafod sie   healle mærre
5 ond gesomnige   side weallas
fæste gefoge,   flint unbræcne,
þæt geond eorð-byrg eall   eagna gesihþe
wundrien to worlde.   Wuldres Ealdor,
gesweotula nu þurh searo-cræft   þin sylfes weorc,
10 soð-fæst, sigor-beorht,   ond sona forlæt
weall wið wealle.   Nu is þam weorce þearf
þæt se cræftga cume   ond se cyning sylfa
ond þonne gebete,   nu gebrosnad is,
hus under hrofe.   He þæt hra gescop,
15 leomo læmena;   nu sceal Lif-Frea
þone wergan heap   wraþum ahreddan,
earme from egsan,   swa he oft dyde.
    Eala þu reccend   ond þu ryht cyning
se þe locan healdeð,   lif ontyneð,
20 eadgum up-wegas,   oþrum forwyrneð
wlitigan wil-siþes   gif his weorc ne deag.
Huru we for þearfe   þas word sprecað
ond myndgiað   þone þe mon gescop
þæt he ne læte   to lose weorðan
25 cearfulra þing,   þe we in carcerne

. . . the king. You are the wall stone which long ago the
workers rejected from the work. It is entirely fitting for you
to be the head of the glorious hall and to join together firmly 5
the wide walls, indestructible flint stone, so that throughout
the cities on earth all, with the sight of their eyes, may mar-
vel forever. Lord of glory, steadfast in truth, victoriously ra- 10
diant, skillfully reveal now your own work, and at once let
wall join with wall. The work needs the craftsman and the
king himself to come and then to restore the house under its
roof, now that it has fallen into ruins. He created the body,
the limbs of clay; now the Lord of life must rescue the griev- 15
ing multitude from their hostile enemies, the wretches from
terror, as he has often done.

O you ruler and just king who guards the locks, who
opens life, the ascent to heaven, to a blessed one and denies 20
to another that glorious longed-for journey if his deeds are
not good enough. Truly we speak these words out of need
and entreat him who created man to be mindful not to allow
us anxious ones to be ruined, who sit in prison sorrowing, 25

sittað sorgende,   sunnan wenað,
hwonne us Lif-Frea   leoht ontyne,
weorðe ussum mode   to mund-boran
ond þæt tydre gewitt   tire bewinde,
30 gedo usic þæs wyrðe,   þe he to wuldre forlet
þa we heanlice   hweorfan sceoldan
on þis enge lond,   eðle bescyrede.
    Forþon secgan mæg   se ðe soð spriceð
þæt he ahredde,   þa forhwyrfed wæs,
35 frum-cyn fira.   Wæs seo fæmne geong,
mægð manes leas,   þe he him to meder geceas;
þæt wæs geworden   butan weres frigum,
þæt þurh bearnes gebyrd   bryd eacen wearð.
Nænig efenlic þam,   ær ne siþþan,
40 in worlde gewearð   wifes gearnung;
þæt degol wæs,   Dryhtnes geryne.
Eal giofu gæstlic   grund-sceat geondspreot;
þær wisna fela   wearð inlihted
lare longsume   þurh lifes fruman
45 þe ær under hoðman   biholen lægon,
witgena woð-song,   þa se waldend cwom
se þe reorda gehwæs   ryne gemiclað
ðara þe geneahhe   noman scyppendes
þurh horscne had   hergan willað.
50   Eala sibbe gesihð,   sancta Hierusalem,
cyne-stola cyst,   Cristes burg-lond,
engla eþel-stol,   ond þa ane in þe
saule soð-fæstra   simle gerestað,
wuldrum hremge.   Næfre wommes tacn
55 in þam eard-gearde   eawed weorþeð,

who hope for the sun, when the Lord of life may open the
light to us, become a protector to our spirits and envelop
our weak understanding in glory, may make us worthy of   30
this, whom he allowed into heaven when we had had to turn
away downcast into this narrow land, deprived of our home-
land.

Therefore anyone who speaks the truth can say that he
rescued the race of men when it had been perverted. The   35
virgin was young, a girl without sin, whom he chose as his
mother; it happened that, without a man's embraces, the
bride became pregnant, bearing a child. There has been no
woman's merit equal to this in the world, before or since;   40
it was incomprehensible, a mystery of the Lord. All that
spiritual grace spread throughout the precincts of the earth;
then many matters were illuminated by the source of life,
the enduring doctrine which had lain hidden under dark-   45
ness, the song of the prophets, when the ruler came who
magnifies the course of every speech uttered by those who
wish to praise, abundantly and wisely, the name of the cre-
ator.

O vision of peace, *sancta* Jerusalem, choicest of royal   50
seats, site of Christ's city, ancient seat of angels, in you shall
the souls of the righteous only rest forever, exulting in glory.
No sign of a blemish shall ever be revealed in that dwelling   55

ac þe firina gehwylc   feor abugeð,
wærgðo ond gewinnes.   Bist to wuldre full
halgan hyhtes,   swa þu gehaten eart.
Sioh nu sylfa þe   geond þas sidan gesceaft,
60   swylce rodores hrof,   rume geondwlitan
ymb healfa gehwone,   hu þec heofones cyning
siðe geseceð   ond sylf cymeð,
nimeð eard in þe,   swa hit ær gefyrn
witgan wis-fæste   wordum sægdon,
65   cyðdon Cristes gebyrd,   cwædon þe to frofre,
burga betlicast!   Nu is þæt bearn cymen,
awæcned to wyrpe   weorcum Ebrea,
bringeð blisse þe,   benda onlyseð
niþum genedde.   Nearo-þearfe conn,
70   hu se earma sceal   are gebidan.

"Eala wifa wynn   geond wuldres þrym,
fæmne freolicast   ofer ealne foldan sceat
þæs þe æfre sund-buend   secgan hyrdon,
arece us þæt geryne   þæt þe of roderum cwom,
75   hu þu eacnunge   æfre onfenge
bearnes þurh gebyrde,   ond þone gebedscipe
æfter mon-wisan   mod ne cuðes.
Ne we soðlice   swylc ne gefrugnan
in ær-dagum   æfre gelimpan,
80   þæt ðu in sundur-giefe   swylce befenge,
ne we þære wyrde   wenan þurfon
toweard in tide.   Huru treow in þe
weorðlicu wunade,   nu þu wuldres þrym
bosme gebære   ond no gebrosnad wearð

place but every sin, punishment and tribulation will turn far away from you. You shall be gloriously full of holy joy, just as you are named. Look now for yourself all over this spacious creation, over the roof of heaven also, to survey far and wide 60 on every side, look how the king of heaven is seeking you out on his journey and is coming in person, taking up his abode in you, just as long ago wise prophets declared in their utterances, proclaimed the birth of Christ and spoke to 65 comfort you, best of cities! Now that child has come, has been born to alleviate the sufferings of the Hebrews, bringing happiness to you, releasing you from the bonds forced upon you by evil. He knows the dire need, how the wretched 70 must wait for mercy.

"O joy of women throughout the glory of heaven, the most noble virgin over all the expanse of the earth as far as mankind has ever heard tell, explain to us the mystery which came to you from heaven, how you ever conceived, bearing 75 a child, without having intercourse according to human ideas. Truly we never heard of anything like this happening in former days, anything like how you, by special grace, contained within you a conception such as this, nor need we expect that event to happen in time to come. A noble faith has indeed dwelt in you, now that you have carried the glory of heaven in your womb without your celebrated virginity

85 mægðhad se micla.   Swa eal manna bearn
sorgum sawað,   swa eft ripað,
cennað to cwealme."

     Cwæð sio eadge mæg
symle sigores full,   sancta Maria:
"Hwæt is þeos wundrung   þe ge wafiað
90 ond geomrende   gehþum mænað,
sunu Solimæ   somod his dohtor?
Fricgað þurh fyrwet   hu ic fæmnan had,
mund minne geheold,   ond eac modor gewearð
mære meotudes Suna.   Forþan þæt monnum nis
95 cuð geryne,   ac Crist onwrah
in Dauides   dyrre mægan
þæt is Euan scyld   eal forpynded,
wærgða aworpen,   ond gewuldrad is
se heanra had.   Hyht is onfangen
100 þæt nu bletsung mot   bæm gemæne
werum ond wifum   a to worulde forð
in þam uplican   engla dreame
mid Soð-Fæder   symle wunian."

   Eala earendel,   engla beorhtast,
105 ofer middan-geard   monnum sended,
ond soð-fæsta   sunnan leoma,
torht ofer tunglas,   þu tida gehwane
of sylfum þe   symle inlihtes.
Swa þu, God of Gode   gearo acenned,
110 Sunu soþan Fæder,   swegles in wuldre
butan anginne   æfre wære,
swa þec nu for þearfum   þin agen geweorc
bideð þurh byldo,   þæt þu þa beorhtan us
sunnan onsende,   ond þe sylf cyme

being corrupted. Just as all the children of men sow in sor- 85
row, so do they reap likewise, giving birth for death."

The blessed woman, *sancta* Mary, forever triumphant,
spoke: "What sort of astonishment is this which amazes
you, sons and daughters of Salem, though mourning you la- 90
ment your sorrow? You ask out of curiosity how I preserved
my virginity, my virtue, and also became the glorious mother
of the creator's Son. For that is not a mystery that is made 95
known to mankind, but Christ revealed, in the person of
David's beloved kinswoman, that Eve's guilt is all annulled,
the curse removed, and the weaker sex is glorified. They
have received hope that happiness may now last forever for 100
both men and women alike world without end in the heav-
enly joy of the angels with the Father of truth."

O rising sun, brightest of angels, sent to people all over 105
the earth, and true radiance of the sun, more splendid than
the stars, you by your own person always illuminate every
age. Just as you, God born of old from God, Son of the true 110
Father, always existed without beginning in the glory of
heaven, so now your own creation, in its need, confidently
entreats you to send us that bright sun and to come yourself

115 þæt ðu inleohte   þa þe longe ær
þrosme beþeahte   ond in þeostrum her,
sæton sin-neahtes;   synnum bifealdne
deorc deaþes sceadu   dreogan sceoldan.
     Nu we hyhtfulle   hælo gelyfað
120 þurh þæt word Godes   weorodum brungen,
þe on frymðe wæs   Fæder ælmihtigum
efen-ece mid God,   ond nu eft gewearð
flæsc firena leas,   þæt seo fæmne gebær
geomrum to geoce.   God wæs mid us,
125 gesewen butan synnum;   somod eardedon
mihtig meotudes bearn   ond se monnes sunu
geþwære on þeode.   We þæs þonc magon
secgan Sige-Dryhtne   symle bi gewyrhtum,
þæs þe he hine sylfne us   sendan wolde.
130   Eala gæsta God,   hu þu gleawlice
mid noman ryhte   nemned wære
Emmanuhel,   swa hit engel gecwæð
ærest on Ebresc!   Þæt is eft gereht,
rume bi gerynum: "Nu is rodera weard,
135 God sylfa mid us."   Swa þæt gomele gefyrn
ealra cyninga cyning   ond þone clænan eac
sacerd soðlice   sægdon toweard,
swa se mæra iu,   Melchisedech,
gleaw in gæste   god-þrym onwrah
140 eces alwaldan.   Se wæs æ bringend,
lara lædend,   þam longe his
hyhtan hidercyme   swa him gehaten wæs
þætte Sunu meotudes   sylfa wolde
gefælsian   foldan mægðe

that you may enlighten those who for a long time already 115
have sat enveloped in smoke and in darkness here, in per-
petual night; entangled in sins, they have had to endure the
dark shadow of death.

Full of hope now, we believe in the salvation brought to 120
the multitudes by the word of God, which was coeternal
with God, the almighty Father, in the beginning, and has
now subsequently become flesh without sin, which the vir-
gin bore as a comfort to the sorrowful. God was seen to be 125
without sins among us; the powerful son of the creator and
the son of a human lived in union together among the peo-
ple. For this we can say thanks forever to the Lord of victory,
according to our merits, because he was willing to send him-
self to us.

O God of souls, how discerningly you were rightly named 130
by the name Emmanuel, as an angel originally said it in He-
brew! That was afterward fully interpreted by its hidden
meaning: "Now the guardian of heaven, God himself, is with 135
us." Just as men of old long ago truly prophesied him who
was the king of all kings and the pure priest, so the great
Melchisedech, wise in spirit, once revealed the divine maj-
esty of the eternal almighty. He was the lawgiver, the bringer 140
of precepts, to those who for a long time hoped for his com-
ing just as it had been promised to them that the Son of
the creator would himself purify the people of the earth

145 swylce grundas eac Gæstes mægne
   siþe gesecan. Nu hie softe þæs
   bidon in bendum hwonne Bearn Godes
   cwome to cearigum. Forþon cwædon swa,
   suslum geslæhte:
         "Nu þu sylfa cum,
150 heofones heah-cyning. Bring us hælo lif,
   werigum wite-þeowum, wope forcymenum,
   bitrum bryne-tearum. Is seo bot gelong
   eal æt þe anum for ofer-þearfum;
   hæftas hyge-geomre hider geseces.
155 Ne læt þe behindan þonne þu heonan cyrre
   mænigo þus micle ac þu miltse on us
   gecyð cynelice, Crist nergende,
   wuldres æþeling; ne læt awyrgde ofer us
   onwald agan. Læf us ecne gefean
160 wuldres þines þæt þec weorðien,
   weoroda wuldor-cyning, þa þu geworhtes ær
   hondum þinum. Þu in heannissum
   wunast wide-ferh mid waldend Fæder."

    "Eala Ioseph min, Iacobes bearn,
165 mæg Dauides mæran cyninges,
   na þu freode scealt fæste gedælan,
   alætan lufan mine. Ic lungre eam
   deope gedrefed, dome bereafod,
   forðon ic worn for þe worda hæbbe
170 sidra sorga ond sar-cwida,
   hearmes gehyred, ond me hosp sprecað,
   torn-worda fela. Ic tearas sceal
   geotan geomor-mod. God eaþe mæg

and would also seek out the abyss on his expedition, by the 145
power of his Spirit. Calmly now they waited in their fetters
for the time when the Son of God would come to the sor-
rowful ones. Therefore, weakened by torments, they spoke
in this way:

"Come now in person, high king of heaven. Bring the life 150
of salvation to us, who are weary and reduced to slavery,
overcome by weeping, by bitter scalding tears. Deliverance
is entirely dependent on you alone for us who are in dire
need; you will seek out the sad captives in this place. Do not 155
leave behind you such a great multitude when you return
from here but royally show mercy on us, Christ savior,
prince of glory; do not allow the cursed ones have power
over us. Leave us the eternal joy of your glory so that they, 160
whom you once made with your own hands, may honor you,
glorious king of hosts. You live always with the ruler, the Fa-
ther, on high."

"O my Joseph, son of Jacob, kinsman of the glorious king 165
David, you must not sever a firm affection, forsake love of
me. I am suddenly deeply troubled, robbed of my honor, be-
cause on your account I have heard many words of enor- 170
mous pain and reproach, of harm, and they utter insults
to me, many cruel words. Sad at heart, I must shed tears.

gehælan hyge-sorge   heortan minre,
175 afrefran fea-sceaftne."
                      "Eala fæmne geong,
mægð Maria,   hwæt bemurnest ðu,
cleopast cearigende?   Ne ic culpan in þe,
incan ænigne,   æfre onfunde,
womma geworhtra,   ond þu þa word spricest
180 swa þu sylfa sie   synna gehwylcre
firena gefylled.   Ic to fela hæbbe
þæs byrdscypes   bealwa onfongen!
Hu mæg ic ladigan   laþan spræce,
oþþe ondsware   ænige findan
185 wraþum towiþere?   Is þæt wide cuð
þæt ic of þam torhtan   temple Dryhtnes
onfeng freolice   fæmnan clæne,
womma lease,   ond nu gehwyrfed is
þurh nathwylces.   Me nawþer deag,
190 secge ne swige.   Gif ic soð sprece,
þonne sceal Dauides   dohtor sweltan,
stanum astyrfed.   Gen strengre is
þæt ic morþor hele;   scyle man-swara,
laþ leoda gehwam   lifgan siþþan,
195 fracoð in folcum."
                      Þa seo fæmne onwrah
ryht-geryno   ond þus reordade:
"Soð ic secge   þurh Sunu meotudes,
gæsta geocend,   þæt ic gen ne conn
þurh gemæcscipe   monnes ower,
200 ænges on eorðan.   Ac me eaden wearð,
geongre in geardum,   þæt me Gabrihel,
heofones heag-engel,   hælo gebodade.

God can easily cure the anxiety of my heart, comfort the 175
wretched one."

"O young girl, virgin Mary, why are you lamenting, crying
out in sorrow? I never found a fault in you, any suspicion of
sins you had committed, yet you speak these words as if you 180
yourself were filled with every sin and wicked deed. I have
received too much pain because of this pregnancy! How can
I clear myself against this hateful talk or find any answer
against my enemies? It is widely known that I willingly re- 185
ceived a pure virgin from the bright temple of the Lord, free
from stain, and yet that has been changed by someone un-
known. Neither speech nor silence will do me any good. If I 190
tell the truth, then David's daughter will have to die, stoned
to death. It is even worse if I conceal the crime; I would
have to live afterward as a perjurer, hateful to every people,
despicable to mankind." 195

Then the virgin revealed the true mystery and spoke
thus: "By the creator's Son, the comforter of souls, I am tell-
ing the truth that, now as before, I have not had intercourse
with any man anywhere on earth. But it was granted to me, a 200
young woman at home, that Gabriel, heaven's archangel,

Sægde soðlice   þæt me swegles Gæst
leoman onlyhte,   sceolde ic lifes þrym
205 geberan, beorhtne Sunu,   bearn eacen Godes,
torhtes tir-fruman.   Nu ic his tempel eam
gefremed butan facne   —in me frofre Gæst
geeardode—   nu þu ealle forlæt
sare sorg-ceare.   Saga ecne þonc
210 mærum meotodes Sunu   þæt ic his modor gewearð,
fæmne forð seþeah,   ond þu fæder cweden
woruld-cund bi wene;   sceolde witedom
in him sylfum beon   soðe gefylled."
    Eala þu soða   ond þu sibsuma
215 ealra cyninga cyning,   Crist ælmihtig,
hu þu ær wære   eallum geworden
worulde þrymmum   mid þinne Wuldor-Fæder
cild acenned   þurh his cræft ond meaht!
Nis ænig nu   eorl under lyfte,
220 secg searo-þoncol,   to þæs swiðe gleaw
þe þæt asecgan mæge   sund-buendum,
areccan mid ryhte,   hu þe rodera weard
æt frymðe genom   him to Freo-Bearne.
Þæt wæs þara þinga   þe her þeoda cynn
225 gefrugnen mid folcum   æt fruman ærest
geworden under wolcnum,   þæt witig God,
lifes ord-fruma,   leoht ond þystro
gedælde dryhtlice,   ond him wæs domes geweald,
ond þa wisan abead   weoroda Ealdor:
230 "Nu sie geworden forþ   a to widan feore
leoht, lixende gefea,   lifgendra gehwam
þe in cneorissum   cende weorðen."
Ond þa sona gelomp,   þa hit swa sceolde.

greeted me. He said truthfully that the Spirit of heaven would illuminate me with his radiance, that I would have to 205 bear the glory of life, the bright Son, the mighty child of God, of the radiant prince of glory. Now that I am his temple, made without a flaw—in me the Spirit of consolation has dwelt—let go of all your painful sorrow. Say eternal thanks to the splendid Son of the creator that I have be- 210 come his mother, although still a virgin, and that you are called his father, in the opinion of the world; the prophecy was destined to be truly fulfilled in his own person."

O you true and peace-loving king of all kings, almighty 215 Christ, how you existed before all the world's multitudes, with your glorious Father, born as an infant through his power and might! There is now no man on earth, no inge- 220 nious person, who is so very wise that he can declare to mankind, explain correctly how heaven's guardian in the beginning took you as his true Son. First among those things of which humankind might have heard tell here among the 225 people, it happened at the beginning under the skies that the wise God, the source of life, majestically divided light and darkness, and he had authority and power, and the Lord of the heavenly hosts decreed the matter: "Let there be 230 light, a radiant joy, now and forever henceforth, for all of the living who may be born in their generations." And then it happened straightaway, as it had to. The radiance, splendid

Leoma leohtade   leoda mægþum,
235 torht mid tunglum,   æfter þon tida bigong.
Sylfa sette   þæt þu Sunu wære
efen-eardigende   mid þinne engan Frean
ærþon oht þisses   æfre gewurde.
Þu eart seo snyttro   þe þas sidan gesceaft
240 mid þi waldende   worhtes ealle.
Forþon nis ænig þæs horsc,   ne þæs hyge-cræftig,
þe þin from-cyn mæge   fira bearnum
sweotule geseþan.
                    Cum nu, sigores weard,
meotod mon-cynnes,   ond þine miltse her
245 ar-fæst ywe!   Us is eallum neod
þæt we þin medren-cynn   motan cunnan,
ryht-geryno,   nu we areccan ne mægon
þæt fædren-cynn   fier owihte.
Þu þisne middan-geard   milde geblissa
250 þurh ðinne her-cyme,   hælende Crist,
ond þa gyldnan geatu,   þe in gear-dagum
ful longe ær   bilocen stodan,
heofona Heah-Frea,   hat ontynan,
ond usic þonne gesece   þurh þin sylfes gong
255 eað-mod to eorþan.   Us is þinra arna þearf!
Hafað se awyrgda   wulf tostenced,
deor dæd-scua,   Dryhten, þin eowde,
wide towrecene.   Þæt ðu, waldend, ær
blode gebohtes,   þæt se bealofulla
260 hyneð heardlice,   ond him on hæft nimeð
ofer usse nioda lust.   Forþon we, nergend, þe
biddað geornlice   breost-gehygdum
þæt þu hrædlice   helpe gefremme

18

among the stars, has given light to generations of people 235
throughout the course of the ages. He himself ordained that
you, the Son, were co-dwelling with your only Lord before
any of this had ever come to pass. You are the wisdom who,
with the ruler, made all of this spacious creation. For this 240
reason, there is no one so quick-witted nor so knowledge-
able in mind who can clearly prove your origin to the chil-
dren of men.

Come now, guardian of victory, creator of mankind, and,
compassionate one, show your mercy here! It is necessary 245
for us all to know your descent on your mother's side, the
true mystery, now that we cannot explain your descent on
your father's side any further at all. Mercifully gladden this
earth through your advent, savior Christ, and, high Lord of 250
heaven, command these golden gates to be opened, which in
days of old already stood locked for a very long time, and
then, with humility, seek us out through your own journey 255
to the earth. We have need of your mercies! The cursed wolf,
the fierce agent of darkness, has driven your flock apart,
Lord, and scattered it far and wide. The evil being cruelly
oppresses and takes captive, contrary to our desire and long-
ing, that which you, the ruler, formerly bought with your 260
blood. Therefore, savior, we eagerly pray to you in our inner-
most thoughts that you may quickly help us weary exiles, so

wergum wreccan,   þæt se wites bona
265 in helle grund   hean gedreose,
ond þin hond-geweorc,   hæleþa scyppend,
mote arisan   ond on ryht cuman
to þam up-cundan   æþelan rice.
Þonan us ær þurh syn-lust   se swearta gæst
270 forteah ond fortylde,   þæt we, tires wone,
a butan ende   sculon ermþu dreogan,
butan þu usic þon ofostlicor,   ece Dryhten,
æt þam leod-sceaþan,   lifgende God,
helm al-wihta,   hreddan wille.

275   Eala þu mæra   middan-geardes,
seo clæneste   cwen ofer eorþan
þara þe gewurde   to widan feore,
hu þec mid ryhte   ealle reord-berend
hata∂ ond secga∂   hæle∂ geond foldan
280 bliþe mode   þæt þu bryd sie
þæs selestan   swegles Bryttan!
Swylce þa hyhstan   on heofonum eac,
Cristes þegnas,   cweþa∂ ond singa∂
þæt þu sie hlæfdige   halgum meahtum
285 wuldor-weorudes   ond world-cundra
hada under heofonum   ond helwara.
Forþon þu þæt ana   ealra monna
geþohtest þrymlice,   þrist-hycgende,
þæt þu þinne mæg∂had   meotude brohtes,
290 sealdes butan synnum.   Nan swylc ne cwom
ænig oþer   ofer ealle men,
bryd beaga hroden,   þe þa beorhtan lac
to heofon-hame   hlutre mode

that the torturing slayer may fall, despised, into the abyss of 265 hell and so that your handiwork, creator of men, may rise and rightly come into the noble heavenly kingdom. From there the dark spirit formerly led us astray and seduced us 270 through our desire for sin so that we, devoid of glory, will have to suffer torments forever without end, unless you, eternal Lord, living God, protector of all creation, are willing to rescue us the more speedily from the enemy of the people.

O you glory of the world, purest queen of those who have 275 ever existed on earth, how rightly all speech-bearing people throughout the world, with joyful minds name you and 280 say that you are the bride of heaven's most generous Lord! Likewise the highest in heaven, Christ's attendants, also declare and sing that you, with your holy virtues, are the lady of the heavenly host and of the earthly orders under the 285 heavens and of the inhabitants of hell. For you alone of all people gloriously and boldly resolved to bring your virginity to the creator, gave it without sin. No one like you, no 290 other bride adorned with treasure, has since come from all mankind who has sent this radiant offering to the heavenly

siþþan sende.   Forðon heht sigores fruma
295   his heah-bodan   hider gefleogan
of his mægen-þrymme   ond þe meahta sped
snude cyðan,   þæt þu Sunu Dryhtnes
þurh clæne gebyrd   cennan sceolde
monnum to miltse,   ond þe, Maria, forð
300   efne unwemme   a gehealdan.
    Eac we þæt gefrugnon,   þæt gefyrn bi þe
soð-fæst sægde   sum woð-bora
in eald-dagum,   Esaias,
þæt he wære gelæded   þær he lifes gesteald
305   in þam ecan ham   eal sceawode.
Wlat þa swa wis-fæst   witga geond þeod-land
oþ þæt he gestarode   þær gestaþelad wæs
æþelic ingong.   Eal wæs gebunden
deoran since   duru ormæte,
310   wundur-clommum bewriþen.   Wende swiðe
þæt ænig elda   æfre ne meahte
swa fæstlice   fore-scyttelsas
on ecnesse   o inhebban,
oþþe ðæs ceaster-hlides   clustor onlucan,
315   ær him Godes engel   þurh glædne geþonc
þa wisan onwrah   ond þæt word acwæð:
"Ic þe mæg secgan"   —þæt soð gewearð—
"þæt ðas gyldnan gatu   giet sume siþe
God sylf wile   Gæstes mægne
320   gefælsian,   Fæder ælmihtig,
ond þurh þa fæstan locu   foldan neosan,
ond hio þonne æfter him   ece stondað
simle singales   swa beclysed

home with a pure mind. Because of that the ruler of victory commanded his archangel to fly here from his heavenly host 295 and quickly make known to you the abundance of his powers, that you would have to bear the Son of the Lord in a virgin birth, out of compassion for mankind, and from then on keep yourself, Mary, equally unblemished always. 300

We have also learned that a certain true prophet in former days, Isaiah, said about you long ago that he had been brought to where he saw the entire abode of life in the eter- 305 nal home. Then this exceedingly wise prophet looked all over that region until he saw where a magnificent entrance was placed. The huge door was all covered with precious treasure, bound round with marvelous bonds. He was con- 310 vinced that no man could ever in eternity lift up those bars, so firmly fixed in place, or unlock the bolt of the city gate, before God's angel, with joyous spirit, explained the matter 315 and spoke these words: "I can tell you"—that came true— "that God himself, the almighty Father, intends to pass through these golden gates by the power of the Spirit at 320 some time in the future and will visit the earth through these secure locks and then, after him, they will always and forever stand eternally closed in the same way so that no

þæt nænig oþer,   nymðe nergend God,
325 hy æfre ma   eft onluceð."
Nu þæt is gefylled   þæt se froda þa
mid eagum þær   on wlatade.
Þu eart þæt weall-dor;   þurh þe waldend Frea
æne on þas eorðan   ut siðade,
330 ond efne swa þec gemette,   meahtum gehrodene,
clæne ond gecorene,   Crist ælmihtig,
swa ðe æfter him   engla Þeoden
eft unmæle   ælces þinges
lioþu-cægan bileac,   lifes brytta.
335   Iowa us nu þa are   þe se engel þe,
Godes spel-boda,   Gabriel brohte.
Huru þæs biddað   burg-sittende
þæt ðu þa frofre   folcum cyðe,
þinre sylfre sunu.   Siþþan we motan
340 an-modlice   ealle hyhtan
nu we on þæt bearn foran   breostum stariað.
Geþinga us nu   þristum wordum
þæt he us ne læte   leng owihte
in þisse deað-dene   gedwolan hyran,
345 ac þæt he usic geferge   in Fæder rice,
þær we sorg-lease   siþþan motan
wunigan in wuldre   mid weoroda God.
    Eala þu halga   heofona Dryhten,
þu mid Fæder þinne   gefyrn wære
350 efen-wesende   in þam æþelan ham.
Næs ænig þa giet   engel geworden,
ne þæs miclan   mægen-þrymmes nan
ðe in roderum up   rice biwitigað,

one else, except God the savior, will ever unlock them 325
again." Now what the wise man looked on with his own eyes
has been fulfilled. You are the door in the wall; through you
the ruling Lord on that one occasion journeyed out into this
earth and, just as almighty Christ found you, adorned with 330
virtues, pure and distinguished, so the Lord of angels, the
giver of life, closed you behind him with a key to your limbs,
immaculate afterward in every respect.

Show us now the grace which the angel, God's messenger, 335
Gabriel, brought to you. For this especially we citizens of
earth pray that you reveal to the people that consolation,
your own son. Then we all with one accord may rejoice when 340
we gaze upon the child at your breast. Intercede for us now
boldly that he not allow us to follow error any longer in this
valley of death but that he bring us into his Father's king- 345
dom, where, free from sorrow, we may then live in glory with
the God of the heavenly hosts.

O you holy Lord of the heavens, you were coexistent with
your Father long ago in that glorious home. No angel had 350
yet been created, not one of the great mighty host which
stands guard over the celestial kingdom, the glorious abode

Þeodnes þryð-gesteald   ond his þegnunga,
355   þa þu ærest wære   mid þone ecan Frean
sylf settende   þas sidan gesceaft,
brade bryten-grundas.   Bæm inc is gemæne
Heah-Gæst hleo-fæst.   We þe, hælend Crist,
þurh eað-medu   ealle biddað
360   þæt þu gehyre   hæfta stefne,
þinra nied-þiowa,   nergende God,
hu we sind geswencte   þurh ure sylfra gewill.
Habbað wræc-mæcgas   wergan gæstas,
hetlen hel-sceaþa,   hearde genyrwad,
365   gebunden bealo-rapum.   Is seo bot gelong
eall æt þe anum,   ece Dryhten.
Hreow-cearigum help,   þæt þin hider-cyme
afrefre fea-sceafte,   þeah we fæhþo wið þec
þurh firena lust   gefremed hæbben.
370   Ara nu onbehtum   ond usse yrmþa geþenc,
hu we tealtrigað   tydran mode,
hwearfiað heanlice.   Cym nu, hæleþa cyning,
ne lata to lange!   Us is lissa þearf,
þæt þu us ahredde   ond us hælo-giefe
375   soð-fæst sylle,   þæt we siþþan forð
þa sellan þing   symle moten
geþeon on þeode,   þinne willan.

    Eala seo wlitige,   weorð-mynda full,
heah ond halig,   heofon-cund Þrynes,
380   brade geblissad   geond bryten-wongas
þa mid ryhte sculon   reord-berende,
earme eorð-ware   ealle mægene
hergan healice,   nu us hælend God

of the Lord and his attendants, when you yourself, with the 355
eternal Lord, were establishing this vast creation in the be-
ginning, these broad and spacious lands. The sheltering
Holy Spirit is one with you both. Savior Christ, God of sal-
vation, we all humbly pray to you that you may hear the 360
voice of the captives, of your slaves, how we are oppressed
through our own will. The cursed spirits, hostile foes out of
hell, have cruelly confined us exiles, bound us with perni- 365
cious ropes. Eternal Lord, deliverance is completely depen-
dent on you alone. Help us in our sorrow and anxiety, so that
your advent may comfort the wretched, although through
our sinful desires we have conducted a feud against you.
Have mercy now on your servants and be mindful of our 370
miseries, how we stumble, weak in spirit, roam about miser-
ably. Come now, king of men, do not delay too long! We have
need of mercy, that you should rescue us and, righteous one, 375
give us your saving grace, so that ever afterward among the
people we may always do what is better, your will.

O beautiful heavenly Trinity, abounding in honors, ex-
alted and holy, blessed far and wide all over the spacious 380
plains, whom all speech-bearing people, wretched inhabi-
tants of earth, must rightly praise highly with all their might,
now that God the savior, true to his promise, has revealed to

wær-fæst onwrah   þæt we hine witan moton.
385 Forþon hy, dæd-hwæte,   dome geswiðde,
þæt soð-fæste   seraphinnes cynn,
uppe mid englum   a bremende,
unaþreotendum   þrymmum singað
ful healice   hludan stefne,
390 fægre feor ond neah.   Habbaþ folgoþa
cyst mid cyninge.   Him þæt Crist forgeaf,
þæt hy motan his ætwiste   eagum brucan
simle singales,   swegle gehyrste,
weorðian waldend   wide ond side,
395 ond mid hyra fiþrum   frean ælmihtges
onsyne wreað   ecan Dryhtnes,
ond ymb þeoden-stol   þringað georne
hwylc hyra nehst mæge   ussum nergende
flihte lacan   frið-geardum in.
400 Lofiað leoflicne   ond in leohte him
þa word cweþað,   ond wuldriað
æþelne ord-fruman   ealra gesceafta:
    "Halig eart þu, halig,   heah-engla brego,
soð sigores Frea;   simle þu bist halig,
405 dryhtna Dryhten!   A þin dom wunað
eorðlic mid ældum   in ælce tid
wide geweorþad.   Þu eart weoroda God,
forþon þu gefyldest   foldan ond rodoras,
wigendra hleo,   wuldres þines,
410 helm al-wihta.   Sie þe in heannessum
ece hælo,   ond in eorþan lof,
beorht mid beornum.   Þu gebletsad leofa,

us that we may know him. Because of that, the true race of 385
seraphim, brave in their deeds, confirmed in glory, exulting
always on high among the angels, sing in their untiring hosts
with loud voices, very sublimely and beautifully, far and near. 390
They have the best position with the king. Christ granted
them that, so that they may enjoy his presence with their
own eyes, may always and forever, brilliantly adorned, honor
the ruler far and wide, and with their wings they cover the 395
face of the almighty ruler, the eternal Lord, and eagerly
throng about his princely throne, whichever of them can fly
nearest to our savior in the dwellings of peace. They praise 400
the beloved one and in that brightness say these words to
him and glorify the noble source of all created things:

"You are holy, holy, ruler of archangels, true Lord of vic-
tory; you will be forever holy, Lord of lords! Your earthly 405
glory will live always among men in every age, honored far
and wide. You are the God of hosts, for you have filled the
earth and the skies with your glory, protector of warriors,
defender of all creatures. Let there be eternal greeting to 410
you in the highest and praise on earth, glorious among men.
May you live praised by us, you who, in the name of the

þe in Dryhtnes noman   dugeþum cwome
heanum to hroþre.   Þe in heahþum sie
a butan ende   ece herenis."

    Eala, hwæt þæt is wrætlic wrixl   in wera life,
þætte moncynnes   milde scyppend
onfeng æt fæmnan   flæsc unwemme,
ond sio weres friga   wiht ne cuþe,
ne þurh sæd ne cwom   sigores Agend
monnes ofer moldan;   ac þæt wæs ma cræft
þonne hit eorð-buend   ealle cuþan
þurh geryne,   hu he, rodera þrim,
heofona Heah-Frea,   helpe gefremede
monna cynne   þurh his modor hrif.
Ond swa forð-gongende   folca nergend
his forgifnesse   gumum to helpe
dæleð dogra gehwam,   Dryhten weoroda.
Forþon we hine dom-hwate   dædum ond wordum
hergen holdlice.   Þæt is healic ræd
monna gehwylcum   þe gemynd hafað,
þæt he symle oftost   ond inlocast
ond geornlicost   God weorþige.
He him þære lisse   lean forgildeð,
se gehalgoda   hælend sylfa,
efne in þam eðle   þær he ær ne cwom,
in lifgendra   londes wynne,
þær he gesælig   siþþan eardað,
ealne widan feorh   wunað butan ende.
Amen.

Lord, came to mankind, as a solace to the lowly. To you on high be eternal praise, forever without end." 415

O, how wondrous an exchange it is in the life of men, that the merciful creator of mankind received immaculate flesh from a woman, and she knew nothing of a man's embraces, nor did the triumphant Lord come through the seed of any 420 man on earth; but that was a more ingenious power than all the world's inhabitants could understand because of its mystery, how he, the majesty of the skies, the high Lord of the heavens, helped mankind through his mother's womb. And, 425 coming forth like this, the savior of the peoples, the Lord of the hosts, distributes his grace every day to help men. Therefore let us, who are eager for glory, praise him devoutly in deeds and in words. It is noble wisdom in every 430 person who has understanding that he should most often and most sincerely and most eagerly honor God always. He will give him the reward of his mercy, the blessed savior him- 435 self, in that very homeland into which he never came before, in the joy of the land of the living, where, blessed, he will dwell from then on for evermore and will live without end. Amen.

CHRIST IN JUDGMENT

Ðonne mid fere   fold-buende
se micla dæg   meahtan Dryhtnes
æt midre niht   mægne bihlæmeð,
scire gesceafte,   swa oft sceaða fæcne,
5   þeof þristlice,   þe on þystre fareð,
on sweartre niht,   sorg-lease hæleð
semninga forfehð   slæpe gebundne,
eorlas ungearwe   yfles genægeð.
Swa on Syne beorg   somod up cymeð
10   mægen-folc micel,   meotude getrywe,
beorht ond bliþe   —him weorþeð blæd gifen.
Þonne from feowerum   foldan sceatum,
þam ytemestum   eorþan rices,
englas æl-beorhte   on efen blawað
15   byman on brehtme.   Beofað middan-geard,
hruse under hæleþum.   Hlydað tosomne,
trume ond torhte,   wið tungla gong,
singað ond swinsiaþ   suþan ond norþan,
eastan ond westan,   ofer ealle gesceaft.
20   Weccað of deaðe   dryht-gumena bearn,
eall monna cynn,   to meotud-sceafte
egeslic of þære ealdan moldan,   hatað hy upp astandan
sneome of slæpe þy fæstan.   Þær mon mæg sorgende folc
gehyran hyge-geomor,   hearde gefysed,

34

Then, unexpectedly, in the middle of the night, the great day of the mighty Lord will resound powerfully over the world's inhabitants, over the bright creation, just as a deceitful robber, a thief, boldly making his way in darkness, in the black night, often suddenly takes careless, sleep-bound men by surprise and evilly attacks unprepared men. Likewise a great and mighty company will come up together to Mount Sion, faithful to the creator, radiant and happy—to them shall glory be given. Then from the four outermost corners of the world, of the kingdom of earth, resplendent angels will blow trumpets all together with a loud sound. The earth, the ground underneath men, will tremble. They will sound together, strong and clear, sing and make melody in the direction of the stars' course, from the south and north, from the east and west, over all creation. They will awaken the children of men, the terrified human race, from death, out of the ancient earth, to the decree of destiny, will command them to stand up immediately from that deep sleep. There grieving people, sad in mind, driven harshly on,

25   cearum cwiþende   cwicra gewyrhtu,
forhte afærde.   Þæt bið fore-tacna mæst
þara þe ær oþþe sið   æfre gewurde
monnum oþywed,   þær gemengde beoð
onhælo gelac   engla ond deofla,
30   beorhtra ond blacra;   weorþeð bega cyme,
hwitra ond sweartra,   swa him is ham sceapen
ungelice,   englum ond deoflum.

     Þonne semninga   on Syne beorg
suþan-eastan   sunnan leoma
35   cymeð of scyppende   scynan leohtor
þonne hit men mægen   modum ahycgan,
beorhte blican,   þonne bearn Godes
þurh heofona gehleodu   hider oðyweð.

     Cymeð wundorlic   Cristes onsyn,
40   æþel-cyninges wlite,   eastan fram roderum,
on sefan swete   sinum folce,
biter bealofullum,   gebleod wundrum,
eadgum ond earmum   ungelice.

     He bið þam godum   glæd-mod on gesihþe,
45   wlitig, wynsumlic,   weorude þam halgan,
on gefean fæger,   freond ond leof-tæl,
lufsum ond liþe   leofum monnum
to sceawianne   þone scynan wlite,
weðne mid willum,   waldendes cyme,
50   mægen-cyninges,   þam þe him on mode ær
wordum ond weorcum   wel gecwemdun.

     He bið þam yflum   egeslic ond grimlic
to geseonne,   synnegum monnum,
þam þær mid firenum cumað   forð forworhte.
55   Þæt mæg wites to wearninga   þam þe hafað wisne geþoht,

afraid, terrified, will be heard lamenting their sorrows, the 25
deeds they did while they were alive. This will be the great-
est portent ever shown to mankind before or since, where
entire throngs of angels and devils will be mixed, the bright 30
and the dark; both will come, the white and the black, as dif-
ferent as the homes that have been created for them, for an-
gels and devils.

Then suddenly on Mount Sion the radiance of the sun
will come from the southeast, from the creator, shining 35
more brightly than people can imagine in their minds, glori-
ously radiating light, when the Son of God will appear here
through the vault of the heavens. The wonderful sight of
Christ, the beautiful form of the glorious king, will come 40
from the east out of the heavens, dear to the hearts of his
own people, bitter to those full of evil, wondrously varied,
different for the blessed and the wretched.

He will be pleasant in appearance to the good, beauti- 45
ful and delightful to the holy host, lovely in his joy, friendly
and kind, will be loving and gracious for his beloved people,
those who had previously pleased him well in his heart with
their words and deeds, to behold with pleasure his shining 50
beauty, the gentle coming of the ruler, of the mighty king.

For the evil, for sinful people, for those who will come
there with wicked deeds, condemned henceforth, he will be
terrifying and fierce to behold. For anyone with a wise mind, 55

þæt se him eallunga   owiht ne ondrædeð,
se for ðære onsyne   egsan ne weorþeð
forht on ferðe,   þonne he Frean gesihð
ealra gesceafta   ondweardne faran
60 mid mægen-wundrum   mongum to þinge,
ond him on healfa gehwone   heofon-engla þreat
ymbutan farað,   æl-beorhtra scolu,
hergas haligra,   heapum geneahhe.
Dyneð deop gesceaft,   ond fore Dryhtne færeð
65 wælm-fyra mæst   ofer widne grund.
Hlemmeð hata leg,   heofonas berstað,
trume ond torhte,   tungol ofhreosað.
Þonne weorþeð sunne   sweart gewended
on blodes hiw,   seo ðe beorhte scan
70 ofer ær-woruld   ælda bearnum;
mona þæt sylfe,   þe ær moncynne
nihtes lyhte,   niþer gehreoseð
ond steorran swa some   stredað of heofone,
þurh ða strongan lyft   stormum abeatne.
75   Wile ælmihtig   mid his engla gedryht,
mægen-cyninga meotod,   on gemot cuman,
þrym-fæst þeoden.   Bið þær his þegna eac
hreþ-eadig heap.   Halge sawle
mid hyra Frean farað,   þonne folca weard
80 þurh egsan þrea   eorðan mægðe
sylfa geseceð.   Weorþeð geond sidne grund
hlud gehyred   heofon-byman stefn,
ond on seofon healfa   swogað windas,
blawað brecende   bearhtma mæste,
85 weccað ond woniað   woruld mid storme,
fyllað mid fere   foldan gesceafte.

that can serve as a warning of punishment to come, a warning that he will dread nothing at all if he will not become afraid in his heart at the terror of that sight, when he will see the Lord of all creation physically present, proceeding to judgment with many mighty wonders, and on each side of 60 him throngs of heaven's angels will fly about, a troop of radiant beings, hosts of saints, in abundant bands. The vast creation will resound and the greatest of raging fires will travel 65 over the wide world in front of the Lord. The hot flame will roar, the heavens will burst asunder, the stars, steadfast and radiant, will fall down. Then the sun, which shone brightly over the former world for the children of men, will be turned 70 dark, the color of blood; the moon itself, which formerly gave light to mankind at night, will fall down and so too the stars will be scattered from the sky through the violent air, lashed by storms.

The almighty, with his host of angels, the creator of 75 mighty kings, the glorious prince, will come to that assembly. There will also be an exultant band of his followers. Holy souls will advance with their Lord, when the guardian of mankind himself seeks out the nations of the earth, inflic- 80 ting terror. The loud sound of the heavenly trumpets will be heard all over the wide world and on seven sides the winds will howl and blow, forcing their way with the loudest of uproars, awakening and damaging the world in the storm, 85 filling earth's creatures with fear. Then a violent crash will

Ðonne heard gebrec,　hlud, unmæte,
swar ond swiðlic,　sweg-dynna mæst,
ældum egeslic,　eawed weorþeð.
90　Þær mægen werge　monna cynnes
wornum hweorfað　on widne leg,
þa þær cwice meteð　cwelmende fyr,
sume up, sume niþer,　ældes fulle.
Þonne bið untweo　þæt þær Adames
95　cyn, cearena full,　cwiþeð gesargad,
nales fore lytlum,　leode geomre,
ac fore þam mæstan　mægen-earfeþum,
ðonne eall þreo　on efen nimeð
won fyres wælm　wide tosomne,
100　se swearta lig,　sæs mid hyra fiscum,
eorþan mid hire beorgum,　ond upheofon
torhtne mid his tunglum.　Teon-leg somod
þryþum bærneð　þreo eal on an
grimme togædre.　Grornað gesargad
105　eal middan-geard　on þa mæran tid.

　　Swa se gifra gæst　grundas geondseceð;
hiþende leg　heah-getimbro
fylleð on fold-wong　fyres egsan,
wid-mære blæst　woruld mid ealle,
110　hat, heoro-gifre.　Hreosað geneahhe
tobrocene burg-weallas.　Beorgas gemeltað
ond heah-cleofu,　þa wið holme ær
fæste wið flodum　foldan sceldun,
stið ond stæð-fæst,　staþelas wið wæge,
115　wætre windendum.　Þonne wihta gehwylce,
deora ond fugla,　deað-leg nimeð;

40

be heard, loud, immense, painful and violent, the loudest of dins resounding, terrifying people. The miserable throngs 90 of mankind will go in their multitudes into the vast flame there, where the tormenting fire, full of flames, will meet the living, some up high, some below. Then without doubt the grieving kin of Adam, full of cares, will lament there, 95 a people sad, not about a small thing but about the worst of heavy miseries, when the dark surge of fire, the smoky flame, will seize, at the same time, all three together from 100 their different places, the seas with their fish, the earth with its mountains, and the bright sky above with its stars. The destroying flame will burn all three together at once, fiercely and powerfully. All the earth will mourn, grieving at that 105 awe-inspiring time.

So the devouring spirit will scour the earth; the ravaging flame, the hot blaze, greedy for slaughter, infamous, will fill the tall buildings on the earth, the entire world, with the 110 terror of fire. The broken town walls will fall completely. The mountains will melt away, as will the high cliffs, which, strong and stable, had shielded the earth and its foundations securely from the sea, from the floods, the waves and 115 the encircling water. Then the deadly fire will seize every

færeð æfter foldan   fyr-swearta leg,
weallende wiga.   Swa ær wæter fleowan,
flodas afysde,   þonne on fyr-baðe
120   swelað sæ-fiscas;   sundes getwæfde
wæg-deora gehwylc   werig swelteð;
byrneþ wæter swa weax.   Þær bið wundra ma
þonne hit ænig on mode   mæge aþencan,
hu þæt gestun ond se storm   ond seo stronge lyft
125   brecað brade gesceaft.   Beornas gretað,
wepað wanende   wergum stefnum,
heane, hyge-geomre,   hreowum gedreahte.
Seoþeð swearta leg   synne on fordonum,
ond gold-frætwe   gleda forswelgað,
130   eall ær-gestreon   eþel-cyninga.
Ðær bið cirm ond cearu,   ond cwicra gewin,
gehreow ond hlud wop   bi heofon woman,
earmlic ælda gedreag.   Þonan ænig ne mæg,
firen-dædum fah,   frið gewinnan,
135   leg-bryne losian   londes ower,
ac þæt fyr nimeð   þurh foldan gehwæt,
græfeð grimlice,   georne aseceð
innan ond utan   eorðan sceatas,
oþ þæt eall hafað   ældes leoma
140   woruld-widles wom   wælme forbærned.
      Ðonne mihtig God   on þone mæran beorg
mid þy mæstan   mægen-þrymme cymeð,
heofon-engla cyning;   halig scineð,
wuldorlic ofer weredum,   waldende God,
145   ond hine ymbutan   æþel-duguð betast,
halge here-feðan,   hlutre blicað,
eadig engla gedryht.   In-geþoncum

creature, every animal and bird; the flame, black with smoke, a seething warrior, will travel over the earth. Where waters, rushing floods, had flowed in the past, the fish of the sea will then burn in the bath of fire; separated from the sea, 120 every exhausted sea animal will die; the water will burn like wax. There will be more to marvel at than anyone can imagine, in the way that the crash and the storm and the violent air will break this creation apart, far and wide. Wretched 125 men, sad at heart and oppressed by sorrow, will wail and weep, lamenting with miserable voices. The smoky fire will make those damned by sin seething hot and the flames will swallow the gold adornments, all the ancient treasure of the 130 kings who held sway on the earth. There will be shrieking and sorrow at the terrible noise from the heavens, the struggle of the living, their regret and loud weeping, the wretched uproar of men. No one stained with evil deeds will be able to find refuge away from there or escape the burning anywhere 135 in the land, but the fire will seize everything all over the earth, will delve into it fiercely, will eagerly search the regions of the earth, inside and out, until the glare of fire will 140 have burned up in its surging heat all the defilement of earthly corruption.

Then mighty God, king of the heavenly angels, will come to that renowned mountain in his great majesty; holy and glorious, God the ruler will shine above the hosts and 145 around him the best of noble companies, the holy band, the blessed host of angels, will shine resplendently. In their

forhte beofiað   fore Fæder egsan.

Forþon nis ænig wundor   hu him woruld-monna
150   seo unclæne gecynd,   cearum sorgende,
hearde ondrede,   ðonne sio halge gecynd,
hwit ond heofon-beorht,   heag-engla mægen,
for ðære onsyne beoð   egsan afyrhte;
bidað beofiende   beorhte gesceafte
155   Dryhtnes domes.

               Daga egeslicast
weorþeð in worulde,   þonne wuldor-cyning
þurh þrym þreað   þeoda gehwylce,
hateð arisan   reord-berende
of fold-grafum,   folc anra gehwylc,
160   cuman to gemote   mon-cynnes gehwone.
Þonne eall hraðe   Adames cynn
onfehð flæsce;   wcorþeð fold-ræste
eardes æt ende.   Sceal þonne anra gehwylc
fore Cristes cyme   cwic arisan,
165   leoðum onfon   ond lic-homan,
edgeong wesan.   Hafað eall on him
þæs þe he on foldan   in fyrn-dagum,
godes oþþe gales,   on his gæste gehlod,
geara gongum,   hafað ætgædre bu,
170   lic ond sawle.   Sceal on leoht cuman
sinra weorca wlite   ond worda gemynd
ond heortan gehygd   fore heofona cyning.
    Ðonne biþ geyced   ond geedniwad
mon-cyn þurh meotud.   Micel ariseð
175   dryht-folc to dome,   siþþan deaþes bend
toleseð lif-fruma.   Lyft bið onbærned,
hreosað heofon-steorran,   hyþað wide

innermost thoughts they will tremble with fear in their terror of the Father. It is no wonder, then, that the impure human race, grieving and anxious, should be exceedingly afraid 150 when that holy race, radiant and heavenly bright, the host of archangels, will be frightened and awed in his presence; the bright creatures, trembling, will await the judgment of the 155 Lord.

It will be the most terrifying day in the world, when the glorious king in his majesty will rebuke every people and will command speech-bearing men, each and every nation, every one of mankind, to rise from their graves and to come to 160 the assembly. Then all of Adam's kin will immediately take on flesh; there will be an end of their rest and their sojourn in the earth. Then each and every one will have to rise alive as a result of Christ's coming, take on limbs and body, become young again. He will retain within himself everything, 165 both good and evil, with which he had filled his spirit in his former days on earth, over the course of the years, and he will have both body and soul together. The form of his deeds 170 and the memory of his words and the thoughts of his heart will have to come to light before the king of heaven.

Then mankind will be replenished and renewed by the creator. A great multitude will arise to judgment, when the 175 source of life dissolves the bonds of death. The sky will burn, the stars of heaven will fall, the voracious flames will rav-

gifre glede,   gæstas hweorfað
on ecne eard.   Opene weorþað
180 ofer middan-geard   monna dæde.
Ne magun hord weras,   heortan geþohtas,
fore waldende   wihte bemiþan.
Ne sindon him dæda dyrne,   ac þær bið Dryhtne cuð
on þam miclan dæge,   hu monna gehwylc
185 ær earnode   eces lifes,
ond eall ondweard   þæt hi ær oþþe sið
worhtun in worulde.   Ne bið þær wiht forholen
monna gehygda,   ac se mæra dæg
hreþer-locena hord,   heortan geþohtas,
190 ealle ætyweð.   Ær sceal geþencan
gæstes þearfe,   se þe Gode mynteð
bringan beorhtne wlite,   þonne bryne costað,
hat, heoru-gifre,   hu gehealdne sind
sawle wið synnum   fore sige-deman.
195 Ðonne sio byman stefen   ond se beorhta segn
ond þæt hate fyr   ond seo hea duguð
ond se engla þrym   ond se egsan þrea
ond se hearda dæg   ond seo hea rod,
ryht aræred   rices to beacne,
200 folc-dryht wera   biforan bonnað,
sawla gehwylce   þara þe sið oþþe ær
on lic-homan   leoþum onfengen.
Ðonne weoroda mæst   fore waldende,
ece ond edgeong,   ondweard gæð
205 neode ond nyde,   bi noman gehatne,
berað breosta hord   fore Bearn Godes,
feores frætwe.   Wile Fæder eahtan
hu gesunde suna   sawle bringen

age far and wide and spirits will go to their eternal dwelling
place. People's deeds will be exposed all over the world. Men 180
will not in the least be able to hide their hoards, the thoughts
of their hearts, in the presence of the ruler. Their deeds will
not be hidden from him, but there, on that great day, the 185
extent to which each person has merited life everlasting will
be known to the Lord and all that they did at any time in the
world will be present in witness. There people's thoughts
will not be hidden in the least, but that great day will com-
pletely reveal the treasure of their breasts, the thoughts of 190
their hearts. Anyone who intends to bring a radiant form to
God, when the hot slaughter-greedy fire, in the presence of
the victorious judge, will test how souls have been protected
from sin, will have to think beforehand of his spirit's need.

Then the sound of the trumpet and the bright standard 195
and the hot fire and the exalted troop and the host of angels
and the terror inflicted and the cruel day and the high cross,
raised upright as a symbol of power, will summon the host of 200
people forward, every one of the souls who at any time re-
ceived limbs in their bodies. Then the greatest of hordes,
called by name, everlasting and young again, will make its
way into the presence of the ruler, either willingly or under 205
compulsion, and they will bring the hoards of their hearts,
the treasures of their lives, into the presence of the Son of
God. The Father will want to assess how sound are the souls

of þam eðle   þe hi on lifdon.

210 Ðonne beoð bealde   þa þe beorhtne wlite
meotude bringað.   Bið hyra meaht ond gefea
swiðe gesæliglic   sawlum to gielde,
wuldor-lean weorca.   Wel is þam þe motun
on þa grimman tid   Gode lician.

215   Þær him sylfe geseoð   sorga mæste,
syn-fa men,   sarig-ferðe.
Ne bið him to are   þæt þær fore ell-þeodum
usses Dryhtnes rod   ondweard stondeð,
beacna beorhtast,   blode bistemed,
220 heofon-cyninges   hlutran dreore,
biseon mid swate   þæt ofer side gesceaft
scire scineð.   Sceadu beoð bidyrned
þær se leohta beam   leodum byrhteð.
Þæt þeah to teonum   geteod weorþeð,
225 þeodum to þrea,   þam þe þonc Gode
wom-wyrcende   wihte ne cuþun,
þæs he on þone halgan beam   ahongen wæs
fore mon-cynnes   man-forwyrhtu,
þær he leoflice   lifes ceapode,
230 þeoden mon-cynne,   on þam dæge,
mid þy weorðe,   þe no wom dyde
his lic-homa   leahtra firena,
mid þy usic alysde.   Þæs he eft-lean wile
þurh eorneste   ealles gemonian,
235 ðonne sio reade   rod ofer ealle
swegle scineð   on þære sunnan gyld.
On þa forhtlice   firenum fordone,
swearte syn-wyrcend,   sorgum wlitað,

48

his children bring from that land in which they lived. Then 210
those who bring a radiant form to the creator will be confi-
dent. Their power and their joy will be entirely blessed as
a recompense for their souls, a glorious reward for their
deeds. It will be well for those who will be able to please
God in that terrible time.

There sin-stained people, sad at heart, will see for them- 215
selves the greatest of sorrows. It will be of no help to them
that the cross of our Lord will stand in the presence of the
nations of the world, will shine brightly over the spacious 220
creation, the brightest of symbols, wet with blood, with the
pure blood of the king of heaven, drenched with his gore.
Shadows will disappear where that luminous tree will shine
on the people. Yet that will be made a reproach and a rebuke 225
to people, to the sinners who gave no thanks at all to God
for his being hung on that holy tree in atonement for man-
kind's evil deeds, when the prince lovingly bought life for 230
mankind, on that day for that price, he whose body, with
which he redeemed us, did no evil, committed no vicious
sins. For all of this he will want to demand recompense
sternly when the red cross will shine brightly over every- 235
thing in place of the sun. The dark sinners, damned by their
sins, will look fearfully and anxiously at it and will perceive

       geseoð him to bealwe   þæt him betst bicwom,
240   þær hy hit to gode   ongietan woldan.
    Ond eac þa ealdan wunde   ond þa openan dolg
       on hyra Dryhtne geseoð   dreorig-ferðe,
       swa him mid næglum þurhdrifan   nið-hycgende
       þa hwitan honda   ond þa halgan fet,
245   ond of his sidan swa some   swat forletan,
       þær blod ond wæter   bu tu ætsomne
       ut bicwoman   fore eagna gesyhð,
       rinnan fore rincum,   þa he on rode wæs.
       Eall þis magon him sylfe   geseon þonne,
250   open, orgete,   þæt he for ælda lufan,
       firen-fremmendra,   fela þrowade.
       Magun leoda bearn   leohte oncnawan
       hu hine lygnedon   lease on geþoncum,
       hysptun hearm-cwidum,   ond on his hleor somod
255   hyra spatl speowdon.   Spræcon him edwit,
       ond on þone eadgan   ondwlitan swa some
       hel-fuse men   hondum slogun,
       folmum areahtum   ond fystum eac,
       ond ymb his heafod   heardne gebigdon
260   beag þyrnenne,   blinde on geþoncum,
       dysge ond gedwealde.
                 Gesegun þa dumban gesceaft,
      eorðan eal-grene   ond uprodor,
      forhte gefelan   Frean þrowinga,
      ond mid cearum cwiðdun,   þeah hi cwice næron,
265   þa hyra scyppend   sceaþan onfengon
      syngum hondum.   Sunne wearð adwæsced,
      þ̄ream aþrysmed;   þa sio þeod geseah

as their destruction that which should have been most ben-
eficial for them, had they been willing to perceive it as good.   240
And, wretched in spirit, they will also see the old wounds
and the open sores on their Lord, where men with malice in
their hearts drove nails through him, through his white
hands and holy feet, and likewise shed blood from his side,   245
where blood and water both came out together before their
eyes, running in the sight of men when he was on the cross.

They will be able to see all this for themselves then, plain   250
and manifest, how he suffered much for the love of men, of
evildoers. The false children of men will easily be able to un-
derstand how they denied him in their thoughts, mocked
him with insults and spat their spittle at his face too. They   255
declared their contempt to him and hell-bound men also
struck the blessed face with their hands, with open palms
and with fists as well, and, blind in their thoughts, foolish   260
and deceived, they bent a hard crown of thorns around his
head.

They saw the dumb creation fearful, saw the earth, all
green, and the heavens above, feel for the sufferings of
the Lord and lament them sorrowfully, although they were
not alive, when his enemies seized their creator with sin-   265
ful hands. The sun was extinguished and obscured by his

in Hierusalem   god-webba cyst,
þæt ær ðam halgan   huse sceolde
270   to weorþunga   weorud sceawian,
ufan eall forbærst,   þæt hit on eorþan læg
on twam styccum.   Þæs temples segl,
wundor-bleom geworht   to wlite þæs huses,
sylf slat on tu,   swylce hit seaxes ecg
275   scearp þurhwode.   Scire burstan
muras ond stanas   monge æfter foldan,
ond seo eorðe eac,   egsan myrde,
beofode on bearhtme,   ond se brada sæ
cyðde cræftes meaht   ond of clomme bræc
280   up yrringa   on eorþan fæðm,
ge on stede scynum   steorran forleton
hyra swæsne wlite.   On þa sylfan tid
heofon hluttre ongeat   hwa hine healice
torhtne getremede   tungol-gimmum;
285   forþon he his bodan sende,   þa wæs geboren ærest
gesceafta scir-cyning.   Hwæt eac scyldge men
gesegon to soðe,   þy sylfan dæge
þe on þrowade,   þeod-wundor micel,
þætte eorðe ageaf   þa hyre on lægun!
290   Eft lifgende   up astodan
þa þe heo ær fæste   bifen hæfde,
deade bibyrgde,   þe Dryhtnes bibod
heoldon on hreþre.   Hell eac ongeat,
scyld-wreccende,   þæt se scyppend cwom,
295   waldende God,   þa heo þæt weorud ageaf,
hloþe of ðam hatan hreþre.   Hyge wearð mongum blissad,
sawlum sorge toglidene.   Hwæt eac sæ cyðde
hwa hine gesette   on sidne grund,

suffering; in Jerusalem, when the people were looking at the best of cloths, the ornament of the holy house at which the multitude used to gaze respectfully, it all broke apart from the top so that it lay on the ground in two pieces. The veil of the temple, made with wonderful colors to adorn that house, tore itself in two, as if the sharp blade of a knife had cut through it. Many shining walls and rocks broke apart across the earth and the ground also, thrown into confusion by terror, shook loudly and the vast sea showed the power of its strength and fiercely broke away from its bonds, up onto the bosom of the earth, and the stars, shining in their appointed places, lost their gracious beauty. At that same time heaven clearly recognized who it was who had fixed it in its place on high, bright with starry jewels; for it sent its messenger when the radiant king of creation was first born. How great a wonder did even guilty men truly see, on that same day on which he suffered, that the earth gave up those who lay within it! Alive again, they arose, those whom it had tightly confined, the buried dead who had kept the Lord's command in their hearts. Hell, which punishes the guilty, also recognized that the creator had come, the ruling God, when it surrendered its band, its troop, out of its hot bosom. Many people's minds were gladdened, sorrow dispelled from their souls. How clearly even the sea showed who had set it

tir-meahtig cyning,   forþon he hine tredne him
300   ongean gyrede,   þonne God wolde
ofer sine yðe gan!   Eah-stream ne dorste
his Frean fet   flode bisencan,
ge eac beamas onbudon   hwa hy mid bledum sceop,
—monge, nales fea—   ða mihtig God
305   on hira anne gestag   þær he earfeþu
geþolade fore þearfe   þeod-buendra,
laðlicne deað   leodum to helpe.
Ða wearð beam monig   blodigum tearum
birunnen under rindum,   reade ond þicce;
310   sæp wearð to swate.   Þæt asecgan ne magun
fold-buende   þurh frod gewit,
hu fela þa onfundun   þa gefelan ne magun
Dryhtnes þrowinga,   deade gesceafte.
Þa þe æþelast sind   eorðan gecynda,
315   ond heofones eac   heah-getimbro,
eall fore þam anum   unrot gewearð,
forht afongen.   Þeah hi ferð-gewit
of hyra æþelum   ænig ne cuþen,
wendon swa þeah wundrum,   þa hyra waldend for
320   of lic-homan.
                Leode ne cuþon,
mod-blinde men,   meotud oncnawan,
flintum heardran,   þæt hi Frea nerede
fram hell-cwale   halgum meahtum,
alwalda God.   Þæt æt ærestan
325   fore-þoncle men   from fruman worulde
þurh wis gewit,   witgan Dryhtnes,
halge hige-gleawe,   hæleþum sægdon,
oft, nales æne,   ymb þæt æþele bearn,

in its place in the spacious earth, the king of glorious might,
for it made itself firm for him to walk on when God wished   300
to walk over its waves! The sea did not dare to submerge
its Lord's feet in the water and the trees—many of them,
not just a few—also proclaimed who had created them with
their fruit, when mighty God mounted on one of them, on   305
which he suffered hardships for the benefit of mankind, a
horrible death to help people. There, under its bark, many a
tree was wet all over with bloody tears, red and abundant;
the sap was turned to blood. Human beings, with their wise   310
understanding, cannot tell how much these dead creatures,
which cannot feel, experienced the sufferings of the Lord.
The noblest of earth's species and also of heaven's high halls   315
all became sorrowful, gripped by fear on account of that one
man. Although they did not have any spiritual understand-
ing as their birthright, they nevertheless apprehended it mi-
raculously when their ruler departed from his body.   320

But people, men whose minds were blind, harder than
flint, did not know how to acknowledge their creator, did
not know that the Lord, the all-ruling God, had saved them
from the torment of hell with his holy powers. From the
beginning, from the origin of the world, men with fore-   325
thought, the prophets of the Lord, with their wise under-
standing, their holy and discerning minds, told people of-
ten, not just once, about that noble child, told them that

ðæt se earcnan-stan   eallum sceolde
330   to hleo ond to hroþer   hæleþa cynne
weorðan in worulde,   wuldres agend,
eades ord-fruma,   þurh þa æþelan cwenn.

Hwæs weneð se   þe mid gewitte nyle
gemunan þa mildan   meotudes lare,
335   ond eal ða earfeðu   þe he fore ældum adreag,
forþon þe he wolde   þæt we wuldres eard
in ecnesse   agan mosten?
Swa þam bið grorne   on þam grimman dæge
domes þæs miclan,   þam þe Dryhtnes sceal,
340   deað-firenum forden,   dolg sceawian,
wunde ond wite.   On werigum sefan
geseoð sorga mæste,   hu se sylfa cyning
mid sine lic-homan   lysde of firenum
þurh milde mod,   þæt hy mostun man-weorca
345   tome lifgan,   ond tires blæd
ecne agan.   Hy þæs eðles þonc
hyra waldende   wihte ne cuþon;
forþon þær to teonum   þa tacen geseoð
orgeatu on Gode,   ungesælge,
350   þonne Crist siteð   on his cynestole,
on heah-setle,   heofon-mægna God,
Fæder ælmihtig.   Folca gehwylcum
scyppend scinende   scrifeð bi gewyrhtum,
eall æfter ryhte,   rodera waldend.

355   Ðonne beoð gesomnad   on þa swiþran hond
þa clænan folc,   Criste sylfum
gecorene bi cystum,   þa ær sinne cwide georne
lustum læstun   on hyra lif-dagum,

that precious stone was destined to become a shelter and a   330
comfort for all mankind in the world, the lord of glory, the
author of happiness, through that noble queen.

What is he thinking of, who is not willing to bear in mind
the gentle teaching of the creator and all of the hardships   335
which he endured for the sake of men, because he wished
that we might obtain a dwelling in heaven forever? On that
terrible day of the great judgment it will be wretched for the
man who, corrupted by deadly sins, will have to look upon   340
the sores, wounds and torment of the Lord. Sad at heart,
they will see the greatest of sorrows, how the king himself,
out of his merciful heart, redeemed them from sins with his
body, so that they might live free from wicked deeds and ob-   345
tain the eternal happiness of glory. They did not give thanks
at all to their ruler for this home; therefore the wretched
ones will see these signs there, plainly visible on God, as
reproaches to them, when Christ sits on his royal seat, his   350
throne, God of the heavenly powers, the almighty Father.
The shining creator, ruler of the heavens, will pass sentence
on each one of the people according to their merits, all in
accordance with justice.

Then the pure people will be assembled on the right-hand   355
side, chosen by Christ himself according to their excellence,
those who had eagerly and gladly fulfilled his commands in

ond þær wom-sceaþan   on þone wyrsan dæl
360   fore scyppende   scyrede weorþað;
hateð him gewitan   on þa winstran hond,
sigora soð-cyning,   synfulra weorud.
Þær hy arasade   reotað ond beofiað
fore Frean forhte,   swa fule swa gæt,
365   unsyfre folc,   arna ne wenað.
    Ðonne bið gæsta dom   fore Gode sceaden
wera cneorissum,   swa hi geworhtun ær.
Þær bið on eadgum   eð-gesyne
þreo tacen somod,   þæs þe hi hyra þeodnes wel
370   wordum ond weorcum   willan heoldon.
An is ærest   orgeate þær
þæt hy fore leodum   leohte blicaþ,
blæde ond byrhte   ofer burga gesetu.
Him on scinað   ær-gewyrhtu,
375   on sylfra gehwam   sunnan beorhtran.
Oþer is to eacan   ondgete swa some,
þæt hy him in wuldre witon   waldendes giefe,
ond on seoð,   eagum to wynne,
þæt hi on heofon-rice   hlutre dreamas
380   eadge mid englum   agan motun.
Ðonne bið þridde,   hu on þystra bealo
þæt gesælige weorud   gesihð þæt fordone
sar þrowian,   synna to wite,
weallendne lig,   ond wyrma slite
385   bitrum ceaflum,   byrnendra scole.
Of þam him aweaxeð   wynsum gefea,
þonne hi þæt yfel geseoð   oðre dreogan,
þæt hy þurh miltse   meotudes genæson.
Ðonne hi þy geornor   Gode þonciað

their lifetimes, and there before the creator the evildoers
will be assigned to the worse part; the true king of victories   360
will command them, the troop of sinners, to go to his left-
hand side. Exposed there, they will wail and tremble, fearful
before the Lord, unclean people as foul as goats, despairing   365
of mercy.

Then, in the presence of God, the judgment of souls of
generations of mankind will be decided, as they had de-
served. There, upon the blessed, three signs of how they
fully observed their prince's will in their words and in their
deeds will be easily visible, all together. The first one evident   370
there is that they will shine with light, glory and radiance
over the city dwellings, there in front of the people. Their
former deeds will shine in each of them, brighter than the   375
sun. The second is also obvious in the same way, that in their
glory they will be conscious of the ruler's grace in them-
selves and will see, to their eyes' delight, that they are al-
lowed to possess bright joys in heaven, blessed among the   380
angels. Then the third will be that the blessed company will
see how the damned are suffering pain in the torment of
darkness, as a punishment for their sins, will see the rag-
ing flame, the serpents biting with fierce jaws, the host   385
of those who are burning. From that a delightful happi-
ness will spring up in them when they see others endure
that misery from which they, by the creator's mercy, were
preserved. Then they will thank God all the more eagerly

390 blædes ond blissa   þe hy bu geseoð,
þæt he hy generede   from nið-cwale
ond eac forgeaf   ece dreamas;
bið him hel bilocen,   heofon-rice agiefen.
Swa sceal gewrixled   þam þe ær wel heoldon
395 þurh mod-lufan   meotudes willan.
      Ðonne bið þam oþrum   ungelice
willa geworden.   Magon weana to fela
geseon on him selfum,   synne genoge,
atol-earfoða   ær gedenra.
400 Þær him sorgendum   sar oðclifeð,
þroht þeod-bealu,   on þreo healfa.
An is þara   þæt hy him yrmþa to fela,
grim helle fyr,   gearo to wite
ondweard seoð;   on þam hi awo sculon,
405 wræc winnende,   wærgðu dreogan.
Ðonne is him oþer   earfeþu swa some
scyldgum to sconde,   þæt hi þær scoma mæste
dreogað fordone.   On him Dryhten gesihð
nales feara sum   firen-bealu laðlic,
410 ond þæt æll-beorhte   eac sceawiað
heofon-engla here,   ond hæleþa bearn,
ealle eorð-buend   ond atol deofol,
mircne mægen-cræft,   man-womma gehwone
magun þurh þa lic-homan,   leahtra firene,
415 geseon on þam sawlum.   Beoð þa syngan flæsc
scandum þurhwaden   swa þæt scire glæs,
þæt mon yþæst mæg   eall þurhwlitan.
Ðonne bið þæt þridde   þearfendum sorg
cwiþende cearo,   þæt hy on þa clænan seoð,
420 hu hi fore god-dædum   glade blissiað,

for their glory and happiness because they will see both that 390
he has rescued them from violent destruction and also that
he has given them eternal joys; hell will be closed to them
and the kingdom of heaven given to them. This is how those
who had fully observed the will of the creator out of deep 395
love shall be recompensed.

Then for those others his will shall come to pass in a dif-
ferent way. They will be able to see too many evils in them-
selves, sins in abundance, the horror of the iniquities they
had committed. Pain, dire, terrible torment, will cling fast 400
to them in their sorrow there, in three ways. One of them
is that they will see before them innumerable miseries, the
fierce fire of hell, ready to punish them; in it they will have
to endure damnation forever, undergoing punishment. 405
Then there is a second tribulation likewise, ignominious for
the guilty, that the damned will endure there the greatest of
shames. The Lord will see in them many a repulsive sinful
evil, and the radiant host of heavenly angels and the children 410
of men, all the inhabitants of earth, and the terrible devil
will also examine their dark strength, will be able to see
through their bodies every guilty stain, the wicked sinful
deeds on their souls. Their sinful flesh will be ignominiously 415
penetrated like that clear glass through which one can see
completely with the greatest of ease. Then the third cause
of distress for those miserable people will be the plaintive
sorrow, that they will look upon the pure, how the joyous 420

þa hy, unsælge,   ær forhogdun
to donne   þonne him dagas læstun,
ond be hyra weorcum   wepende sar
þæt hi ær freolice   fremedon unryht.

425 Geseoð hi þa betran   blæde scinan;
ne bið him hyra yrmðu   an to wite,
ac þara oþerra   ead to sorgum,
þæs þe hy swa fægre gefeon   on fyrn-dagum
ond swa ænlice   anforletun,

430 þurh leaslice   lices wynne,
earges flæsc-homan   idelne lust.
Þær hi ascamode,   scondum gedreahte,
swiciað on swiman;   syn-byrþenne,
firen-weorc berað,   on þæt þa folc seoð.

435   Wære him þonne betre   þæt hy bealo-dæde,
ælces unryhtes,   ær gescomeden
fore anum men,   eargra weorca,
Godes bodan sægdon   þæt hi to gyrne wiston
firen-dæda on him.   Ne mæg þurh þæt flæsc se scrift

440 geseon on þære sawle,   hwæþer him mon soð þe lyge
sagað on hine sylfne,   þonne he þa synne bigæð.
Mæg mon swa þeah gelacnigan   leahtra gehwylcne,
yfel unclæne,   gif he hit anum gesegð,
ond nænig bihelan mæg   on þam heardan dæge

445 wom unbeted,   ðær hit þa weorud geseoð.
    Eala, þær we nu magon   wraþe firene
geseon on ussum sawlum,   synna wunde,
mid lic-homan   leahtra gehygdu,
eagum unclæne   in-geþoncas,

450 ne þæt ænig mæg   oþrum gesecgan
mid hu micle elne   æghwylc wille

62

exult because of the good deeds which the wretched had scorned to do in their lifetimes, and the weeping grief concerning their own deeds, that they had willingly done what was wrong. They will see those better people shining in 425 glory; not only will their own miseries be a torment for them, but the happiness of those others will also be a sorrow because in former days they had lost such delightful and incomparable joys because of the false pleasures of the body, 430 the vain lust of their vile flesh. There, ashamed and oppressed by the ignominy, they will wander around dizzily; they will bear the burden of their sins and wicked deeds, which the people will look at.

It would be better for them then if they had been 435 ashamed of their evil deeds, of every wrong and of their vile actions, earlier, in front of one man, if they had told God's messenger that they knew too well the wicked deeds within them. The confessor cannot see through the flesh into the 440 soul, whether someone is telling him the truth or a lie about himself when he recounts his sins. Nevertheless, every vice and impure evil can be healed, if it is told to just one person, but no one can hide a sinful stain for which he has not atoned on that harsh day when the multitude will see it. 445

O, if we could see now with our bodily eyes the malignant crimes in our souls, the wounds of sin, our vicious intentions, our impure innermost thoughts, no one can tell any- 450 one else how vigorously, with every art, everyone would wish

þurh ealle list   lifes tiligan,
feores forhtlice,   forð aðolian,
syn-rust þwean   ond hine sylfne þrean,
455   ond þæt wom ærran   wunde hælan,
þone lytlan fyrst   þe her lifes sy,
þæt he mæge fore eagum   eorð-buendra
unscomiende   eðles mid monnum
brucan bysmer-leas,   þendan bu somod
460   lic ond sawle   lifgan mote.

Nu we sceolon georne   gleawlice þurhseon
usse hreþer-cofan   heortan eagum,
innan uncyste.   We mid þam oðrum ne magun,
heafod-gimmum,   hyge-þonces ferð
465   eagum þurhwlitan   ænge þinga,
hwæþer him yfel þe god   under wunige,
þæt he on þa grimman tid   Gode licie,
þonne he ofer weoruda gehwylc   wuldre scineð
of his heah-setle   hlutran lege.
470   Þær he fore englum   ond fore el-þeodum
to þam eadgestum   ærest mæðleð,
ond him swæslice   sibbe gehateð,
heofona heah-cyning;   halgan reorde
frefreð he fægre   ond him friþ beodeð,
475   hateð hy gesunde   ond gesenade
on eþel faran   engla dreames,
ond þæs to widan feore   willum neotan:
"Onfoð nu mid freondum   mines Fæder rice
þæt eow wæs ær woruldum   wynlice gearo,
480   blæd mid blissum,   beorht eðles wlite,
hwonne ge þa lif-welan   mid þam leofstum,

to strive fearfully for life and existence, to persevere longer,
in order to wash away the foulness of sin and to correct him-
self and heal the stain of his earlier wound in the short span   455
of his lifetime here, so that, unashamed before the eyes of
the world, he may be able to enjoy his home among people,
free from dishonor, while body and soul may both live to-   460
gether.

Now we must eagerly and keenly see into our breasts to
the vices within with the eyes of our hearts. With our other
eyes, with the sight of the jewels in our heads, we cannot
penetrate the spirit of our minds' thoughts at all, whether   465
evil or good dwell within, so that it may be pleasing to God
in that terrible time, when he will shine in glory on his
throne, above each of the hosts, with a pure flame. There,   470
before the angels and before the nations of the world, he
will speak first to the most blessed, and the high King of
heaven will kindly promise them peace; in his holy voice he
will gently comfort them and proclaim peace to them, will   475
command them to go, unharmed and blessed, to the home
of angelic joy and to enjoy it forever with delight: "Receive
now, together with your friends, my Father's kingdom, glory   480
and happiness, the radiant beauty of the heavenly home,

swase swegl-dreamas, geseon mosten.

Ge þæs earnedon þa ge earme men,

woruld-þearfende, willum onfengun

485 on mildum sefan. Ðonne hy him þurh minne noman

eað-mode to eow arna bædun,

þonne ge hyra hulpon ond him hleoð gefon,

hingrendum hlaf ond hrægl nacedum;

ond þa þe on sare seoce lagun,

490 æfdon unsofte, adle gebundne,

to þam ge holdlice hyge staþeladon

mid modes myne. Eall ge þæt me dydon,

ðonne ge hy mid sibbum sohtun, ond hyra sefan

trymedon

forð on frofre. Þæs ge fægre sceolon

495 lean mid leofum lange brucan."

Onginneð þonne to þam yflum ungelice

wordum mæðlan þe him bið on þa wynstran hond,

þurh egsan þrea, alwalda God.

Ne þurfon hi þonne to meotude miltse gewenan,

500 lifes ne lissa, ac þær lean cumað

werum bi gewyrhtum worda ond dæda,

reord-berendum; sceolon þone ryhtan dom

anne geæfnan, egsan fulne.

Bið þær seo miccle milts afyrred

505 þeod-buendum, on þam dæge,

þæs ælmihtigan, þonne he yrringa

on þæt fræte folc firene stæleð

laþum wordum, hateð hyra lifes riht

ondweard ywan þæt he him ær forgeaf

510 syngum to sælum.

Onginneð sylf cweðan,

which was joyfully made ready for you before the ages, in anticipation of the time when you might see the riches of life among the most beloved, the sweet joys of heaven. You earned this when you willingly received poor and needy people charitably. When in my name the humble asked you for   485
acts of kindness, you helped them and gave them shelter, bread to the hungry and clothing to the naked; and with all your hearts you kindly strengthened the spirits of those who   490
lay sick in pain, suffering severely, bound by disease. You did all that for me when you visited them with kindness and fortified their spirits with consolation. You shall long enjoy the   495
reward for this, splendidly with my beloved ones."

Then omnipotent God will proceed to speak words to the evil, who will be on his left-hand side, in a different way, inflicting terror. They need not expect mercy then from the creator or life or favor, but rewards will come to speech-   500
bearing men there according to their deserts, their words and deeds; they will have to endure the one just judgment, one full of terror. On that day the great mercy of the al-   505
mighty will be withdrawn from mankind, when, with hostile words, he will angrily accuse the shameful people of their wicked deeds, will command them to give an account of the current state of their lives, those lives which he had given them, the sinners, for their happiness.   510

The almighty Lord himself will begin to speak, as if he

swa he to anum sprece,   ond hwæþre ealle mæneð,
firen-synnig folc,   Frea ælmihtig:
"Hwæt ic þec mon   minum hondum
ærest geworhte,   ond þe ondgiet sealde!
515 Of lame ic þe leoþe gesette,   geaf ic ðe lifgendne gæst,
arode þe ofer ealle gesceafte,   gedyde ic þæt þu onsyn
                                                            hæfdest,
mæg-wlite me gelicne.   Geaf ic þe eac meahta sped,
welan ofer wid-londa gehwylc;   nysses þu wean ænigne
                                                            dæl,
ðystra þæt þu þolian sceolde.   Þu þæs þonc ne wisses.
520 Þa ic ðe swa scienne   gesceapen hæfde,
wynlicne geworht,   ond þe welan forgyfen
þæt ðu mostes wealdan   worulde gesceaftum,
ða ic þe on þa fægran   foldan gesette
to neotenne   neorxna-wonges
525 beorhtne blæd-welan,   bleom scinende,
ða þu lifes word   læstan noldes,
ac min bibod bræce   be þines bonan worde.
Fæcnum feonde   furþor hyrdes,
sceþþendum scaþan,   þonne þinum scyppende.
530 Nu ic ða ealdan race   anforlæte,
hu þu æt ærestan   yfle gehogdes,
firen-weorcum forlure   þæt ic ðe to fremum sealde.
Þa ic þe goda swa fela   forgiefen hæfde
ond þe on þam eallum   eades to lyt
535 mode þuhte,   gif þu meahte sped
efen-micle Gode   agan ne moste,
ða þu of þan gefean   fremde wurde,
feondum to willan   feor aworpen.

were speaking to just one person, but he will mean all of them, the wicked people: "It was with my own hands that I made you human in the beginning and gave you understanding! I formed your limbs from clay, I gave you a living spirit, 515 showed favor to you above all other creatures, and I caused you to have a shape and form like mine. I also gave you an abundance of powers and prosperity throughout every spacious land; you knew nothing of any grief or darkness that you would have to suffer. You were not thankful for this. When I had created you so bright, had made you so beauti- 520 ful and had given you prosperity so that you might rule the creatures of the world, when I had set you on the fair earth to enjoy the bright abundant riches of paradise, shining col- 525 orfully, then you were not willing to observe my life-giving words but you broke my command at the bidding of your slayer. You obeyed the deceitful devil, the harmful enemy, more than your creator. Now I will omit the old account of 530 how you resolved upon evil in the beginning and, by your wicked deeds, lost what I had given you for your benefit. When I had given you so many good things and when it seemed to you in your heart that there was too little hap- 535 piness in all these things if you could not possess an abundance of power equal to that of God, then you were deprived of those joys, banished far off, to the delight of the fiends.

Neorxna-wonges wlite   nyde sceoldes
540   agiefan geomor-mod,   gæsta eþel,
      earg ond unrot,   eallum bidæled
      dugeþum ond dreamum,   ond þa bidrifen wurde
on þas þeostran weoruld,   þær þu þolades siþþan
      mægen-earfeþu   micle stunde,
545   sar ond swar gewin   ond sweartne deað,
      ond æfter hin-gonge   hreosan sceoldes
      hean in helle,   helpendra leas.
      Ða mec ongon hreowan   þæt min hond-geweorc
      on feonda geweald   feran sceolde,
550   mon-cynnes tuddor   man-cwealm seon,
      sceolde uncuðne   eard cunnian,
      sare siþas.   Þa ic sylf gestag,
      maga in modor,   þeah wæs hyre mægden-had
      æghwæs onwalg.   Wearð ic ana geboren
555   folcum to frofre.   Mec mon folmum biwond,
bipeahte mid þearfan wædum,   ond mec þa on þeostre
                                            alegde
      biwundenne mid wonnum claþum.   Hwæt ic þæt for
                                       worulde geþolade!
Lytel þuhte ic leoda bearnum;   læg ic on heardum stane,
cild-geong on crybbe.   Mid þy ic þe wolde cwealm afyrran,
560   hat helle bealu,   þæt þu moste halig scinan
      eadig on þam ecan life,   forðon ic þæt earfeþe wonn.

      "Næs me for mode,   ac ic on magu-geoguðe
      yrmþu geæfnde,   arleas lic-sar,
      þæt ic þurh þa   wære þe gelic,
565   ond þu meahte   minum weorþan
      mæg-wlite gelic,   mane bidæled.

70

Sad at heart, wicked and sorrowful, you were compelled to   540
give up the beauty of paradise, the homeland of souls, de-
prived of all its blessings and joys, and then you were driven
into this dark world where since then you have suffered
great hardships for a long time, pain and heavy toil and dark   545
death, and after your departure you have had to fall, humili-
ated, into hell, bereft of helpers. Then I began to regret that
my handiwork would have to pass into the power of fiends,
that the offspring of mankind would have to see death, ex-   550
perience an unknown dwelling place and painful fortunes.
Then I myself descended as a son into his mother, yet her
virginity was altogether uncorrupted. I alone was born as a   555
consolation to mankind. I was wrapped by people's hands,
clothed in the garments of a pauper, and then laid in dark-
ness, wrapped in dark clothes. How I suffered that for the
sake of the world! I seemed small to people; I lay on a hard
stone, childlike in the manger. By doing this I intended to
take death, the fiery torment of hell, away from you so that   560
you might shine, holy and blessed, in eternal life, because I
had suffered that hardship.

"It was not because of pride in me, but, as a young
man, I endured miseries, merciless pain in my body so
that, through it, I might be like you and you might become   565
like me in appearance, released from guilt. And my head

Ond fore monna lufan   min þrowade
heafod hearm-slege,   hleor geþolade;
oft ondlata   ar-leasra spatl
570   of muðe onfeng,   man-fremmendra.
Swylce hi me geblendon   bittre tosomne
unswetne drync   ecedes ond geallan.
Ðonne ic fore folce onfeng   feonda geniðlan;
fylgdon me mid firenum,   fæhþe ne rohtun,
575   ond mid sweopum slogun.   Ic þæt sar for ðe
þurh eað-medu   eall geþolade,
hosp ond heard-cwide.   Þa hi hwæsne beag
ymb min heafod   heardne gebygdon,
þream biþrycton,   se wæs of þornum geworht.
580   Ða ic wæs ahongen   on heanne beam,
rode gefæstnad;   ða hi ricene mid spere
of minre sidan   swat ut guton,
dreor to foldan,   þæt þu of deofles þurh þæt
nyd-gewalde   genered wurde.
585   Ða ic, womma leas,   wite þolade,
yfel earfeþu,   oþ þæt ic anne forlet
of minum lic-homan   lifgendne gæst.
      "Geseoð nu þa feorh-dolg   þe ge gefremedun ær
on minum folmum   ond on fotum swa some,
590   þurh þa ic hongade   hearde gefæstnad;
meaht her eac geseon   orgete nu gen
on minre sidan   swatge wunde.
Hu þær wæs unefen racu   unc gemæne!
Ic onfeng þin sar   þæt þu gesælig moste
595   mines eþel-rices   eadig neotan,
    ond þe mine deaðe   deore gebohte
þæt longe lif   þæt þu on leohte siþþan,

suffered and my cheek endured harmful blows for love of
men; my face was often subjected to spitting from the 570
mouths of the impious and the sinful. Moreover they cruelly
mixed a bitter drink of vinegar and gall for me. Then in front
of that people I endured the hatred of my enemies; they
hounded me violently, had no misgivings about their hostil-
ity, and they beat me with whips. I humbly endured all that 575
pain for you, the scorn and abuse. Then they bent a sharp
hard crown around my head, pressed it on painfully; it was
made of thorns. Then I was hung on a high tree, fastened to 580
the cross; then straightaway with a spear they shed blood
from my side, made my blood flow to the ground, so that by
this you would be rescued from the devil's tyranny. Then, 585
sinless, I endured torments, evil sufferings, until I released
my one living soul from my body.

"Now look at the deadly wounds which you formerly
made in my hands and also in my feet, by which I hung cru- 590
elly fastened; you can also see here, still plainly visible in my
side, the bloody wound. How unequal the reckoning was
there between the two of us! I took on your pain so that you
might enjoy my homeland, happy and blessed, and with my 595
death I paid dearly for long life for you so that you might

      wlitig, womma leas,   wunian mostes.

      Læg min flæsc-homa   in foldan bigrafen,

600   niþre gehyded,   se ðe nængum scod,

in byrgenne,   þæt þu meahte beorhte uppe

      on roderum wesan,   rice mid englum.

      "For hwon forlete þu   lif þæt scyne

      þæt ic þe for lufan   mid mine lic-homan

605   heanum to helpe   hold gecypte?

      Wurde þu þæs gewit-leas   þæt þu waldende

      þinre alysnesse   þonc ne wisses?

      Ne ascige ic nu   owiht bi þam bitran

      deaðe minum   þe ic adreag fore þe,

610   ac forgield me þin lif,   þæs þe ic iu þe min

      þurh woruld-wite   weorð gesealde;

      ðæs lifes ic manige   þe þu mid leahtrum hafast

      ofslegen synlice   sylfum to sconde.

      For hwan þu þæt sele-gescot   þæt ic me swæs on þe

615   gehalgode,   hus to wynne,

      þurh firen-lustas,   fule synne,

      unsyfre bismite   sylfes willum?

      Ge þu þone lic-homan   þe ic alysde me

      feondum of fæðme,   ond þa him firene forbead,

620   scyld-wyrcende   scondum gewemdest.

    For hwon ahenge þu mec hefgor   on þinra honda rode

      þonne iu hongade?   Hwæt me þeos heardra þynceð!

      Nu is swærra mid mec   þinra synna rod

      þe ic unwillum   on beom gefæstnad,

625   þonne seo oþer wæs   þe ic ær gestag,

      willum minum,   þa mec þin wea swiþast

      æt heortan gehreaw,   þa ic þec from helle ateah,

      þær þu hit wolde sylfa   siþþan gehealdan.

then live in the light, beautiful and sinless. My body, which harmed no one, lay buried in the ground, hidden below in 600 the grave, so that you could be up in heaven, radiantly exalted among the angels.

"Why have you lost that bright life which, for love of you, I graciously bought with my body to help you in your 605 wretched plight? Did you become so foolish that you were not thankful to your ruler for your salvation? I ask nothing now for that bitter death of mine which I suffered for you but pay me back for your life, that life for which I once gave 610 mine as the price, in my torment on earth; I demand the life which you have sinfully killed with your vices, to your own shame. Why did you, with your sinful desires, with foul sin, filthily and of your own free will, defile the tabernacle, the 615 house, which I had consecrated in you as my own, for my delight? And, with your evildoing, you shamefully defiled the body which I had redeemed for myself from the fiends' 620 clutches and which I had then forbidden to sin. Why did you hang me more heavily on the cross of your hands than I once hung? How much harder this seems to me! The cross of your sins, on which I am unwillingly fastened, is heavier for me now than was that other one on which I willingly as- 625 cended before, when your misery most grieved my heart, when I led you out of hell, provided that you yourself were

Ic wæs on worulde wædla   þæt ðu wurde welig in
                                        heofonum;
630   earm ic wæs on eðle þinum   þæt þu wurde eadig on
                                        minum.
    Þa ðu þæs ealles   ænigne þonc
    þinum nergende   nysses on mode.
    Bibead ic eow   þæt ge broþor mine
    in woruld-rice   wel aretten
635   of þam æhtum   þe ic eow on eorðan geaf,
    earmra hulpen.   Earge ge þæt læstun;
    þearfum forwyrndon   þæt hi under eowrum þæce
                                        mosten
    in gebugan,   ond him æghwæs oftugon,
    þurh heardne hyge,   hrægles nacedum,
640   moses mete-leasum.   Þeah hy him þurh minne noman
    werge, won-hale,   wætan bædan,
    drynces gedreahte,   duguþa lease,
    þurste geþegede,   ge him þriste oftugon.
    Sarge ge ne sohton,   ne him swæslic word
645   frofre gespræcon,   þæt hy þy freoran hyge
    mode gefengen.   Eall ge þæt me dydan,
to hynþum heofon-cyninge.   Þæs ge sceolon hearde
                                        adreogan
    wite to widan ealdre,   wræc mid deoflum geþolian."
    Ðonne þær ofer ealle   egeslicne cwide
650   sylf sigora weard,   sares fulne,
    ofer þæt fæge folc   forð forlæteð,
    cwið to þara synfulra   sawla feþan:
    "Farað nu, awyrgde,   willum biscyrede
    engla dreames,   on ece fir
655   þæt wæs Satane   ond his gesiþum mid,

willing to preserve that subsequently. I was a pauper in the world, so that you might be wealthy in heaven; I was wretched in your homeland, so that you might be blessed in mine. Then you were not at all thankful to your savior in your heart for all this. I commanded you to comfort my brothers well on earth with those worldly possessions which I gave you, commanded you to help the wretched. You have fulfilled that very badly; you denied to the poor that they might enter under your roof and, in your hardheartedness, you withheld everything from them, clothing from the naked and food from those who had none. Even when the weary and the sick, with no means and tormented by the need for a drink, consumed by thirst, asked for water in my name, you shamelessly withheld it from them. You did not visit the grieving nor did you speak a kind word of consolation to them, so that they might gain a happier state of mind in their hearts. You did all that in contempt of me, the heavenly king. For that you will have to suffer punishment painfully forever and ever, endure exile among the devils."

Then the guardian of victories himself will pass a terrifying sentence there, full of pain, upon them all, upon that damned people, and will say to the band of sinful souls: "Depart now, you cursed, deprived by your own will of the joy of angels, into the eternal fire that was prepared for Satan and

630

635

640

645

650

655

77

deofle gegearwad   ond þære deorcan scole,
hat ond heoro-grim.   On þæt ge hreosan sceolan!"
   Ne magon hi þonne gehynan   heofon-cyninges bibod,
rædum birofene.   Sceolon raþe feallan
660 on grimne grund   þa ær wiþ Gode wunnon.
Bið þonne rices weard   reþe ond meahtig,
yrre ond egesful.   Ondweard ne mæg
on þissum fold-wege   feond gebidan.

   Swapeð sige-mece   mid þære swiðran hond
665 þæt on þæt deope dæl   deofol gefeallað
in sweartne leg,   synfulra here
under foldan sceat,   fæge gæstas
on wraþra wic,   womfulra scolu
werge to forwyrde   on wite-hus,
670 deað-sele deofles.   Nales Dryhtnes gemynd
siþþan gesecað,   synne ne aspringað,
þær hi leahtrum fa,   lege gebundne,
swylt þrowiað.   Bið him syn-wracu
ondweard undyrne;   þæt is ece cwealm.
675 Ne mæg þæt hate dæl   of heoloð-cynne
in sin-nehte   synne forbærnan
to widan feore,   wom of þære sawle,
ac þær se deopa seað   dreorge fedeð,
grund-leas giemeð   gæsta on þeostre,
680 æleð hy mid þy ealdan lige,   ond mid þy egsan forste,
wraþum wyrmum   ond mid wita fela,
frecnum feorh-gomum,   folcum scendeð.
   Þæt we magon eahtan   ond on an cweþan,
soðe secgan,   þæt se sawle weard,
685 lifes wisdom,   forloren hæbbe,

his companions, for the devil and that evil troop, flaming and fierce. You will have to sink down into that!"

Then, deprived of anything that might benefit them, they will not be able to scorn the command of the heavenly king. Those who formerly fought against God will be forced 660 to fall quickly into the terrible abyss. The guardian of the kingdom will be stern and mighty then, angry and terrible. No enemy on this earth will be able to remain in his presence.

With his right hand he will swing the sword of victory so that the devils will fall into that deep pit, into the dark 665 flame, the multitude of the sinful down under the surface of the earth, the damned spirits into the dwelling of the evil ones, the accursed troop of the defiled into damnation, into the house of torment, the devil's hall of death. Afterward 670 they will never come into the Lord's recollection at all, nor will they cease from sin in that place where, stained by vice and hemmed in by fire, they will suffer death. The punishment for their sins will be clearly revealed before them; that is eternal torment. That flaming abyss will nevermore, in the 675 eternal night, be able to burn the sin out of the dwellers in hell, the defilement out of their souls, but there the deep bottomless pit will feed the sorrowful with affliction, will care for the spirits in the darkness, will consume them with 680 the ancient flame and with the terror of extreme cold and will injure the multitude with fierce serpents and with many torments, with its fearful, fatal jaws.

We can reflect on this and say with one accord, telling the truth, that he who is not concerned now about whether his 685

se þe nu ne giemeð   hwæþer his gæst sie
earm þe eadig,   þær he ece sceal
æfter hin-gonge   ham-fæst wesan.
Ne bisorgað he   synne to fremman,
690   won-hydig mon,   ne he wihte hafað
hreowe on mode   þæt him Halig Gæst
losige þurh leahtras   on þas lænan tid.
Ðonne man-sceaða   fore meotude forht,
deorc on þam dome standeð,   ond deaðe fah,
695   wommum awyrged,   bið se wær-loga
fyres afylled.   Feores unwyrðe,
egsan geþread,   ondweard Gode
won ond wlite-leas   hafað werges bleo,
facen-tacen feores.
                        Ðonne firena bearn
700   tearum geotað,   þonne þæs tid ne biþ,
synne cwiþað;   ac hy to sið doð
gæstum helpe,   ðonne þæs giman nele
weoruda waldend,   hu þa wom-sceaþan
hyra eald-gestreon   on þa openan tid
705   sare greten.   Ne biþ þæt sorga tid
leodum alyfed,   þæt þær læcedom
findan mote,   se þe nu his feore nyle
hælo strynan   þenden her leofað.
Ne bið þær ængum godum   gnorn ætywed,
710   ne nængum yflum wel,   ac þær æghwæþer
anfealde gewyrht   ondweard wigeð.
Forðon sceal onettan,   se þe agan wile
lif æt meotude,   þenden him leoht ond gæst
somod-fæst seon.   He his sawle wlite
715   georne bigonge   on Godes willan,

spirit will be wretched or blessed, about where he will have
to establish his home eternally after his death, has lost the
guardian of his soul, the wisdom of life. That reckless man
does not regret committing sins, nor does he have any sor- 690
row at all in his heart that the Holy Spirit is lost to him
through his vices in this transitory time. Then the dark evil
sinner will stand frightened before God at the judgment,
and, marked by death, cursed with sins, that traitor will be 695
filled with fire. Unworthy of life, overwhelmed by terror,
dark and ugly in the presence of the creator, he will have the
appearance of a criminal, a sign of the evil of his life.

Then, when it is the wrong time for it, the children of 700
wickedness will shed tears and will lament their sins; but
they will do it too late to help their spirits, when the ruler
of hosts will not care about how the evildoers may bitterly
weep for the treasure they had of old, at that time when ev- 705
erything will be revealed. That time of sorrows will not be
granted to people in order that he, who is not willing to gain
salvation for his spirit now while he is living here, may find a
remedy. No good person will show sorrow there, or an evil
one pleasure, but each of them present will get just what he
deserves.

Therefore he who may wish to obtain life from the cre-
ator must hurry, while life and spirit are joined together
in him. Let him eagerly look after the beauty of his soul in 715
accordance with the will of God and be careful of his words

ond wær weorðe   worda ond dæda,
þeawa ond geþonca,   þenden him þeos woruld,
sceadum scriþende,   scinan mote,
þæt he ne forleose   on þas lænan tid
720   his dreames blæd   ond his dagena rim,
ond his weorces wlite   ond wuldres lean,
þætte heofones cyning   on þa halgan tid
soð-fæst syleð   to sigor-leanum
þam þe him on gæstum   georne hyrað.
725   Þonne heofon ond hel   hæleþa bearnum,
fira feorum,   fylde weorþeð.
Grundas swelgað   Godes ondsacan,
lacende leg   laðwende men,
þreað þeod-sceaþan,   ond no þonan læteð
730   on gefean faran   to feorhnere,
ac se bryne bindeð   bid-fæstne here,
feoð firena bearn.   Frecne me þinceð
þæt þas gæst-berend   giman nellað,
men on mode,   þonne man fremmað,
735   hwæt him se waldend   to wrace gesette,
laþum leodum.   Þonne lif ond deað
sawlum swelgað.   Bið susla hus
open ond oðeawed   að-logum ongean;
ðæt sceolon fyllan   firen-georne men
740   sweartum sawlum.   Þonne synna to wrace
scyldigra scolu   ascyred weorþeð
heane from halgum   on hearm-cwale.
Ðær sceolan þeofas   ond þeod-sceaþan,
lease ond forlegene,   lifes ne wenan,
745   ond man-sworan   morþor-lean seon,
heard ond heoro-grim.   Þonne hel nimeð

and deeds, his conduct and his thoughts, while this world, wandering in the shadows, may shine for him, so that in this transitory time he may not lose the glory of his joy and the number of his days and the splendor of his deeds and the glorious reward that the true king of heaven will give in that holy time as the rewards of victory to those who eagerly obey him in their spirits. 720

Then heaven and hell will be filled with the children of men, with people's souls. The depths and the leaping flame will swallow up God's enemies, the evil people, will punish his archenemies, and will never let them go from there joyfully to their salvation, but the burning will imprison the multitude, fix them in their places, and persecute the children of wickedness. It seems dangerous to me that people possessed of spirits are not willing to be concerned in their hearts, when they commit a crime, about what the ruler has ordained as retribution for them, for evil people. Then life and death will swallow up the souls. The house of torments will be open and revealed to receive those who break their oaths; sin-loving people shall fill it with their dark souls. Then in punishment for their sins the troop of the guilty and the despised will be separated from the holy, banished into painful destruction. That is where thieves and arch-criminals must go, the false and the adulterers, with no hope of life, and where perjurers will see the cruel and deadly fierce reward of sin. Then hell will take the throng of 725 730 735 740 745

wær-leasra weorud,   ond hi waldend giefeð
feondum in forwyrd;   fa þrowiað
ealdor-bealu egeslic.   Earm bið se þe wile
750 firenum gewyrcan,   þæt he fah scyle
from his scyppende   ascyred weorðan
æt dom-dæge   to deaðe niþer,
under helle cinn   in þæt hate fyr,
under liges locan,   þær hy leomu ræcað
755 to bindenne   ond to bærnenne
ond to swingenne   synna to wite.
Ðonne Halig Gæst   helle biluceð,
morþer-husa mæst,   þurh meaht Godes,
fyres fulle,   ond feonda here,
760 cyninges worde.   Se bið cwealma mæst
deofla ond monna!   Þæt is dream-leas hus,
ðær ænig ne mæg   ower losian
caldan clommum.   Hy bræcon cyninges word,
beorht boca bibod;   forþon hy abidan sceolon
765 in sin-nehte,   sar ende-leas,
firen-dædum fa,   forð þrowian,
ða þe her forhogdun   heofon-rices þrym.
    Þonne þa gecorenan   fore Crist berað
beorhte frætwe.   Hyra blæd leofað
770 æt dom-dæge,   agan dream mid Gode
liþes lifes,   þæs þe alyfed bið
haligra gehwam   on heofon-rice.
Ðæt is se eþel   þe no geendad weorþeð,
ac þær symle forð   synna lease
775 dream weardiað,   Dryhten lofiað,
leofne lifes weard,   leohte biwundne,
sibbum bisweðede,   sorgum biwerede,

faithless people and the ruler will hand them over to the fiends, damning them; accursed, they will suffer terrible deadly torment. That man will be wretched who is willing to 750 deserve by his sins that, accursed, he will have to be banished from his creator on the day of judgment to death below, subject to the race of hell, into that fierce fire, under locks of flame, where they will present their limbs to be 755 bound and burned and whipped as punishment for their sins. Then, by the power of God, at the word of the king, the Holy Spirit will shut up hell, the greatest of torment houses, filled with fire, and the troop of fiends. That will be the 760 greatest of torments for devils and people! That is a joyless house, where no one can ever escape from its cold clutches. They broke the word of the king, the clear command of books; therefore they who scorned the glory of the heavenly 765 kingdom here will have to dwell in eternal night, stained with sinful deeds, suffer endless pain continually.

Then the chosen ones will bring their radiant treasures before Christ. Their glory will endure on judgment day and 770 they will obtain the joy of a peaceful life with God, which will be granted to each of the holy in the kingdom of heaven. That is the homeland which will never come to an end but there, from then on, free of sin, they will possess heavenly 775 joy, will praise the Lord, the beloved guardian of life, encircled by light, enfolded in peace, protected against sorrows,

dreamum gedyrde,　　Dryhtne gelyfde.

Awo to ealdre　　engla gemanan

780　　brucað mid blisse,　　beorhte mid lisse,

freogað folces weard.　　Fæder ealra geweald

hafað ond healdeð　　haligra weorud.

Ðær is engla song,　　eadigra blis;

þær is seo dyre　　Dryhtnes onsien

785　　eallum þam gesælgum　　sunnan leohtra.

Ðær is leofra lufu,　　lif butan deaðe,

glæd gumena weorud,　　gioguð butan ylde,

heofon-duguða þrym,　　hælu butan sare,

ryht-fremmendum　　ræst butan gewinne,

790　　dom-eadigra　　dæg butan þeostrum,

beorht blædes full,　　blis butan sorgum,

frið freondum bitweon　　forð butan æfestum,

gesælgum on swegle,　　sib butan niþe

halgum on gemonge.　　Nis þær hungor ne þurst,

795　　slæp ne swar leger,　　ne sunnan bryne,

ne cyle ne cearo,　　ac þær cyninges giefe

awo brucað　　eadigra gedryht,

weoruda wlite-scynast,　　wuldres mid Dryhten.

honored with joy, dear to the Lord. Forever they will enjoy
the fellowship of angels in bliss, radiant in delight, and will   780
love the guardian of mankind. The Father will have power
over all and will rule the host of the holy ones.

There will be the singing of angels there, the happiness of
the blessed; there will be the dear face of the Lord, brighter   785
than the sun for all of those fortunate ones. There will be
the love of dear ones, life without death, a joyous troop of
men, youth without age, the glory of the heavenly hosts,
health without sickness, rest without toil for those who
have acted rightly, the bright day of the glorious ones with   790
no darkness, full of splendor, happiness without sorrows,
peace among friends with no envy from then on, blessed in
the heavens, love without hostility among the saints. There
will be no hunger or thirst there, or sleep or painful illness or   795
the burning of the sun or cold or sorrow but there the host
of the blessed, the most beautiful of multitudes, will forever
enjoy the grace of the king, glory with the Lord.

GUTHLAC A

Se bið gefeana fægrast   þonne hy æt frymðe gemetað,
engel ond seo eadge sawl.   Ofgiefeþ hio þas eorþan wynne,
forlæteð þas lænan dreamas   ond hio wiþ þam lice
                                        gedæleð.
Ðonne cwið se engel   —hafað yldran had—
5 greteð gæst oþerne,   abeodeð him Godes ærende:
   "Nu þu most feran   þider þu fundadest
   longe ond gelome;   ic þec lædan sceal.
   Wegas þe sindon weþe,   ond wuldres leoht
   torht ontyned.   Eart nu tid-fara
10 to þam halgan ham."
                     Þær næfre hreow cymeð,
   eder-gong fore yrmþum,   ac þær biþ engla dream,
   sib ond gesælignes,   ond sawla ræst,
   ond þær a to feore   gefeon motun,
   dryman mid Dryhten,   þa þe his domas her
15 æfnað on eorþan.   He him ece lean
   healdeð on heofonum,   þær se hyhsta
   ealra cyninga cyning   ceastrum wealdeð.
   Ðæt sind þa getimbru   þe no tydriað,
   ne þam fore yrmþum   þe þær in wuniað
20 lif aspringeð,   ac him bið lenge hu sel;
   geoguþe brucað   ond Godes miltsa.
   Þider soð-fæstra   sawla motun
   cuman æfter cwealme,   þa þe her Cristes æ

That will be the most delightful of joys when they meet at first, the angel and the blessed soul. It will give up earth's pleasures, abandon these transitory joys, and part from the body. Then the angel will speak—he has the older and senior rank—one spirit will welcome the other, proclaim God's message to it: "Now you may go to that place toward which you have been striving constantly for a long time; I shall lead you. The paths will be pleasant for you and the bright light of heavenly glory will be revealed. You are now a timely traveler to that holy home."

Sorrow, departure forced by miseries, will never occur there, but the joy of angels will be there, peace and happiness and a resting-place for souls, and those who fulfill his laws here on earth may be happy there for evermore, rejoicing with the Lord. He keeps an eternal reward for them in the heavens, where the highest king of all kings rules the cities. Those are the buildings that will never decay, nor does life fail because of miseries for those who dwell there, but for them the longer they are there, the better; they enjoy youth and God's favor. The souls of the just, those who teach and carry out Christ's law and praise him, will be

lærað ond læstað   ond his lof rærað;

25 oferwinnað þa awyrgdan gæstas,   bigytað him wuldres
                                                                    ræste,

hwider sceal þæs monnes   mod astigan,
ær oþþe æfter,   þonne he his ænne her
gæst bigonge,   þæt se Gode mote,
womma clæne,   in geweald cuman.

30   Monge sindon   geond middan-geard
hadas under heofonum   þa þe in haligra
rim arisað.   We þæs ryht magun
æt æghwylcum   anra gehyran,
gif we halig bebodu   healdan willað;

35 mæg no snottor guma   sæle brucan
godra tida   ond his gæste forð
weges willian.   Woruld is onhrered;
colaþ Cristes lufu.   Sindan costinga
geond middan-geard   monge arisene,

40 swa þæt geara iu   Godes spel-bodan
wordum sægdon   ond þurh witedom
eal anemdon,   swa hit nu gongeð.
Ealdað eorþan blæd   æþela gehwylcre,
ond of wlite wendað   wæstma gecyndu;

45 bið seo siþre tid   sæda gehwylces
mætræ in mægne.   Forþon se mon ne þearf
to þisse worulde   wyrpe gehycgan,
þæt he us fægran   gefean bringe
ofer þa niþas   þe we nu dreogað,

50 ærþon endien   ealle gesceafte
ða he gesette   on siex dagum,
ða nu under heofonum   hadas cennað,

permitted to come there after death; they will overcome the   25
accursed spirits and attain for themselves the repose of
heaven, that place to which a person's spirit is destined to
ascend, sooner or later, when he cares for his one and only
soul here, so that he may come, free from defilements, into
the power of God.

There are many ranks throughout the world under the   30
heavens which appear among the number of the saints. Ac-
cordingly, we can rightly belong to any one of them, if we
are willing to observe the holy commandments; a wise man   35
cannot enjoy the happiness of good times now and desire
the journey onward for his spirit. The world is disturbed;
love of Christ grows cold. Many tribulations have appeared
throughout the world, just as long ago God's messengers de-   40
clared and announced in their prophecies all that is happen-
ing now. The earth's abundance is growing old in every one
of its excellent qualities, and all kinds of fruit decrease in
beauty; everything that grows is weaker in strength in this   45
later time. Therefore a person need not hope for improve-
ment in this world, that it may bring us pleasant joys af-
ter the troubles which we now endure, before all creatures,   50
big and small, which he formed in six days and which now
reproduce their kinds under the heavens, reach the end of

micle ond mæte.　Is þes middan-geard
dalum gedæled.　Dryhten sceawað
55　hwær þa eardien　þe his æ healden;
gesihð he þa domas　dogra gehwylce
wonian ond wendan　of woruld-ryhte
ða he gesette　þurh his sylfes word.
He fela findeð;　fea beoð gecorene.
60　Sume him þæs hades　hlisan willað
wegan on wordum　ond þa weorc ne doð.
Bið him eorð-wela　ofer þæt ece lif
hyhta hyhst,　se gehwylcum sceal
fold-buendra　fremde geweorþan.
65　Forþon hy nu hyrwað　haligra mod,
ða þe him to heofonum　hyge staþeliað,
witon þæt se eðel　ece bideð
ealra þære mengu　þe geond middan-geard
Dryhtne þeowiað　ond þæs deoran ham
70　wilniað bi gewyrhtum.　Swa þas woruld-gestreon
on þa mæran god　bimutad weorþað,
ðonne þæt gegyrnað　þa þe him Godes egsa
hleonaþ ofer heafdum.　Hy þy hyhstan beoð
þrymme geþreade,　þisses lifes
75　þurh bibodu brucað　ond þæs betran forð
wyscað ond wenaþ.　Wuldres bycgað:
sellað ælmessan,　earme frefrað,
beoð rum-mode　ryhtra gestreona,
lufiað mid lacum　þa þe læs agun,
80　dæghwam Dryhtne þeowiaþ;　he hyra dæde sceawað.
Sume þa wuniað　on westennum,
secað ond gesittað　sylfra willum
hamas on heolstrum;　hy ðæs heofon-cundan

their lives. This earth is divided into parts. The Lord observes where people who uphold his law dwell; every day he 55 sees judgments weakening and departing from the justice of the world which he established by his own words. He finds many; few will be chosen.

Some people want to obtain the fame of this status by 60 means of their words but do not do the deeds. Earthly wealth, which must become alien to every human being, is the highest hope for them, above eternal life. Therefore 65 they now despise the spirits of the saints who fix their minds on heaven, who know that the eternal home awaits all the multitude who serve the Lord throughout the world and desire to go to that dear home deservedly. So these worldly 70 treasures will be exchanged for that sublime good when they, who are guided by the fear of God, yearn for it. They are chastised by that highest majesty, live in accordance with his commandments, and continually wish and hope for the 75 better life. They buy heavenly glory: give alms, console the wretched, are liberal in giving of their lawful wealth, show love by gifts to those who have less, serve the Lord daily; he 80 observes their deeds.

Some who dwell in the wilderness seek out and occupy homes in hidden places of their own accord; they await the heavenly abode. He who begrudges them their

boldes bidað.   Oft him brogan to
85   laðne gelædeð   se þe him lifes ofonn,
eaweð him egsan,   hwilum idel wuldor;
brægd-wis bona   hafað bega cræft,
eahteð an-buendra.   Fore him englas stondað,
gearwe mid gæsta wæpnum,   beoþ hyra geoca gemyndge,
90   healdað haligra feorh,   witon hyra hyht mid Dryhten.
Þæt synd þa gecostan cempan   þa þam cyninge þeowað,
se næfre þa lean alegeð   þam þe his lufan adreogeð.

Magun we nu nemnan   þæt us neah gewearð
þurh haligne   had gecyþed,
95   hu Guðlac his   in Godes willan
mod gerehte,   man eall forseah,
eorðlic æþelu,   upp gemunde
ham in heofonum.   Him wæs hyht to þam,
siþþan hine inlyhte   se þe lifes weg
100   gæstum gcarwað,   ond him giefe sealde
engel-cunde,   þæt he ana ongan
beorg-seþel bugan,   ond his blæd Gode
þurh eað-medu   ealne gesealde,
ðone þe he on geoguðe   bigan sceolde
105   worulde wynnum.   Hine weard biheold
halig of heofonum,   se þæt hluttre mod
in þæs gæstes god   georne trymede.
Hwæt we hyrdon oft   þæt se halga wer
in þa ærestan   ældu gelufade
110   frecnessa fela!   Fyrst wæs swa þeana
in Godes dome,   hwonne Guðlace
on his ondgietan   engel sealde
þæt him sweðraden   synna lustas.

lives often brings evil danger to them, sometimes presenting 85
them with something to terrify them, at other times with
the danger of vain glory; the deceitful killer has skill in both
and persecutes hermits. Angels stand before them, equipped
with spiritual weapons, guarding the lives of the saints,
mindful of their safety, knowing that their hope is in the 90
Lord. Those are the tried champions who serve the king,
whose rewards for those who show their love for him are
never ending.

Now we can tell what was made known near to us in a
holy manner, how Guthlac directed his spirit according to 95
the will of God, rejected all evil and earthly nobility, was
mindful of his home up in heaven. That was the object of
his hope after he who prepares the way of life for souls had
enlightened him and had given him angelic grace so that 100
he began to inhabit a hill-dwelling alone and with humility
gave to God all the wealth which in his youth he was accus-
tomed to devote to the pleasures of the world. A holy guard- 105
ian from heaven watched over him, who eagerly strength-
ened that pure heart in spiritual goodness.

How often have we heard that the holy man loved many
dangerous things in his youth! However, that period of time 110
was in God's power, until he should grant Guthlac an angel
in his mind so that his sinful desires should cease. That time

Tid wæs toweard;   hine twegen ymb
115   weardas wacedon,   þa gewin drugon,
engel Dryhtnes   ond se atela gæst.
Nalæs hy him gelice   lare bæron
in his modes gemynd   mongum tidum.
Oþer him þas eorþan   ealle sægde
120   læne under lyfte,   ond þa longan god
herede on heofonum,   þær haligra
sawla gesittað   in sigor-wuldre
Dryhtnes dreamas;   he him dæda lean
georne gieldeð,   þam þe his giefe willað
125   þicgan to þonce   ond him þas woruld
uttor lætan   þonne þæt ece lif.
Oþer hyne scyhte,   þæt he sceaðena gemot
nihtes sohte   ond þurh neþinge
wunne æfter worulde,   swa doð wræc-mæcgas
130   þa þe ne bimurnað   monnes feore
þæs þe him to honda   huþe gelædeð,
butan hy þy reafe   rædan motan.
    Swa hy hine trymedon   on twa healfa
oþ þæt þæs gewinnes   weoroda Dryhten
135   on þæs engles dom   ende gereahte.
Feond wæs geflymed;   siþþan frofre gæst
in Guðlaces   geoce gewunade,
lufade hine ond lærde   lenge hu geornor,
þæt him leofedan   londes wynne,
140   bold on beorhge.   Oft þær broga cwom
egeslic ond uncuð,   eald-feonda nið,
searo-cræftum swiþ.   Hy him sylf hyra
onsyn ywdon,   ond þær ær fela
setla gesæton,   þonan sið tugon

98

was approaching; two guardians who struggled against each 115
other watched over him, the angel of the Lord and the terri-
ble demon. Many times they brought totally different teach-
ings into his mind's thoughts. One told him that all the earth
under the sky was transitory and praised the lasting good 120
in heaven where in triumphant glory the souls of the saints
possess the joys of the Lord; he gladly gives a reward for
their deeds to those who are willing to receive his grace 125
gratefully and to give up this world more totally than that
eternal life. The other urged him that he should seek out
bands of thieves by night and through daring strive for
worldly things, as outcasts do who do not care about the life 130
of the man who brings plunder into their hands, unless
thereby they may have possession of the spoils.

In this manner they urged him on both sides until the
Lord of hosts directed an end to the contest as the angel de- 135
creed. The fiend was put to flight; after that the comfort-
ing spirit continued as a help to Guthlac, showed him love,
and instructed him ever more diligently so that the plea-
sures of that land delighted him, his dwelling on the hill. 140
Terror often showed itself there, frightening and strange,
the hostility of the old enemies, powerful in their treacher-
ous arts. They displayed their own forms to him, for they
had previously occupied many dwelling places there, from
which they had made their way in flight through the air,

145 wide waðe, wuldre byscyrede,
  lyft-lacende. Wæs seo londes stow
  bimiþen fore monnum, oþ þæt meotud onwrah
  beorg on bearwe, þa se bytla cwom
  se þær haligne ham arærde,
150 nales þy he giemde þurh gitsunga
  lænes lif-welan, ac þæt lond Gode
  fægre gefreoþode, siþþan feond oferwon
  Cristes cempa.
       He gecostad wearð
  in gemyndigra monna tidum,
155 ðara þe nu gena þurh gæstlicu
  wundor weorðiað ond his wisdomes
  hlisan healdað, þæt se halga þeow
  elne geeode, þa he ana gesæt
  dygle stowe. Ðær he Dryhtnes lof
160 reahte ond rærde; oft þurh reorde abead,
  þam þe þrowera þeawas lufedon,
  Godes ærendu, þa him gæst onwrah
  lifes snyttru, þæt he his lic-homan
  wynna forwyrnde ond woruld-blissa,
165 seftra setla ond symbel-daga,
  swylce eac idelra eagena wynna,
  gierelan gielplices. Him wæs Godes egsa
  mara in gemyndum þonne he menniscum
  þrymme æfter þonce þegan wolde.

170   God wæs Guðlac! He in gæste bær
  heofon-cundne hyht, hælu geræhte
  ecan lifes. Him wæs engel neah,
  fæle freoðu-weard, þam þe feara sum

wandering far and wide, cut off from heavenly glory. That spot in the country had been concealed from people until the creator revealed the hill in the wood, when the builder came who constructed his holy home there, not out of greed, because he cared for transitory earthly wealth, but so that he might defend that land well for God after Christ's champion had overcome the fiend. 145 150

He was tested in the times of people who remember, people who still, on account of his spiritual miracles, honor and preserve the fame of his wisdom, which the holy servant won courageously when he occupied that remote place alone. There he recited and glorified praise of God; he often proclaimed God's message in speech to those who loved the martyrs' way of life when the spirit had revealed the wisdom of life to him so that he denied his body pleasures and worldly joys, comfortable seats and days of banqueting, as well as the vain pleasures of the eyes and of ostentatious dress. There was too great a fear of God in his thoughts for him to wish to devote himself to human glory for the sake of pleasure. 155 160 165

Guthlac was good! In his spirit he possessed heavenly hope and he attained the salvation of eternal life. An angel, a faithful guardian of peace, was close by him, when, one of 170

mearc-lond gesæt.   Þær he mongum wearð
175 bysen on Brytene,   siþþan biorg gestah
eadig oretta,   ondwiges heard.
Gyrede hine georne   mid gæstlicum
wæpnum ond wædum,   wong bletsade,
him to ætstælle   ærest aræerde
180 Cristes rode.   Þær se cempa oferwon
frecnessa fela,   frome wurdun monge
Godes þrowera;   we þæs Guðlace
deor-wyrðne dæl   Dryhtne cennað.
He him sige sealde   ond snyttru-cræft,
185 mund-byrd meahta,   þonne mengu cwom
feonda fær-scytum   fæhðe ræran.
Ne meahton hy æfeste   anforlætan,
ac to Guðlaces   gæste gelæddun
frasunga fela.   Him wæs fultum neah;
190 engel hine elne trymede,   þonne hy him yrre hweopan
frecne fyres wylme.   Stodan him on feðe-hwearfum,
cwædon þæt he on þam beorge   byrnan sceolde
ond his lic-homan   lig forswelgan,
þæt his earfeþu   eal gelumpe
195 mod-cearu mægum,   gif he monna dream
of þam orlege   eft ne wolde
sylfa gesecan,   ond his sibbe ryht
mid moncynne   maran cræfte
willum bewitigan,   lætan wræce stille.
200   Swa him yrsade,   se for ealle spræc
feonda mengu.   No þy forhtra wæs
Guðlaces gæst,   ac him God sealde
ellen wiþ þam egsan   þæt þæs eald-feondes

only a few, he occupied the borderlands. He was an example   175
to many in Britain when the blessed warrior climbed the hill
there, strong in resistance. He eagerly armed himself with
spiritual weapons and armor and consecrated the place, first
raising up Christ's cross as his standard. Where the war-   180
rior overcame many dangers, many of God's martyrs have
become strong; in respect to that, we declare in Guthlac a
share precious to the Lord. He gave him victory and wis-
dom, the protection of his power, when a throng of fiends   185
came to stir up a feud with their unexpected shots. They
could not let go of their malice, but brought many temp-
tations to Guthlac's spirit. Help was close by him; the an-   190
gel strengthened him with courage when, in their anger,
they threatened him with fierce surging flames. They stood
around him in droves, said that he would have to burn on
that hill and that flame would devour his body, so that all his
suffering and sorrow would fall upon his kinsmen, if he him-   195
self was not willing to seek out earthly happiness again, away
from this battle, and willingly attend to his kinship duties
among mankind with greater ability, giving up the hostility.

So the one who spoke for all the throng of fiends raged   200
at him. Guthlac's spirit was not any the more frightened at
this, but God gave him courage against the terror so that

scyldigra scolu   scome þrowedon;
205   wæron teon-smiðas   tornes fulle,
cwædon þæt him Guðlac   eac Gode sylfum
earfeþa mæst   ana gefremede,
siþþan he for wlence   on westenne
beorgas bræce,   þær hy bidinge,
210   earme ondsacan,   æror mostun
æfter tintergum   tidum brucan,
ðonne hy of waþum   werge cwoman
restan ryne-þragum,   rowe gefegon;
wæs him seo gelyfed   þurh lytel fæc.
215   Stod seo dygle stow   Dryhtne in gemyndum;
idel ond æmen,   eþel-riehte feor,
bad bisæce   betran hyrdes.
To þon eald-feondas   ondan noman,
swa hi singales   sorge dreogað.
220   Ne motun hi on eorþan   eardes brucan,
ne hy lyft swefeð   in leoma ræstum,
ac hy hleo-lease   hama þoliað,
in cearum cwiþað,   cwealmes wiscað,
willen þæt him Dryhten   þurh deaðes cwealm
225   to hyra earfeða   ende geryme.
Ne mostun hy Guðlaces   gæste sceþþan,
ne þurh sar-slege   sawle gedælan
wið lic-homan,   ac hy lige-searwum
ahofun hearm-stafas,   hleahtor alegdon,
230   sorge seofedon,   þa hi swiðra oferstag
weard on wonge.   Sceoldon wræc-mæcgas
ofgiefan gnornende   grene beorgas.
Hwæþre hy þa gena,   Godes ondsacan,
sægdon sar-stafum,   swiþe geheton,

the old enemy's guilty troop was put to shame; the evildoers   205
were full of fury, said that Guthlac alone, besides God him-
self, had inflicted the greatest hardship upon them, after he,
out of arrogance, had taken by storm the hills in the wilder-
ness, where formerly the wretched enemies had sometimes   210
been allowed to possess an abode after their torments,
when, weary from their wandering, they came to rest for a
while and were glad of the quiet; it was permitted to them
for a short period.

That remote spot was in the Lord's thoughts; empty and   215
desolate, far from his rightful homeland, it awaited the
claim of a better guardian. The old enemies became envi-
ous at that since they continually endure sorrow. They are   220
not permitted to possess a home on earth nor does the air
lull them into resting their limbs, but, shelterless, they lack
homes, lament amid their sorrows, wish for death, desire
that the Lord, by means of the penalty of death, should clear   225
the way to an end to their sufferings. They were not permit-
ted to harm Guthlac's spirit nor to part his soul from his
body with a painful blow but they stirred up troubles with
their lying tricks, put an end to laughter, sighed in sorrow   230
when the more powerful guardian defeated them in that
place. Lamenting, the outcasts had to leave the green hills.

Yet God's opponents still spoke with bitter words, vowed

235 þæt he deaþa gedal   dreogan sceolde,
gif he leng bide   laþran gemotes,
hwonne hy mid mengu   maran cwome,
þa þe for his life   lyt sorgedon.
Guðlac him ongean þingode,   cwæð þæt hy gielpan ne
                þorftan
240 dædum wið Dryhtnes meahtum.   "Þeah þe ge me deað
                gehaten,
mec wile wið þam niþum genergan   se þe eowrum nydum
                wealdeð.
An is ælmihtig God,   se mec mæg eaðe gescyldan;
he min feorg freoþað.   Ic eow fela wille
soþa gesecgan.   Mæg ic þis setl on eow
245 butan earfeðum   ana geðringan.
Ne eam ic swa fea-log,   swa ic eow fore stonde,
monna weorudes,   ac me mara dæl
in god-cundum   gæst-gerynum
wunað ond weaxeð,   se me wraþe healdeð.
250 Ic me anum her   eaðe getimbre
hus ond hleonað;   me on heofonum sind
lare gelonge.   Mec þæs lyt tweoþ
þæt me engel to   ealle gelædeð
spowende sped   spreca ond dæda.
255 Gewitað nu, awyrgde,   werig-mode,
from þissum earde   þe ge her on stondað,
fleoð on feor-weg.   Ic me frið wille
æt Gode gegyrnan;   ne sceal min gæst mid eow
gedwolan dreogan,   ac mec Dryhtnes hond
260 mundað mid mægne.   Her sceal min wesan
eorðlic eþel,   nales eower leng."

fiercely that he would have to suffer death if he were to wait 235
any longer for a more hostile encounter when they should
come with a bigger company who would care little for his
life. Guthlac addressed them, said that they need not boast
of their deeds against the Lord's powers. "Though you 240
threaten me with death, he who ordains the hardships you
suffer will save me from these attacks. There is one almighty
God, who can easily protect me; he will preserve my life. I
intend to tell you many true things. Without difficulty and 245
on my own I can gain this place from you by force. As I stand
before you, I am not lacking in a host of men, for a greater
force dwells and grows within me, in a spiritual mystery
which preserves me with its support. Here I shall easily 250
build a house and shelter for myself alone; instruction comes
from the heavens to me. I have little doubt that an angel will
bring me in abundance every success in words and deeds.
Depart now, you who are accursed and downcast, from 255
where you are standing here, flee to distant parts! I intend to
ask God eagerly for protection; my spirit shall not commit
error with you, but the Lord's hand will guard me with its 260
power. My earthly home shall be here, yours no longer."

Ða wearð breahtm hæfen.   Beorg ymbstodan
hwearfum wræc-mæcgas.   Woð up astag,
cearfulra cirm.   Cleopedon monige,
265 feonda fore-sprecan,   firenum gulpon:
"Oft we ofersegon   bi sæm tweonum
þeoda þeawas,   þræce modigra,
þara þe in gelimpe   life weoldon.
No we ofer-hygdu   anes monnes
270 geond middan-geard   maran fundon.
Ðu þæt gehatest   þæt ðu ham on us
gegan wille,   eart ðe Godes yrming.
Bi hwon scealt þu lifgan,   þeah þu lond age?
Ne þec mon hider   mose fedeð;
275 beoð þe hungor ond þurst   hearde gewinnan,
gif þu gewitest   swa wilde deor
ana from eþele.   Nis þæt onginn wiht!
Geswic þisses setles!   Ne mæg þec sellan ræd
mon gelæran   þonne þeos mengu eall.
280 We þe beoð holde   gif ðu us hyran wilt,
oþþe þec ungearo   eft gesecað
maran mægne,   þæt þe mon ne þearf
hondum hrinan,   ne þin hra feallan
wæpna wundum.   We þas wic magun
285 fotum afyllan;   folc inðriceð
meara þreatum   ond mon-farum.
Beoð þa gebolgne,   þa þec breodwiað,
tredað þec ond tergað,   ond hyra torn wrecað,
toberað þec blodgum lastum;   gif þu ure bidan þencest,
290 we þec niþa genægað.   Ongin þe generes wilnian,
far þær ðu freonda wene   gif ðu þines feores recce."

108

Then an outcry rose up. The outcasts surrounded the hill
in troops. A cry went up, the shriek of the sorrowful. Many
of them, the fiends' spokesmen, called out and boasted with   265
evil intent: "We have often observed peoples' customs on
earth, the power of proud men, of those who have led their
lives in prosperity. We have never encountered greater arro-
gance in any man throughout the world. You who vow that   270
you will take this home from us by force, you are God's pau-
per. Even if you possess the land, how will you live? No one
will feed you here; hunger and thirst will be cruel opponents   275
if, like the wild animals, you go away from your home alone.
That enterprise is worthless! Give up this place! No one can
give you better advice than all this multitude. We will be gra-   280
cious toward you if you will obey us, or else we will seek you
out again with a greater force, when you are unprepared, in
such a way that it will not be necessary to strike you with our
hands nor for your corpse to fall from weapons' wounds. We
can level this dwelling with our feet; an army will come   285
pushing in with troops of horses and of men. Then they will
be enraged , will strike you down, trample on you and insult
you and vent their anger, will carry you off, leaving bloody
tracks; if you intend to wait for us, we will attack you vio-   290
lently. Start wishing for a refuge for yourself, go where you
can expect friends if you care about your life."

Gearo wæs Guðlac;   hine God fremede
on ondsware   ond on elne strong.
Ne wond he for worde,   ac his wiþerbreocum
295 sorge gesægde,   cuðe him soð genog:
"Wid is þes westen,   wræc-setla fela,
eardas onhæle   earmra gæsta;
sindon wær-logan   þe þa wic bugað.
Þeah ge þa ealle   ut abonne,
300 ond eow eac gewyrce   widor sæce,
ge her ateoð   in þa torn-wræce
sige-leasne sið.   No ic eow sweord ongean
mid gebolgne hond   oðberan þence,
worulde wæpen,   ne sceal þes wong Gode
305 þurh blod-gyte   gebuen weorðan,
ac ic minum Criste   cweman þence
leofran lace.   Nu ic þis lond gestag,
fela ge me earda   þurh idel word
aboden habbað.   Nis min breost-sefa
310 forht ne fæge,   ac me friðe healdeð
ofer monna cyn   se þe mægna gehwæs
weorcum wealdeð.   Nis me wiht æt eow
leofes gelong,   ne ge me laþes wiht
gedon motun.   Ic eom Dryhtnes þeow;
315 he mec þurh engel   oft afrefreð.
Forðon mec longeþas   lyt gegretað,
sorge sealdun,   nu mec sawel-cund
hyrde bihealdeð.   Is min hyht mid God,
ne ic me eorð-welan   owiht sinne,
320 ne me mid mode   micles gyrne,
ac me dogra gehwam   Dryhten sendeð
þurh monnes hond   mine þearfe."

Guthlac was prepared; God made him strong in his answer and in his courage. He did not hesitate for words, but announced sorrow in store for his enemies; he knew the full truth: "Vast is this wilderness, its many places of exile, the secret homes of wretched spirits; those who inhabit these dwellings are traitors. Even if you were to summon all of them out and even extend the conflict more widely, in your fierce vengeance you will be setting out on an expedition that has no hope of victory here. I do not intend to carry a sword, a worldly weapon, against you with enraged hand nor shall this place be occupied for God by means of bloodshed, but I intend to please my Christ with a gift dearer to him. Since I came up into this region, you have offered me, with your empty words, many dwelling places. The mind in my breast is neither afraid nor doomed but he who indeed controls every power protects me more than the rest of mankind. Nothing that I value depends on you nor are you permitted to do anything evil to me. I am the Lord's servant; he often comforts me through an angel. Therefore desires torment me little, sorrows seldom, now that my spiritual guardian watches over me. My hope is in God and I do not care anything for earthly wealth, nor in my heart do I yearn for much for myself but every day the Lord sends me what I need by the hand of man."

Swa modgade,   se wið mongum stod,
awreðed weorðlice   wuldres cempa
325   engla mægne.   Gewat eal þonan
feonda mengu.   Ne wæs se fyrst micel
þe hi Guðlace   forgiefan þohtan.
He wæs on elne   ond on eað-medum,
bad on beorge;   wæs him botles neod,
330   forlet longeþas   lænra dreama.
No he hine wið monna   miltse gedælde,
ac gesynta bæd   sawla gehwylcre
þonne he to eorðan   on þam anade
hleor onhylde.   Him of heofonum wearð
335   onbryrded breost-sefa   bliðe gæste.
Oft eahtade   —wæs him engel neah—
hu þisse worulde   wynna þorfte
mid his lic-homan   læsast brucan.
No him fore egsan   earmra gæsta
340   treow getweode,   ne he tid forsæt
þæs þe he for his Dryhtne   dreogan sceolde
þæt hine æreste   elne binoman
slæpa sluman   oþþe sæne mod.
Swa sceal oretta   a in his mode
345   Gode compian   ond his gæst beran
oft on ondan   þam þe eahtan wile
sawla gehwylcre   þær he gesælan mæg.
   Symle hy Guðlac   in Godes willan
fromne fundon,   þonne flyge-reowe
350   þurh nihta genipu   neosan cwoman,
þa þe onhæle   eardas weredon,
hwæþre him þæs wonges   wyn sweðrade;

So he expressed his bravery, the glorious champion, who
stood against the many, fittingly supported by the power of   325
angels. All the crowd of fiends departed from there. It was
not a long respite which they intended to grant to Guthlac.
He was courageous and humble and remained on the hill;
his earnest desire was for his dwelling, and he renounced any   330
longings for transitory joys. He did not at all detach himself
from compassion toward people, but he prayed for the sal-
vation of every soul when he bowed his face to the ground in
the wilderness. The heart in his breast was inspired from   335
heaven with a joyful spirit. He often considered—the angel
was near him—how necessary it was to enjoy the pleasures
of this world with his body as little as possible. His faith did   340
not falter for fear of the wretched spirits, nor did he neglect
the time when he had to be active for his Lord so that the
slumbers of sleep or a sluggish heart took away from his ris-
ing vigorously. A warrior must always fight like this for God   345
in his heart and often be angrily opposed in his spirit to him
who wishes to act with evil intent toward every soul, if he
can succeed in it.

They always found Guthlac zealous in the will of God
when, wild in flight, they who held the hidden dwelling   350
places came through the darkness of night to find out
whether his pleasure in that place was coming to an end;
they wished that he would become sorrowful in his mind

woldun þæt him to mode   fore mon-lufan
sorg gesohte,   þæt he siþ tuge
355   eft to eþle.   Ne wæs þæt ongin swylc,
ðonne hine engel   on þam anade
geornast grette   ond him giefe sealde,
þæt hine ne meahte   meotudes willan
longað gelettan,   ac he on þæs lareowes
360   wære gewunade.   Oft worde bicwæð:
"Huru, þæs bihofað,   se ðe him Halig Gæst
wisað on willan   ond his weorc trymað,
laþað hine liþum wordum,   gehateð him lifes ræste,
þæt he þæs lat-teowes   larum hyre,
365   ne lete him eald-feond   eft oncyrran
mod from his meotude.   Hu sceal min cuman
gæst to geoce,   nemne ic Gode sylle
hyrsumne hige,   þæt him heortan geþonc . . .

". . . ær oþþe sið   ende geweorðe,
370   þæt ge mec to wundre   wægan motun.
Ne mæg min lic-homa   wið þas lænan gesceaft
dead gedælan,   ac he gedreosan sceal,
swa þeos eorðe eall   þe ic her on stonde.
Ðeah ge minne flæsc-homan   fyres wylme
375   forgripen grom-hydge   gifran lege,
næfre ge mec of þissum wordum onwendað   þendan mec
        min gewit gelæsteð.
Þeah þe ge hine sarum forsæcen,   ne motan ge mine sawle
        gretan,
ac ge on betran gebringað.   Forðan ic gebidan wille
þæs þe me min Dryhten demeð.   Nis me þæs deaþes sorg.
380   Ðeah min ban ond blod   bu tu geweorþen

out of love of human company so that he would journey
back to his homeland. Such was not his intent after the an- 355
gel had addressed him most gladly in that wilderness and
had granted him grace so that discontent could not hin-
der him from the will of the creator, but he remained in his 360
teacher's protection. He often declared: "Truly, he whose
will is directed by the Holy Spirit and whose deeds he
strengthens, whom he calls with gentle words and to whom
he promises rest after life, has good reason to listen to the
teachings of this guide and not to allow the old enemy to 365
turn his heart back, away from his creator. How shall my
spirit attain divine help unless I give an obedient heart to
God so that to him the thoughts of my heart . . .

". . . early or late there will be an end to your being able 370
to harass me so remarkably. It is not possible for my body to
avoid death in this transitory creation but it will have to per-
ish like all this earth on which I am standing here. Even
if you hostile beings were to overwhelm my body with surg- 375
ing fire, with greedy flames, you will never turn me aside
from these words, while my intellect serves me. Even if
you attack it painfully, you will not be permitted to harm
my soul but instead you will make it better. I will await,
therefore, whatever my Lord determines for me. I have no
anxiety about death. Even if both my bones and blood be 380

eorþan to eacan, min se eca dæl
in gefean fareð, þær he fægran
botles bruceð. Nis þisses beorges setl
meodumre ne mara þonne hit men duge
385   se þe in þrowingum þeodnes willan
dæghwam dreogeð. Ne sceal se Dryhtnes þeow
in his mod-sefan mare gelufian
eorþan æht-welan þonne his anes gemet,
þæt he his lic-homan lade hæbbe."
390   Ða wæs eft swa ær eald-feonda nið,
wroht onwylled; woð oþerne
lyt-hwon leoðode, þonne in lyft astag
cear-gesta cirm. Symle Cristes lof
in Guðlaces godum mode
395   weox ond wunade, ond hine weoruda God
freoðade on foldan, swa he feora gehwylc
healdeð in hælo, þær se hyra gæst
þihð in þeawum. He wæs þeara sum;
ne won he æfter worulde, ac he in wuldre ahof
400   modes wynne. Hwylc wæs mara þonne se?
An oretta ussum tidum
cempa gecyðeð þæt him Crist fore
woruldlicra ma wundra gecyðde.

He hine scilde wið sceðþendra
405   eglum onfengum, earmra gæsta;
wæron hy reowe to ræsanne
gifrum grapum. No God wolde
þæt seo sawl þæs sar þrowade
in lic-homan; lyfde seþeana
410   þæt hy him mid hondum hrinan mosten,

added to the earth, the eternal part of me will go into a place of joy where it will enjoy a beautiful abode. This hill-dwelling is neither smaller nor larger than what suffices for a man who in his sufferings daily carries out his Lord's will. The 385 Lord's servant must not in his heart love any more of this world's wealth than that portion allotted to him to provide sustenance for his body."

Then again, just as before, the ill will and animosity of the 390 old enemies boiled up again; the uproar unloosed for a while a second outburst of hate when the cry of the sorrowful demons rose into the air. Praise of Christ constantly grew and dwelt in Guthlac's good heart and the God of hosts pro- 395 tected him on earth, just as he keeps every living creature in safety whose higher spirit grows in virtues. He was one of those; he did not strive after the world, but his heart's delight was directed up to heavenly glory. Who was greater 400 than he? A unique warrior, a champion, reveals to our own times that Christ performed more miracles on earth for his sake.

He shielded himself against the terrible clutches of his 405 enemies, the wretched spirits; they rushed fiercely, with greedy grasps. God was not willing that the soul in his body should suffer pain from this; he permitted, however, that they might strike him with their hands but that his soul's 410

ond þæt frið wið hy   gefreoþad wære.
Hy hine þa hofun   on þa hean lyft,
sealdon him meahte   ofer monna cynn,
þæt he fore eagum   eall sceawode
415   under haligra   hyrda gewealdum
in mynsterum   monna gebæru,
þara þe hyra lifes   þurh lust brucan,
idlum æhtum   ond ofer-wlencum,
gierelum gielplicum,   swa bið geoguðe þeaw,
420   þær þæs ealdres   egsa ne styreð.
No þer þa feondas   gefeon þorfton,
ac þæs blædes hraðe   gebrocen hæfdon
þe him alyfed wæs   lytle hwile,
þæt hy his lic-homan   leng ne mostan
425   witum wælan;   ne him wiht gescod
þæs þe hy him to teonan   þurhtogen hæfdon.
Læddun hine þa of lyfte   to þam leofestan
earde on eorðan,   þæt he eft gestag
beorg on bearwe.   Bonan gnornedon,
430   mændon murnende   þæt hy monnes bearn
þream oferþunge,   ond swa þearfendlic
him to earfeðum   ana cwome,
gif hy him ne meahte   maran sarum
gyldan gyrn-wræce.   Guðlac sette
435   hyht in heofonas,   hælu getreowde,
hæfde feonda feng   feore gedyged.
   Wæs seo æreste   earmra gæsta
costung ofercumen.   Cempa wunade
bliþe on beorge;   wæs his blæd mid God.
440   Ðuhte him on mode   þæt se mon-cynnes
eadig wære   se þe his anum her

safety would be safeguarded. They lifted him up high in the air, gave him powers beyond that of mankind, so that, before his eyes, he saw all the behavior of men in the monasteries under the rule of holy shepherds, who enjoyed their 415 lives in pleasure, with empty possessions and excessive riches, in ostentatious garments, as is the custom of youth when fear of a superior does not restrain them. The fiends 420 had no cause to rejoice there, but they had soon used up the success which was permitted to them for a short while, so that they might not harass his body with torments any 425 longer; nor did anything injure him, of what they had done to hurt him. Then they brought him from the air to the dearest dwelling on earth, so that he climbed the hill in the wood again. The killers lamented, complaining sorrowfully 430 that a son of man should have surpassed them in inflicting misery and should have come, alone and poor, to cause hardship to them, if they could not pay him back with greater pains to avenge their injuries. Guthlac set his hope in heaven 435 and trusted in his salvation, having escaped with his life from the grasp of the fiends.

The first temptation of the wretched spirits had been overcome. The joyful warrior remained on the hill; his happiness was in God. It seemed to him in his heart that he who 440 defended his one and only life here would be blessed among

feore gefreoðade,   þæt him feondes hond
æt þam ytmestan   ende ne scode,
þonne him se Dryhtnes   dom wisade
445   to þam nyhstan   nyd-gedale.
Hwæþre him þa gena   gyrna gemyndge
edwit-sprecan   ermþu geheton
tornum teon-cwidum.   Treow wæs gecyþed,
þætte Guðlace   God leanode
450   ellen mid arum,   þæt he ana gewon.

Him se werga gæst   wordum sægde:
"No we þe þus swiðe   swencan þorftan,
þær þu fromlice   freonda larum
hyran wolde,   þa þu hean ond earm
455   on þis orlege   ærest cwome,
ða þu gehete   þæt þec Halig Gæst
wið earfeþum   eaðe gescilde,
for þam myrcelse   þe þec monnes hond
from þinre onsyne   æþelum ahwyrfde.
460   In þam mæg-wlite   monge lifgað,
gyltum forgiefene;   nales Gode þigað,
ac hy lic-homan   fore lufan cwemað
wista wynnum.   Swa ge weorð-myndu
in dolum dreame   Dryhtne gieldað.
465   Fela ge fore monnum miþað   þæs þe ge in mode gehycgað;
ne beoð eowre dæda dyrne,   þeah þe ge hy in dygle
                                        gefremme.
We þec in lyft gelæddun,   oftugon þe londes wynna,
woldun þu þe sylfa gesawe   þæt we þec soð onstældun.
Ealles þu þæs wite awunne;   forþon þu hit onwendan ne
                                        meahtes."

mankind so that the fiend's hand would not harm him at the
very end, when the Lord's decree would direct him to the fi- 445
nal inevitable parting. However, yet again the jeerers, mind-
ful of their misfortunes, promised him miseries in their bit-
ter insults. His faith was revealed, that God had rewarded
Guthlac's courage with his favor, so that he triumphed 450
alone.

The damned spirit spoke to him in these words: "We
would not have needed to torment you so violently if you
had been willing to listen eagerly to your friends' teachings,
when you first came, poor and wretched, into this battle, 455
when you vowed that the Holy Spirit would easily protect
you against hardships out of regard for that sign which
would turn a man's hand away from you, from the grace of
your countenance. That is the form of life of many who are 460
given to sin; they do not devote themselves to God at all,
but out of love for their bodies they gratify them with the
pleasures of feasts. This is how you pay respect to the Lord
in stupid happiness. You conceal from people much of what 465
you are thinking in your hearts; your deeds are not hidden,
even if you do them in secret. We brought you up into the
air, deprived you of the pleasures of the land, wanted you to
see for yourself that what we accuse you of is true. You have
endured torment for all this, because you were not able to
change it."

470 Ða wæs agongen   þæt him God wolde
     æfter þrowinga   þonc gegyldan
     þæt he martyrhad   mode gelufade;
     sealde him snyttru   on sefan gehygdum,
     mægen-fæste gemynd.   He wið mongum stod
475 eald-feonda,   elne gebylded,
     sægde him to sorge   þæt hy sige-lease
     þone grenan wong   ofgiefan sceoldan:
     "Ge sind forscadene;   on eow scyld siteð!
     Ne cunnon ge Dryhten   duguþe biddan,
480 ne mid eað-medum   are secan,
     þeah þe eow alyfde   lytle hwile,
     þæt ge min onwald   agan mosten;
     ne ge þæt geþyldum   þicgan woldan,
     ac mec yrringa   up gelæddon,
485 þæt ic of lyfte   londa getimbru
     geseon meahte.   Wæs me swegles leoht
     torht ontyned,   þeah ic torn druge.
     Setton me in edwit   þæt ic eaðe forbær
     rume regulas   ond reþe mod
490 geongra monna   in Godes templum;
     woldan þy gehyrwan   haligra lof,
     sohtun þa sæmran,   ond þa sellan no
     demdan æfter dædum.   Ne beoð þa dyrne swa þeah.
     Ic eow soð wiþ þon   secgan wille.
495 God scop geoguðe   ond gumena dream;
     ne magun þa æfter-yld   in þam ærestan
     blæde geberan,   ac hy blissiað
     worulde wynnum,   oð ðæt wintra rim
     gegæð in þa geoguðe   þæt se gæst lufað
500 onsyn ond ætwist   yldran hades,

Then it came about that God wished to pay thanks to   470
him after his sufferings because he loved martyrdom in his
heart; he gave him wisdom in his mind's thoughts, a stead-
fast purpose. He stood against the multitude of old enemies,   475
emboldened by courage, told them to their sorrow that they
would have to quit that green place without victory: "You
have been routed; guilt weighs heavily on you! You do not
know how to entreat the Lord for salvation nor seek grace   480
with humility, even though he permitted you for a short
while to have power over me; you were not willing to ac-
cept that patiently, but you lifted me up angrily, so that I   485
could see from the air the buildings on land. The radiant
light of the sky was revealed to me, even though I was en-
during pain. You blamed me for willingly putting up with
the lax rules and the harsh minds of the young men in God's   490
temples; by that you wanted to pour scorn on praise of holy
men, looking for the worse ones and not valuing the better
ones according to their deeds. Nevertheless, they are not
hidden. I, on the contrary, want to tell you the truth. God   495
created youthfulness and men's happiness; they cannot pro-
duce mature fruit in their first bloom, but they rejoice in the
pleasures of the world, until a number of years passes in
youthfulness so that the spirit loves the form and substance   500

ðe gemete monige   geond middan-geard
þeowiað in þeawum.   Þeodum ywaþ
wisdom weras,   wlencu forleosað,
siððan geoguðe   geað gæst aflihð.

505   Þæt ge ne scirað,   ac ge scyldigra
synne secgað,   soþ-fæstra no
mod ond mon-þeaw   mæran willað.
Gefeoð in firenum,   frofre ne wenað,
þæt ge wræc-siða   wyrpe gebiden.

510   Oft ge in gestalum stondað;   þæs cymeð steor of
heofonum.
Me þonne sendeð   se usic semon mæg,
se þe lifa gehwæs   lengu wealdeð."
Swa hleoþrade   halig cempa;
wæs se martyre,   from mon-cynnes

515   synnum asundrad.   Sceolde he sares þa gen
dæl adreogan,   ðeah þe Dryhten his
witum weolde.   Hwæt þæt wundra sum
monnum þuhte,   þæt he ma wolde
afrum onfengum   earme gæstas

520   hrinan leton,   ond þæt hwæþre gelomp!
Wæs þæt gen mara   þæt he middan-geard
sylfa gesohte   ond his swat ageat
on bonena hond;   ahte bega geweald
lifes ond deaðes   þa he lustum dreag

525   eað-mod on eorðan   ehtendra nið.
Forþon is nu arlic   þæt we æ-fæstra
dæde demen,   secgen Dryhtne lof
ealra þara bisena   þe us bec fore
þurh his wundra geweorc   wisdom cyþað.

of a more mature state which many throughout the earth fittingly serve in their way of life. These men display their wisdom to the people and abandon their arrogance once their spirits flee the folly of youth. You do not declare this, but you relate the sins of the guilty and are never willing to celebrate the spirits and practices of the righteous. You rejoice in wicked deeds and have no hope of relief, that you might experience a change for the better in your exile. You keep on making accusations; punishment will come from heaven for them. That is why he sends me, he who can settle the dispute between us, he who ordains the length of every life." 505 510

So spoke the holy warrior; he was a martyr, cut off from mankind's sins. Then he still had to endure a great deal more of pain, although the Lord had power over his torments. How astonishing a thing it seemed to people that he was willing to permit the wretched spirits to lay hold of him any longer with their fierce clutches, and yet that happened! What was even greater was that he himself came into this world and poured out his blood at his killers' hands; he had power over both life and death, when, in humility, he willingly endured his persecutors' violence on earth. Therefore it is now fitting that we should hold the deeds of devout people in high esteem, declare praise to the Lord for all the examples by which books teach us wisdom through his miraculous deeds. 515 520 525

530   Geofu wæs mid Guðlac,   in god-cundum
    mægne gemeted.   Micel is to secgan
    eall æfter orde   þæt he on elne adreag
    —ðone foregengan   Fæder ælmihtig
    wið onhælum   ealdor-gewinnum
535   sylfa gesette,   þær his sawl wearð
    clæne ond gecostad.   Cuð is wide
    geond middan-geard   þæt his mod geþah
    in Godes willan;   is þæs gen fela
    to secgenne   þæs þe he sylfa adreag
540   under nyð-gista   nearwum clommum.
    He þa sar forseah,   a þære sawle wel
    gemunde þæs mund-boran   þe þæt mod geheold,
    þæt him ne getweode   treow in breostum,
    ne him gnornunga   gæste scodun,
545   ac se hearda hyge   halig wunade,
    oþ þæt he þa bysgu   oferbiden hæfde.
    Þrea wæron þearle,   þegnas grimme;
    ealle hy þam feore   fyl gehehton.
    No hy hine to deað   deman moston,
550   synna hyrdas,   ac seo sawul bad
    in lic-homan   leofran tide.
    Georne hy ongeaton   þæt hyne God wolde
    nergan wið niþum   ond hyra nyd-wræce
    deope deman.   Swa Dryhten mæg,
555   ana ælmihtig,   eadigra gehwone
    wið earfeþum   eaðe gescildan.
      Hwæðre hine gebrohton   bolgen-mode,
    wraðe wræc-mæcgas,   wuldres cempan,

Grace, found in divine power, was with Guthlac. It is a   530
great undertaking to tell everything that he courageously
endured from start to finish—the almighty Father himself
appointed this forerunner against his secret deadly enemies,
there where his soul was made pure and proved by trial. It is   535
widely known throughout the world that his spirit thrived
by the will of God; there is much more still to tell of what
he himself endured in the imprisoning clutches of the mali-   540
cious spirits. Then he scorned the suffering, always remem-
bered well in his soul that protector who guarded his spirit,
so that the faith in his breast did not falter nor did com-
plaining harm his spirit, but his brave heart persisted in ho-   545
liness until he had survived these troubles. The misery they
inflicted was severe, the devil's followers cruel; they all
vowed to destroy his life. The guardians of sin were not per-
mitted to condemn him to death, but the soul within his   550
body awaited a more pleasant time. They clearly understood
that God intended to save him from their persecutions and
to condemn their violence severely. So the one almighty
Lord can easily protect each of the blessed against hardship.   555
Yet the enraged, hostile outcasts brought the glorious

halig husul-bearn,   æt hel-dore,
560 þær firenfulra   fæge gæstas
æfter swylt-cwale   secan onginnað
in-gong ærest   in þæt atule hus,
niþer under næssas   neole grundas.
Hy hine bregdon,   budon orlege,
565 egsan ond ondan   ar-leaslice,
frecne fore,   swa bið feonda þeaw,
þonne hy soð-fæstra   sawle willað
synnum beswican   ond searo-cræftum.
Ongunnon grom-heorte   Godes orettan
570 in sefan swencan,   swiþe geheton
þæt he in þone grimman gryre   gongan sceolde,
hweorfan gehyned   to hel-warum,
ond þær in bendum   bryne þrowian.
Woldun hy geteon   mid torn-cwidum,
575 earme aglæcan,   in orwennysse,
meotudes cempan.   Hit ne meahte swa!
Cwædon cearfulle,   Criste laðe,
to Guðlace   mid grimnysse:
"Ne eart ðu gedefe,   ne Dryhtnes þeow
580 clæne gecostad,   ne cempa god,
wordum ond weorcum   wel gecyþed,
halig in heortan.   Nu þu in helle scealt
deope gedufan,   nales Dryhtnes leoht
habban in heofonum,   heah-getimbru,
585 seld on swegle,   forþon þu synna to fela,
facna gefremedes   in flæsc-homan.
We þe nu willað   womma gehwylces
lean forgieldan,   þær þe laþast bið
in ðam grimmestan   gæst-gewinne."

128

champion, the holy communicant, to hell's door, where, af- 560
ter their death pangs, the doomed spirits of sinners first
seek entry into that horrible house, into the deep abyss,
down under the ground. They terrified him, mercilessly
threatened him with battle, horror and hostility, a danger- 565
ous journey, as is the way with fiends when they wish to de-
ceive the souls of the righteous with sins and treacherous
cunning. Cruel at heart, they began to torment God's cham-
pion in his mind, fiercely vowed that he would have to 570
enter into that grim and terrifying place, go, defeated, to
hell's inhabitants, and there in fetters suffer burning. Those 575
wretched enemies wanted to lead the creator's warrior into
despair with their bitter speeches. This could not be so! Full
of sorrow, hateful to Christ, they spoke to Guthlac with fe-
rocity: "You are not worthy nor are you a completely proven
servant of the Lord or a good warrior well known for words 580
and deeds, holy at heart. Now you will have to sink far down
into hell and not have the light of the Lord in the heavens,
the lofty buildings, a seat in the sky, because you have com- 585
mitted too many sins and faults in the flesh. Now we intend
to pay you back for every sin, in the way that will be most
distressing for you, in the cruelest anguish of soul."

590   Him se eadga wer   ondswarode,
         Guðlac in gæste   mid Godes mægne:
         "Doð efne swa,   gif eow Dryhten Crist,
         lifes leoht-fruma   lyfan wylle,
         weoruda waldend,   þæt ge his wer-gengan
595   in þone laðan leg   lædan motan.
         Þæt is in gewealdum   wuldor-cyninges,
         se eow gehynde   ond in hæft bidraf
         under nearone clom,   nergende Crist.
         Eom ic eað-mod his   ombieht-hera,
600   þeow geþyldig.   Ic geþafian sceal
         æghwær ealles   his anne dom,
         ond him geornlice   gæst-gemyndum
         wille wide-ferh   wesan underþyded,
         hyran holdlice   minum hælende
605   þeawum ond geþyncðum,   ond him þoncian
         ealra þara giefena   þe God gescop
         englum ærest   ond eorð-warum;
         ond ic bletsige   bliðe mode
         lifes leoht-fruman,   ond him lof singe
610   þurh gedefne dom   dæges ond nihtes,
         herge in heortan   heofon-rices weard.
         Þæt eow æfre ne bið   ufan alyfed
         leohtes lissum,   þæt ge lof moten
         Dryhtne secgan,   ac ge deaðe sceolon
615   weallendne wean   wope besingan,
         heaf in helle,   nales herenisse
         halge habban   heofon-cyninges.

The blessed man Guthlac answered them with God's 590
power in his spirit: "Do just that if the Lord Christ, life's
source of light, the ruler of the heavenly hosts, is willing to
permit you to lead his follower into that hated flame. That 595
is under the control of the King of glory, the savior Christ,
who defeated you and drove you into captivity in imprison-
ing fetters. I am his humble obedient attendant, his patient 600
servant. I shall in every way submit entirely to the divine au-
thority which is his alone and intend to be eagerly subject
to him in my thoughts forever, graciously to obey my sav-
ior virtuously and honorably and thank him for all the gifts 605
which God created for the angels first and for humankind;
and I will bless life's source of light with a joyful spirit and
sing praise to him day and night with fitting glory, commend 610
the guardian of heaven in my heart. It will never be permit-
ted to you to utter praise to the Lord from on high in the
delight of heaven, but instead in death you will have to la- 615
ment your raging grief in your songs, wail in hell, not experi-
ence at all the holy praise of the heavenly king.

"Ic þone deman   in dagum minum
wille weorþian   wordum ond dædum,
620   lufian in life.   Swa is lar ond ar
to spowendre   spræce gelæded,
þam þe in his weorcum   willan ræfnað.
Sindon ge wær-logan;   swa ge in wræc-siðe
longe lifdon,   lege biscencte,
625   swearte beswicene,   swegle benumene,
dreame bidrorene,   deaðe bifolene,
firenum bifongne,   feores orwenan,
þæt ge blindnesse   bote fundon.
Ge þa fægran gesceaft   in fyrn-dagum,
630   gæstlicne god-dream,   gearo forsegon,
þa ge wiðhogdun   halgum Dryhtne.
Ne mostun ge a wunian   in wyn-dagum,
ac mid scome scyldum   scofene wurdon
fore ofer-hygdum   in ece fyr,
635   ðær ge sceolon dreogan   deað ond þystro,
wop to widan ealdre;   næfre ge þæs wyrpe gebidað.
       "Ond ic þæt gelyfe   in lif-fruman,
ecne onwealdan   ealra gesceafta,
þæt he mec for miltsum   ond mægen-spedum,
640   niðða nergend,   næfre wille
þurh ellen-weorc   anforlætan,
þam ic longe   in lic-homan
ond in minum gæste   Gode campode
þurh monigfealdra   mægna gerynu.
645   Forðon ic getrywe   in þone torhtestan
Þrynesse þrym,   se geþeahtingum
hafað in hondum   heofon ond eorðan,
þæt ge mec mid niþum   næfre motan

"I wish to honor the judge in my words and deeds during my lifetime, love him throughout my life. This is how guidance and grace result in eloquent speech in those who carry out his will in their deeds. You are traitors; accordingly you have long lived in exile, engulfed in flames, miserably deceived, deprived of heaven, bereft of joy, consigned to death, ensnared in sins, despairing of life, of finding a cure for your blindness. Once, in former days, you spurned this fair creation, heavenly happiness in God, when you set yourselves against the holy Lord. You were not permitted to live forever in days of joy but you were thrust, ignominiously and guiltily, into the eternal fire on account of your pride, where you will have to endure death and darkness, lamentation for ever and ever; you will never live to see a change for the better in that.

"And I believe in the giver of life, the eternal ruler of all created things, the savior of men, believe that, on account of his mercy and might, he will never forsake me because of the courageous deeds with which I have fought for God for a long time in body and in soul, by means of the mysteries of his manifold powers. Therefore I trust in the Trinity's most radiant glory, which by its counsels holds heaven and earth in its hands, that you, wicked murderers and evil foes, with rage in your hearts, dark and defeated, will never be allowed

620

625

630

635

640

645

133

torn-mode teon   in tintergu,
650   mine myrðran   ond man-sceaþan,
swearte sige-lease.   Eom ic soðlice
leohte geleafan   ond mid lufan Dryhtnes
fægre gefylled   in minum feorh-locan,
breostum inbryrded   to þam betran ham,
655   leomum inlyhted   to þam leofestan
ecan earde,   þær is eþel-lond
fæger ond gefealic   in Fæder wuldre,
ðær eow næfre   fore nergende
leohtes leoma   ne lifes hyht
660   in Godes rice   agiefen weorþeð,
for þam ofer-hygdum   þe eow in astag
þurh idel gylp   ealles to swiðe.
Wendun ge ond woldun,   wiþerhycgende,
þæt ge scyppende   sceoldan gelice
665   wesan in wuldre.   Eow þær wyrs gelomp,
ða eow se waldend   wraðe bisencte
in þæt swearte susl,   þær eow siððan wæs
ad inæled   attre geblonden,
þurh deopne dom   dream afyrred,
670   engla gemana.   Swa nu awa sceal
wesan wide-ferh,   þæt ge wærnysse
bryne-wylm hæbben,   nales bletsunga.
Ne þurfun ge wenan,   wuldre biscyrede,
þæt ge mec synfulle   mid searo-cræftum
675   under scæd sconde   scufan motan,
ne in bæl-blæsan   bregdon on hinder
in helle hus   þær eow is ham sceapen,
sweart sin-nehte,   sacu butan ende,
grim gæst-cwalu.   Þær ge gnornende

to drag me violently into torment. Truly I am pleasantly 650
filled with the light of faith and with love of the Lord in my
heart, inspired in my breast toward that better home, illu- 655
mined by his rays, toward that most loved eternal dwelling
where the fair and delightful homeland is in the glory of the
Father, where, in the savior's presence, neither the radiance
of light nor the hope of life in God's kingdom will ever be 660
given to you because of the excessive pride which arose in
you through all too much empty boasting. You imagined and
wished, perverse as you are, that you would be like the cre- 665
ator in glory. It turned out worse for you there, when the
ruler furiously plunged you into that dark torment where a
pyre was then kindled for you, tainted with venom, where,
by his solemn judgment, joy, the companionship of angels,
was taken away. Now and forever, it must always be so, that 670
you will be subject to damnation, the surging flame, no
blessing at all. Cut off from glory, you who are full of sins
need not hope that you will be able to thrust me with your 675
treacherous cunning ignominiously into darkness or fling
me in a blaze of fire down into the house of hell where a
home has been made for you, black eternal night, distress
without end, the grim destruction of the soul. Lamenting

680　deað sceolon dreogan,　ond ic dreama wyn
　　agan mid englum　in þam uplican
　　rodera rice,　þær is ryht cyning,
　　help ond hælu　hæleþa cynne,
　　duguð ond drohtað."
　　　　　　　　　　Ða cwom Dryhtnes ar,
685　halig of heofonum,　se þurh hleoþor abead
　　ufan-cundne ege　earmum gæstum;
　　het eft hraðe　unscyldigne
　　of þam wræc-siðe　wuldres cempan
　　lædan lim-halne,　þæt se leofesta
690　gæst gegearwad　in Godes wære
　　on gefean ferde.　Ða wearð feonda þreat
　　acol for ðam egsan.　Ofer-mæcga spræc,
　　dyre Dryhtnes þegn,　dæg-hluttre scan.
　　Hæfde Guðlaces　gæst in gewealdum
695　modig mund-bora　meahtum spedig
　　þeostra þegnas　þrea-niedlum bond,
　　nyd onsette　ond geneahhe bibead:
　　"Ne sy him banes bryce　ne blodig wund,
　　lices læla　ne laþes wiht,
700　þæs þe ge him to dare　gedon motan,
　　ac ge hine gesundne asettaþ　þær ge hine sylfne genoman.
　　He sceal þy wonge wealdan;　ne magon ge him þa wic
　　　　　　　　　　　　　　　　　forstondan.
　　Ic eom se dema　se mec Dryhten heht
　　snude gesecgan　þæt ge him sara gehwylc
705　hondum gehælde　ond him hearsume
　　on his sylfes dom　siþþan wæron.
　　Ne sceal ic mine onsyn　fore eowere
　　mengu miþan.　Ic eom meotudes þegn.

there, you will have to suffer death, and I shall possess the 680
joy of delights among the angels in the celestial kingdom
of the heavens, where the true King is, help and safety for
mankind, blessings and society."

Then from the heavens came the Lord's holy messenger, 685
who by his speech proclaimed terror from above for those
wretched spirits; he commanded them to bring back the
guiltless glorious champion quickly, unharmed from that
journey of exile, so that the most beloved spirit, being pre- 690
pared, might make its way into God's protection, into the
joyful place. Then the band of fiends was frozen with terror.
The illustrious being, the dear servant of the Lord, spoke,
shining brightly as the day. This brave protector with his
abundant powers had Guthlac's spirit in his protection, and 695
he bound the servants of darkness with painful force, bore
down on them violently and strictly charged them: "Let
there be no breaking of his bones nor a bloody wound nor
bruising of his body nor any injury at all from whatever you 700
may do to harm him, but you will set him down unharmed
in that same place from which you seized him. He is des-
tined to rule this place; you cannot defend this dwelling
against him. I am the judge whom the Lord commanded
to say at once that you should heal every wound in him 705
with your hands and then be obedient to him in whatever
he chooses. I shall not conceal my face from your troop. I
am the creator's servant. I am one of the twelve whom he,

Eom ic þara twelfa sum   þe he getreoweste
710   under monnes hiw   mode gelufade.
He mec of heofonum   hider onsende,
geseah þæt ge on eorðan   fore æfstum
on his wer-gengan   wite legdon.
Is þæt min broþor;   mec his bysgu gehreaw.
715   Ic þæt gefremme   þær se freond wunað
on þære socne   —þe ic þa sibbe wið hine
healdan wille,   nu ic his helpan mot—
þæt ge min onsynn   oft sceawiað.
Nu ic his geneahhe   neosan wille;
720   sceal ic his word ond his weorc   in gewitnesse
Dryhtne lædon.   He his dæde conn."

Ða wæs Guðlaces   gæst geblissad,
siþþan Bartholomeus   aboden hæfde
Godes ærendu.   Gearwe stodun
725   hæftas hearsume,   þa þæs halgan word
lyt oferleordun.   Ongon þa leofne sið
dragan dom-eadig   Dryhtnes cempa
to þam onwillan   eorðan dæle.
Hy hine bæron   ond him bryce heoldon,
730   hofon hine hondum   ond him hryre burgun.
Wæron hyra gongas   under Godes egsan
smeþe ond gesefte.   Sige-hreðig cwom
bytla to þam beorge.   Hine bletsadon
monge mæg-wlitas,   meaglum reordum,
735   treo-fugla tuddor,   tacnum cyðdon
eadges eft-cyme.   Oft he him æte heold,
þonne hy him hungrige   ymb hond flugon,
grædum gifre,   geoce gefegon.

in his human form, loved in his heart as most true. He sent 710
me here from the heavens, saw that out of envy you were
tormenting his follower on earth. He is my brother; his dis-
tress has grieved me. I shall bring it about that where that 715
friend—with whom I wish to maintain friendship now that
I am permitted to help him—dwells in his sanctuary, you
will often see my face. Now I intend to visit him frequently;
I shall bring his words and his deeds to the Lord as testi- 720
mony. He will know his deeds."

Then Guthlac's spirit was cheered, once Bartholomew
had proclaimed God's message. The obedient captives, who 725
did not deviate from the saint's command, stood ready.
Then the glorious warrior of the Lord proceeded to go on
the pleasant journey to that desired portion of land. They
carried him and kept him from injury, lifted him up in their 730
hands and saved him from falling. Their movements were
smooth and comfortable, for fear of God. Triumphant, the
builder came to that hill. The many species and breeds of
birds in the trees blessed him with ardent voices, and by 735
these signals announced the blessed man's return. He often
held out food for them, when, hungry, greedily eager, they
flew around his hand, glad of his help. So that gentle spirit

Swa þæt milde mod   wið mon-cynnes
740   dreamum gedælde,   Dryhtne þeowde,
genom him to wildeorum wynne,   siþþan he þas woruld
forhogde.

Smolt wæs se sige-wong   ond sele niwe,
fæger fugla reord,   folde geblowen;
geacas gear budon.   Guþlac moste
745   eadig ond onmod   eardes brucan.

Stod se grena wong   in Godes wære;
hæfde se heorde,   se þe of heofonum cwom,
feondas afyrde.   Hwylc wæs fægerra
willa geworden   in wera life,
750   þara þe yldran   usse gemunde,
oþþe we selfe   siþþan cuþen?
Hwæt we þissa wundra   gewitan sindon!
Eall þas geeodon   in ussera
tida timan.   Forþon þæs tweogan ne þearf
755   ænig ofer eorðan   ælda cynnes,
ac swilc God wyrceð   gæsta lifes
to trumnaþe,   þy læs þa tydran mod
þa gewitnesse   wendan þurfe,
þonne hy in gesihþe   soþes brucað.
760   Swa se ælmihtiga   ealle gesceafte
lufað under lyfte   in lic-homan,
monna mægðe   geond middan-geard.
Wile se waldend   þæt we wisdom a
snyttrum swelgen,   þæt his soð fore us
765   on his giefena gyld   genge weorðe,
ða he us to are   ond to ondgiete
syleð ond sendeð;   sawlum rymeð
liþe lif-wegas   leohte geræhte.

detached itself from the joys of mankind, served the Lord   740
and took pleasure in the wild animals, after he had rejected
this world.

That plain of victory and his new dwelling were tranquil,
the birds' voices delightful, the earth in bloom; cuckoos an-
nounced the new year. Guthlac, blessed and resolute, was   745
able to enjoy his home. The green place remained under
God's protection; the guardian who had come from heaven
had expelled the fiends. What more agreeable pleasure has
ever come to pass in men's lives, among those whom our   750
elders remembered or of whom we ourselves have known
since? How we are witnesses to these wonders! All these
things happened in the age of our times. Therefore no one
of the race of men on earth has cause to doubt this, but God   755
does it to strengthen the life of souls, lest weak spirits would
be obliged to alter their testimony when they enjoy the
truth in plain sight. This is how the Almighty loves all bodily   760
creatures under the heavens, the races of people throughout
the earth. The ruler wishes that we should always imbibe
wisdom intelligently so that through us his truth may come   765
to prevail in return for the gifts which he gives and sends us
for our benefit and our understanding; he clears pleasant
paths through life for our souls, directed to the light. Indeed

Nis þæt huru læsast   þæt seo lufu cyþeð,
770   þonne heo in monnes   mode getimbreð
gæst-cunde gife,   swa he Guðlaces
dagas ond dæde   þurh his dom ahof.
Wæs se fruma fæstlic   feondum on ondan,
geseted wið synnum;   þær he siþþan lyt
775   wære gewonade,   oft his word Gode
þurh eað-medu   up onsende,
let his ben cuman   in þa beorhtan gesceaft,
þoncade þeodne   þæs þe he in þrowingum
bidan moste,   hwonne him betre lif
780   þurh Godes willan   agyfen worde.
      Swa wæs Guðlaces   gæst gelæded
engla fæðmum   in uprodor;
fore onsyne   eces deman
læddon leoflice.   Him wæs lean geseald,
785   setl on swegle,   þær he symle mot
awo to ealdre   eard-fæst wesan,
bliðe bidan.   Is him Bearn Godes
milde mund-bora,   meahtig Dryhten,
halig hyrde,   heofon-rices weard.
790   Swa soð-fæstra   sawla motun
in ecne geard   up gestigan
rodera rice,   þa þe ræfnað her
wordum ond weorcum   wuldor-cyninges
lare longsume,   on hyra lifes tid
795   earniað on eorðan   ecan lifes,
hames in heahþu.   Þæt beoð husul-weras,
cempan gecorene,   Criste leofe,
berað in breostum   beorhtne geleafan,
haligne hyht,   heortan clæne

that is not the least of what that love manifests, when it   770
builds up spiritual grace in a person's heart, just as he exalted
Guthlac's days and deeds through his authority. The ruler
there was firm in his hostility toward the fiends, set against
sins; afterward his commitment to his pledge decreased lit-   775
tle and he often humbly sent his words up to God, let his
prayer enter that bright element, thanked the prince that he
might remain in suffering until such time as a better life
would be given to him through God's will.   780

So Guthlac's soul was brought to heaven in the embrace
of angels; they led him lovingly before the face of the eternal
judge. A reward was given to him, a place in heaven, where   785
he may always reside forever and ever, dwell joyfully. The
Son of God, the mighty Lord, the holy shepherd, the guard-
ian of the kingdom of heaven, is his merciful protector. So   790
may the souls of the righteous ascend up to the eternal
home, the kingdom of heaven, those who carry out here, in
their words and in their deeds, the everlasting teaching of
the king of glory, earn eternal life in their lifetimes on earth,   795
a home in heaven. Those are the communicants, the chosen
warriors, dear to Christ, bearing their radiant faith in their
breasts, their holy hope, with their pure hearts worshipping

800   weorðiað waldend,   habbað wisne geþoht,
        fusne on forð-weg   to Fæder eðle,
        gearwaþ gæstes hus,   ond mid gleawnesse
        feond oferfeohtað   ond firen-lustas
        forberað in breostum,   broþor-sibbe
805   georne bigongað,   in Godes willan
        swencað hi sylfe,   sawle frætwað
        halgum gehygdum,   heofon-cyninges bibod
        fremmað on foldan,   fæsten lufiað,
        beorgað him bealo-niþ   ond gebedu secað,
810   swincað wið synnum,   healdað soð ond ryht.
        Him þæt ne hreoweð   æfter hin-gonge,
        ðonne hy hweorfað   in þa halgan burg,
        gongað gegnunga   to Hierusalem,
        þær hi to worulde   wynnum motun
815   Godes onsyne   georne bihealdan,
        sibbe ond gesihðe,   þær heo soð wunað,
        wlitig, wuldor-fæst,   ealne widan ferh
        on lifgendra   londes wynne.

the ruler, wise in their thoughts, eager to depart for the   800
home of the Father, preparing the house of their spirits and
conquering the fiend with wisdom, restraining sinful desires
in their breasts, eagerly practicing brotherly love, mortify-   805
ing themselves according to the will of God, adorning their
souls with holy thoughts, carrying out on earth the com-
mands of the heavenly king, loving fasting, protecting them-
selves from wickedness and striving to pray, toiling against   810
sins, upholding truth and justice. They will not regret that
after their departure, when they go to the holy city, make
their way directly to Jerusalem, where they may joyously and
eagerly look upon the face of God for ever, upon the peace   815
and the vision, where, beautiful and glorious, it will truly en-
dure forever in the joy of the land of the living.

THE DESCENT
INTO HELL

Ongunnon him on uhtan   æþel-cunde mægð
gierwan to geonge;   wiston gumena gemot
æþelinges lic   eorð-ærne biþeaht.
Woldan werigu wif   wope bimænan
5   æþelinges deað   ane hwile,
reonge bereotan.   Ræst wæs acolad;
heard wæs hin-sið.   Hæleð wæron modge,
þe hy æt þam beorge   bliðe fundon.
Cwom seo murnende   Maria on dæg-red;
10   heht hy oþre mid   eorles dohtor.
Sohton sarigu tu   Sige-Bearn Godes,
ænne in þæt eorð-ærn,   þær hi ær wiston
þæt hine gehyddan   hæleð Iudea;
wendan þæt he on þam beorge   bidan sceolde,
15   ana in þære Easter-niht.   Huru þæs oþer þing
wiston þa wif-menn,   þa hy on weg cyrdon!
Ac þær cwom on uhtan   an engla þreat;
behæfde heapa wyn   hælendes burg.
Open wæs þæt eorð-ærn;   æþelinges lic
20   onfeng feores gæst.   Folde beofode;
hlogan hel-waran.   Hago-steald onwoc
modig from moldan;   mægen-þrym aras
sige-fæst ond snottor.
Sægde Iohannis,

Before daybreak the noble women prepared themselves for the journey; the assembled people knew that the prince's body had been concealed in a tomb. The grieving women wished to lament the prince's death with weeping for a while, to mourn sadly. His resting-place had grown cold; his   5
journey out of this world had been hard. The men whom they met at the barrow were joyful and brave.

Mary, mourning, came at dawn; she had summoned an-   10
other woman with her. The two sorrowing women were seeking the victorious Son of God, alone in that tomb, where they already knew that the Jewish men had hidden him; they thought that he would have had to remain in the barrow, alone on that Easter eve. The women certainly knew   15
otherwise, when they made their way back!

But a host of angels came there in the hour before dawn; the best of companies surrounded the savior's stronghold. The tomb was open; the prince's body received the breath   20
of life. The earth shook; inhabitants of hell laughed. The courageous young warrior awoke from the earth; the majestic one arose, victorious and wise.

John, the brave man, said to the inhabitants of hell, spoke

hæleð hel-warum, hlyhhende spræc
25 modig to þære mengo ymb his mæges sið:
"Hæfde me gehaten hælend user,
þa he me on þisne sið sendan wolde,
þæt he me gesohte ymb siex monað,
ealles folces fruma. Nu is se fyrst sceacen.
30 Wene ic ful swiþe ond witodlice
þæt us to dæge Dryhten wille
sylfa gesecan, Sige-Bearn Godes."
    Fysde hine þa to fore Frea mon-cynnes;
wolde heofona helm helle weallas
35 forbrecan ond forbygan, þære burge þrym
onginnan reafian, reþust ealra cyninga.
Ne rohte he to þære hilde helm-berendra,
ne he byrn-wigend to þam burg-geatum
lædan ne wolde, ac þa locu feollan,
40 clustor of þam ceastrum. Cyning in oþrad,
ealles folces fruma, forð onette,
weoruda wuldor-giefa. Wræccan þrungon
hwylc hyra þæt Syge-Bearn geseon moste —
Adam ond Abraham, Isac ond Iacob,
45 monig modig eorl, Moyses ond Dauid,
Esaias ond Sacharias,
heah-fædra fela, swylce eac hæleþa gemot,
witgena weorod, wif-monna þreat,
fela fæmnena, folces unrim.
50   Geseah þa Iohannis Sige-Bearn Godes
mid þy cyne-þrymme cuman to helle;
ongeat þa geomor-mod Godes sylfes sið.
Geseah he helle duru hædre scinan,
þa þe longe ær bilocen wæron,

laughing to the multitude about his kinsman's expedition: 25
"When he was about to send me on this expedition, our sav-
ior promised me that he, the ruler of all mankind, would
seek me out after six months. Now that time is up. I fer- 30
vently and truly expect that the Lord himself, the victorious
Son of God, will seek us out today."

Then the Lord of mankind hastened on his journey;
heaven's protector, the most righteous of all kings, intended
to demolish and cast down the walls of hell, to carry off the 35
great body of people in that stronghold. He did not care
about helmeted soldiers for that battle nor did he intend
to lead armor-clad warriors to the gates of that stronghold,
but instead the locks and bars dropped off that city. The 40
king, the ruler of all mankind, who gives glory to the hosts,
rode in and hastened on. The exiles thronged forward, to
see which of them might see the victorious Son—Adam and
Abraham, Isaac and Jacob, many a brave man, Moses and 45
David, Isaiah and Zachariah, many patriarchs, likewise an
assembly of men, a host of prophets, a throng of women,
many virgins, a countless number of people.

Then John saw the victorious Son of God coming to hell 50
with royal majesty; sad at heart, he then understood this ex-
pedition of God himself. He saw the doors of hell shining
brightly, those doors which long before had been locked,

55 beþeahte mid þystre;   se þegn wæs on wynne.
    Abead þa bealdlice   burg-warena ord,
    modig fore þære mengo,   ond to his mæge spræc
    ond þa wil-cuman   wordum grette:
    "Þe þæs þonc sie,   Þeoden user,
60 þæt þu us sarige   secan woldest,
    nu we on þissum bendum   bidan sceoldon.
    Þonne mon gebindeð   broþor-leasne
    wræccan ......   —he bið wide fah—
    ne bið he no þæs nearwe   under nið-locan
65 oððe þæs bitre gebunden   under bealu-clommum,
    þæt he þy yð ne mæge   ellen habban,
    þonne he his hlafordes   hyldo gelyfeð,
    þæt hine of þam bendum   bicgan wille.
    Swa we ealle to þe   an gelyfað,
70 Dryhten min se dyra.   Ic adreag fela
    siþþan þu end to me   in siþadest,
    þa þu me gesealdest   sweord ond byrnan,
    helm ond heoro-sceorp   —a ic þæt heold nu giet—
    ond þu me gecyðdest,   cyne-þrymma wyn,
75 þæt þu mund-bora   minum wære.
        "Eala Gabrihel,   hu þu eart gleaw ond scearp,
    milde ond gemyndig   ond mon-þwære,
    wis on þinum gewitte   ond on þinum worde snottor!
    Þæt þu gecyðdest   þa þu þone cnyht to us
80 brohtest in Bethlem.   Bidan we þæs longe,
    setan on sorgum,   sibbe oflyste,
    wynnum ond wenum,   hwonne we word Godes
    þurh his sylfes muð   secgan hyrde.
        "Eala Maria,   hu þu us modigne
85 cyning acendest,   þa þu þæt cild to us

enveloped in darkness; that warrior was joyful. Then the 55
chief of the inhabitants of that stronghold, brave before the
multitude, boldly proclaimed these words, speaking to his
kinsman and greeting the welcome guest: "Thanks be to
you, our Lord, for being willing to seek us out, your sorrow- 60
ful people, since we have had to wait in these bonds. When a
brotherless exile is bound—he is an enemy far and wide—he
will never be so tightly confined in his place of torment, or 65
so cruelly bound in evil fetters, that he may not the more
easily be able to have courage when he believes in his Lord's
kindness, that he intends to redeem him from those bonds.
This is how we all believe in you alone, my dear Lord. I have 70
endured much since that time when you came in to me,
when you gave me a sword and coat of mail, a helmet and
battle dress—I have kept them constantly up to now—and,
pride of kingly glories, you made known to me that you 75
would be my protector.

"O Gabriel, how discerning and sharp-witted you are,
how kind and thoughtful and gentle, wise in your intellect
and prudent in your words! You showed that when you
brought the boy to us in Bethlehem. We had waited for that 80
so long, sitting in sorrows, joys and hopes, filled with the de-
sire for peace, for the time when we might hear the word of
God spoken by his own mouth.

"O Mary, how brave a king you bore for us when you 85

brohtest in Bethlem!   We þæs beofiende
under helle dorum   hearde sceoldon
bidan in bendum.   Bona weorces gefeah;
wæron ure eald-find   ealle on wynnum
90 þonne hy gehyrdon   hu we hreowende
mændon murnende   mæg-burg usse,
oþ þæt þu us sohtest   Sige-Dryhten God.
Bimengdest . . .   . . . modigast ealra cyninga,
   nu us mon modge þe
95 ageaf from usse geogoðe.   We þurh gifre mod
beswican us sylfe;   we þa synne forþon
berað in urum breostum   to bonan honda,
sculon eac to ussum feondum   freoþo wilnian.
   "Eala Hierusalem   in Iudeum,
100 hu þu in þære stowe   stille gewunadest!
Ne mostan þe geondferan   fold-buende
ealle lifgende,   þa þe lof singað.
   "Eala Iordane   in Iudeum,
hu þu in þære stowe   stille gewunadest!
105 Nales meahtest þu geondflowan   fold-buende;
mostan hy þynes wætres   wynnum brucan.
   "Nu ic þe halsie,   hælend user,
deope in gedyrftum   —þu eart Dryhten Crist—
þæt þu us gemiltsie,   monna scyppend.
110 Þu fore monna lufan   þinre modor bosm
sylfa gesohtes,   Sige-Dryhten God,
nales fore þinre þearfe,   þeoda waldend,
ac for þam miltsum   þe þu mon-cynne
oft ætywdest,   þonne him wæs are þearf.
115 Þu meaht ymbfon   eal folca gesetu,
swylce þu meaht geriman,   rice Dryhten,

brought that child to us in Bethlehem! We had had to wait painfully in fetters for that, trembling behind the doors of hell. The killer was delighted with his work; our old enemies all rejoiced when they heard how we lamented, grieving and mourning for our kindred, until you sought us out, victorious Lord God. Bravest of all kings, you joined . . . now that we, brave ones, have been given to you from our youth. We have deceived ourselves by our own greedy minds; therefore we carry the sins in our breasts into the slayer's hands, must even ask for peace from our enemies.

"O Jerusalem in Judea how still you remained in that place! All the living beings dwelling on earth who sing your praises were not allowed to pass through you.

"O Jordan in Judea, how still you remained in that place! You could not flow at all through those dwelling on earth; they were allowed to partake of your waters joyfully.

"Now, deeply troubled, I entreat you, our savior—you who are Christ the Lord—that you have mercy on us, creator of people. You yourself, victorious Lord God, sought out your mother's breast for love of mankind, not in the least because of your own need, ruler of nations, but out of that mercy which you often showed to mankind when it had need of grace. Powerful Lord, best of all kings, you can

sæs sond-grotu,   selast ealra cyninga.

Swylce ic þe halsige,   hælend user,

fore þinum cildhade,   cyninga selast,

120   ond fore þære wunde,   weoruda Dryhten,

ond for þinum æriste,   æþelinga wyn,

ond fore þinre meder,   þære is Marian nama,

þa ealle hell-wara   hergað ond lofiað,

ond fore þam englum   þe þe ymb stondað,

125   þa þu þe lete sittan   on þa swiþran hond,

þa þu us on þisne wræc-sið,   weoroda Dryhten,

þurh þines sylfes geweald   secan woldest,

ond fore Hierusalem   in Iudeum

(sceal seo burg nu þa   bidan efne swaþeah,

130   þeoden leofa,   þines eft-cymes),

ond for Iordane   in Iudeum

(wit unc in þære burnan   baþodan ætgædre),

oferwurpe þu mid þy wætre,   weoruda Dryhten,

bliþe mode   ealle burg-waran,

135   swylce git Iohannis   in Iordane

mid þy fullwihte   fægre onbryrdon

ealne þisne middan-geard.   Sie þæs symle meotude

þonc!"

encompass all the dwellings of mankind, just as you can
count the grains of sand in the sea. Also I entreat you, our
savior, for the sake of your childhood, best of kings, and for   120
the sake of your wounds, Lord of hosts, and for the sake of
your resurrection, joy of princes, and for the sake of your
mother, whose name is Mary and whom all the inhabitants
of hell praise and exalt, and for the sake of the angels who
stand around you and whom you allowed to sit at your right   125
hand when you, Lord of hosts, wished to seek us out in this
exile through your own power, and for the sake of Jerusalem
in Judea (the city must now, nevertheless, await your return,   130
dear prince), and for the sake of Jordan in Judea (the two of
us bathed together in that stream), Lord of hosts, graciously
sprinkle all who live in this city with that water, just as you   135
and John in the Jordan with baptism happily inspired this
entire world. For that may the creator always be thanked!"

THE VISION OF
THE CROSS

Hwæt ic swefna cyst   secgan wylle,
þæt me gemætte   to midre nihte,
syðþan reord-berend   reste wunedon!
   Þuhte me þæt ic gesawe   syllicre treow
5 on lyft lædan,   leohte bewunden,
   beama beorhtost.   Eall þæt beacen wæs
   begoten mid golde.   Gimmas stodon
fægere æt foldan sceatum;   swylce þær fife wæron
uppe on þam eaxle-gespanne.   Beheoldon þær engel
                                          Dryhtnes ealle,
10 fægere þurh forð-gesceaft.   Ne wæs ðær huru fracodes
                                          gealga
      ac hine þær beheoldon   halige gastas,
   men ofer moldan,   ond eall þeos mære gesceaft.
      Syllic wæs se sige-beam,   ond ic synnum fah,
   forwunded mid wommum.   Geseah ic wuldres treow,
15 wædum geweorðode,   wynnum scinan,
   gegyred mid golde.   Gimmas hæfdon
   bewrigene weorðlice   wealdendes treow.
   Hwæðre ic þurh þæt gold   ongytan meahte
   earmra ær-gewin,   þæt hit ærest ongan
20 swætan on þa swiðran healfe.   Eall ic wæs mid sorgum
                                          gedrefed;
   forht ic wæs for þære fægran gesyhðe.   Geseah ic þæt fuse
                                          beacen

How I wish to tell the best of dreams, which I dreamed in the middle of the night when speech-bearing people were in bed asleep!

It seemed to me that I saw a most extraordinary tree raised into the air, encircled by light, the brightest of beams. All that symbol was covered with gold. Beautiful gems shone from the corners of the earth; likewise there were five up on the intersection. All fair beings throughout creation beheld there the angel of the Lord. That was certainly not the gallows of someone despicable, but holy spirits, people all over the earth, and all this glorious creation beheld it there.

The tree of victory was extraordinary, but I was stained with sins, sorely wounded by evil deeds. I saw the tree of glory, honored by its garments, shining splendidly, adorned with gold. Jewels had honorably covered the ruler's tree. Yet through that gold I could distinguish the former struggle of the wretched ones when it first began to bleed on its right side. I was all troubled by cares; I was afraid before that beautiful sight. I saw that restless symbol, changing its

wendan wædum ond bleom;   hwilum hit wæs mid wætan
                                          bestemed,
beswyled mid swates gange,   hwilum mid since gegyrwed.
    Hwæðre ic þær licgende   lange hwile
25   beheold hreow-cearig   hælendes treow,
    oð ðæt ic gehyrde   þæt hit hleoðrode.
    Ongan þa word sprecan   wudu selesta:
    "Þæt wæs geara iu   —ic þæt gyta geman—
    þæt ic wæs aheawen   holtes on ende,
30   astyred of stefne minum.   Genaman me ðær strange
                                          feondas,
    geworhton him þær to wæfer-syne,   heton me heora
                                          wergas hebban.
    Bæron me ðær beornas on eaxlum,   oð ðæt hie me on
                                          beorg asetton;
    gefæstnodon me þær feondas genoge.   Geseah ic þa Frean
                                          man-cynnes
    efstan elne mycle   þæt he me wolde on gestigan.
35   Þær ic þa ne dorste   ofer Dryhtnes word
    bugan oððe berstan,   þa ic bifian geseah
    eorðan sceatas.   Ealle ic mihte
    feondas gefyllan,   hwæðre ic fæste stod.
    "Ongyrede hine þa geong hæleð   —þæt wæs God
                                          ælmihtig—
40   strang ond stiðmod.   Gestah he on gealgan heanne,
    modig on manigra gesyhðe,   þa he wolde man-cyn lysan.
    Bifode ic þa me se beorn ymbclypte.   Ne dorste ic hwæðre
                                          bugan to eorðan,
    feallan to foldan sceatum,   ac ic sceolde fæste standan.
    Rod wæs ic aræred.   Ahof ic ricne cyning,
45   heofona Hlaford,   hyldan me ne dorste.

garments and its appearance; sometimes it was all soaked with liquid, drenched by the flow of blood, sometimes adorned with treasure.

Yet, lying there for a long time, troubled and anxious, I [25] beheld the savior's tree, until I heard it speak. The best wood spoke these words:

"It was long ago—I still remember it—that I was cut down at the edge of a wood, removed from my root. Strong [30] enemies seized me there, made a show of me in public, commanded me to raise up their criminals. Men carried me on their shoulders there, until they set me on a hill; enemies enough fixed me in place there. Then I saw the Lord of mankind hastening with great courage when he was intent on climbing on to me. Then I dared not bend down or break [35] apart there, against the Lord's word, when I saw all of the earth's surfaces shaking. I could have felled all the enemies, yet I stood fast.

"Then the young hero—who was God Almighty— stripped himself, strong and resolute. He climbed onto the [40] high gallows, brave in the sight of many, when he was intent on setting mankind free. I was shaking when the warrior embraced me. Yet I dared not bend to the ground, fall to the earth's surface, but I had to stand fast. I was raised up, a cross. I lifted up the powerful king, the Lord of the heavens, [45]

Þurhdrifan hi me mid deorcan næglum.   On me syndon þa
                                         dolg gesiene,
opene inwid-hlemmas.   Ne dorste ic hira ænigum sceððan.
Bysmeredon hie unc butu ætgædere.   Eall ic wæs mid
                                      blode bestemed,
begoten of þæs guman sidan,   siððan he hæfde his gast
                                onsended.

50   "Feala ic on þam beorge   gebiden hæbbe
       wraðra wyrda.   Geseah ic weruda God
       þearle þenian.   Þystro hæfdon
       bewrigen mid wolcnum   wealdendes hræw,
       scirne sciman;   sceadu forð eode,
55   wann under wolcnum.   Weop eal gesceaft,
       cwiðdon cyninges fyll.   Crist wæs on rode.

       "Hwæðere þær fuse   feorran cwoman
       to þam æðelinge;   ic þæt eall beheold.
Sare ic wæs mid sorgum gedrefed;   hnag ic hwæðre þam
                                     secgum to handa,
60 eað-mod, elne mycle.   Genamon hie þær ælmihtigne God,
ahofon hine of ðam hefian wite.   Forleton me þa hilde-
                                    rincas
standan steame bedrifenne;   eall ic wæs mid strælum
                               forwundod.
Aledon hie ðær lim-werigne,   gestodon him æt his lices
                                heafdum;
beheoldon hie ðær heofenes Dryhten   ond he hine ðær
                                       hwile reste,
65 meðe æfter ðam miclan gewinne.   Ongunnon him þa
                                      mold-ern wyrcan
beornas on banan gesyhðe.   Curfon hie ðæt of beorhtan
                              stane;

not daring to bow down. They drove dark nails through me. The cuts are visible on me, open malicious wounds. I dared not harm any of them. They mocked us both together. I was all soaked with blood, drenched from that man's side, after he had given up his spirit.

"I experienced many cruel events on that hill. I saw the Lord of hosts harshly stretched out. Darkness had covered the ruler's corpse, the shining brightness, with clouds; a dark shadow advanced under the clouds. All creation wept, lamented the fall of the king. Christ was on the cross.

"Yet people came hastening from far off to the prince; I saw it all. I was sorely troubled by my cares; yet I bowed down to the men's hands, humble, with great courage. They took almighty God there, lifted him down from the heavy torment. The warriors left me standing drenched in blood; I was all cruelly wounded by arrows. They laid him down, weary limbed, stood at the head of his body; there they looked at the Lord of heaven, and he rested there for a while, exhausted after his great struggle. The men began to make a sepulcher for him in the sight of his slayer. They

gesetton hie ðæron sigora wealdend.   Ongunnon him þa
                                 sorh-leoð galan,
earme on þa æfen-tide,   þa hie woldon eft siðian,
meðe fram þam mæran þeodne;   reste he ðær mæte
                                 weorode.
70   "Hwæðere we ðær greotende   gode hwile
stodon on staðole,   syððan stefn up gewat
hilde-rinca.   Hræw colode,
fæger feorg-bold.   Þa us man fyllan ongan
ealle to eorðan;   þæt wæs egeslic wyrd!
75 Bedealf us man on deopan seaþe;   hwæðre me þær
                                 Dryhtnes þegnas,
freondas gefrunon,   . . .
gyredon me   golde ond seolfre.
     "Nu ðu miht gehyran,   hæleð min se leofa,
þæt ic bealu-wara weorc   gebiden hæbbe,
80 sarra sorga.   Is nu sæl cumen
þæt me weorðiað   wide ond side
menn ofer moldan   ond eall þeos mære gesceaft,
gebiddaþ him to þyssum beacne.   On me bearn Godes
þrowode hwile;   forþan ic þrym-fæst nu
85 hlifige under heofenum   ond ic hælan mæg
æghwylcne anra   þara þe him bið egesa to me.
Iu ic wæs geworden   wita heardost,
leodum laðost,   ærþan ic him lifes weg
rihtne gerymde,   reord-berendum.
90 Hwæt me þa geweorðode   wuldres Ealdor
ofer holm-wudu,   heofon-rices weard,
swylce swa he his modor eac,   Marian sylfe,
ælmihtig God   for ealle menn
geweorðode   ofer eall wifa cynn!

carved it out of bright stone; they placed the Lord of vic-
tories in it. The wretched men sang a mournful song in
the evening time, when, exhausted, they wished to go away
again from that splendid prince; he remained there with a
small company.

"Yet we stood in our positions there lamenting for a good 70
while longer, after the voices of the warriors had gone. The
corpse grew cold, that beautiful house of life. Then we were
all felled to the ground; that was a terrible thing to happen!
We were buried in a deep pit; yet the followers of the Lord, 75
his friends, learned about me there . . . they adorned me
with gold and silver.

"Now, my dear man, you can hear that I have suffered at
the hands of men steeped in evil, the pain of bitter sorrows. 80
Now the time has come when people throughout the earth
and all this glorious creation honor me far and wide, praying
to this symbol. On me the Son of God suffered for a time;
that is why I tower up now, glorious under the heavens, and 85
I can heal each and everyone who is in awe of me. I was once
the cruelest of punishments, most hateful to people, until I
opened up the right way of life for speech-bearing people.
How the Lord of glory, the guardian of the heavenly king- 90
dom, honored me then above the trees of the forest, just as
he, Almighty God, honored his mother also, Mary herself,
over all womankind for the sake of the human race!

95 "Nu ic þe hate, hæleð min se leofa,
   þæt ðu þas gesyhðe secge mannum,
   onwreoh wordum þæt hit is wuldres beam,
   se ðe ælmihtig God on þrowode
   for man-cynnes manegum synnum
100 ond Adomes eald-gewyrhtum.
   Deað he þær byrigde, hwæðere eft Dryhten aras
   mid his miclan mihte mannum to helpe.
   He ða on heofenas astag. Hider eft fundaþ
   on þysne middan-geard man-cynn secan
105 on dom-dæge Dryhten sylfa,
   ælmihtig God, ond his englas mid,
   þæt he þonne wile deman, se ah domes geweald,
   anra gehwylcum swa he him ærur her
   on þyssum lænum life geearnaþ.
110 Ne mæg þær ænig unforht wesan
   for þam worde þe se wealdend cwyð.
   Frineð he for þære mænige hwær se man sie,
   se ðe for Dryhtnes naman deaðes wolde
   biteres onbyrigan, swa he ær on ðam beame dyde.
115 Ac hie þonne forhtiað, ond fea þencaþ
   hwæt hie to Criste cweðan onginnen.
   Ne þearf ðær þonne ænig unforht wesan
   þe him ær in breostum bereð beacna selest
   ac ðurh ða rode sceal rice gesecan
120 of eorð-wege æghwylc sawl,
   seo þe mid wealdende wunian þenceð."
      Gebæd ic me þa to þan beame bliðe mode,
   elne mycle, þær ic ana wæs

"Now I command you, my dear man, that you tell this vi- 95
sion to people, reveal in words that this is the tree of glory,
on which almighty God suffered for mankind's many sins
and Adam's ancient deeds. He tasted death there, yet the 100
Lord arose again through his great power to help mankind.
He ascended into the heavens. On the day of judgment the
Lord himself, almighty God, with his angels, will journey 105
here again to seek out mankind on this earth, when he who
has the power to judge will wish to pass judgment on each
and every one according as he will have earned for himself
here in this transitory life. No one there can be fearless re- 110
garding the words which the ruler will speak. He will ask, in
front of the multitude, where that person may be who would
be willing to taste bitter death for the sake of the Lord, as he
did formerly on this cross. But then they will be afraid and 115
will scarcely imagine what to say to Christ. Then no one
there need be afraid, no one who will have carried the best
of symbols in his breast beforehand, but every soul that de-
sires to dwell with the ruler must seek out the heavenly 120
kingdom from this world through that cross."

Then I prayed to that tree with a cheerful spirit, with
great courage, there where I was alone with a small com-

mæte werede.   Wæs mod-sefa
125 afysed on forð-wege,   feala ealra gebad
langung-hwila.   Is me nu lifes hyht
þæt ic þone sige-beam   secan mote
ana oftor   þonne ealle men,
well weorþian.   Me is willa to ðam
130 mycel on mode   ond min mund-byrd is
geriht to þære rode.   Nah ic ricra feala
freonda on foldan   ac hie forð heonon
gewiton of worulde dreamum,   sohton him wuldres cyning,
lifiaþ nu on heofenum   mid Heah-Fædere,
135 wuniaþ on wuldre;   ond ic wene me
daga gehwylce   hwænne me Dryhtnes rod,
þe ic her on eorðan   ær sceawode,
on þysson lænan   life gefetige
ond me þonne gebringe   þær is blis mycel,
140 dream on heofonum,   þær is Dryhtnes folc
geseted to symle,   þær is singal blis,
ond me þonne asette   þær ic syþþan mot
wunian on wuldre,   well mid þam halgum
dreames brucan.   Si me Dryhten freond,
145 se ðe her on eorþan   ær þrowode
on þam gealg-treowe   for guman synnum.
He us onlysde   ond us lif forgeaf,
heofonlicne ham.   Hiht wæs geniwad
mid bledum ond mid blisse   þam þe þær bryne þolodan.
150 Se Sunu wæs sigor-fæst   on þam sið-fate,

pany. My mind was filled with eagerness for death, enduring   125
very many times of longing. My life's hope is now that I
alone may seek out the tree of victory more often than all
other people, honor it well. I have an intense desire for that
in my heart and my hope of protection is directed toward   130
the cross. I do not have many powerful friends on earth, but
they have departed from here, from the joys of the world,
have sought out the king of glory for themselves, live now in   135
heaven with the Father on high, dwell in glory; and every
day I look forward to the time when the cross of the Lord,
which I formerly saw here on earth, will fetch me from this
transitory life and bring me to where there is great bliss, joy   140
in heaven, where the Lord's people are seated at the feast,
where there is everlasting bliss, and will set me down where
I may then dwell in glory, participate fully in joy with the
saints. May the Lord be a friend to me, he who formerly   145
suffered on the gallows tree here on earth for the sins of
mankind. He set us free and gave us life, a heavenly home.
Hope was renewed with glory and with bliss for those who
had endured burning there. The Son was victorious on that   150

mihtig ond spedig,   þa he mid manigeo com,
gasta weorode,   on Godes rice,
anwealda ælmihtig,   englum to blisse
ond eallum ðam halgum   þam þe on heofonum ær
155 wunedon on wuldre,   þa heora wealdend cwom,
ælmihtig God,   þær his eðel wæs.

expedition, powerful and successful, when he came with a
multitude, a band of spirits, into God's kingdom, the al-
mighty Lord, bringing bliss to the angels and all the saints
who before that had dwelt in glory in the heavens, when 155
their ruler came, almighty God, to where his homeland was.

THE RUTHWELL CROSS
CRUCIFIXION POEM

I

Ondgeredæ hinæ   God almegttig
þa he walde on galgu gistiga,
modig fore . . . men.
Buga . . .

II
5   . . . ic riicnæ kyniŋc,
heafunæs Hlafard;   hælda ic ni dorstæ.
Bismærædu uŋket men ba ætgadre;   ic . . . miþ blodæ
                                                            bistemid,
bigoten . . .

III
Krist wæs on rodi.
10   Hweþræ þer fusæ   fearran kwomu
æþþilæ til anum.   Ic þæt al biheald.
Saræ ic wæs miþ sorgum gidrœfid,   hnag . . . . . .

IV
miþ strelum giwundad.
Alegdun hiæ hinæ lim-wœrignæ,   gistoddun him . . .
                                                            licæs heafdum;
15   bihealdun hiæ þer . . . .

God almighty stripped himself when he was intent on climbing onto the gallows, brave before . . . people. [I did not dare] bend . . .

. . . a powerful king, the Lord of heaven; I dared not bow down. People mocked us both together; I . . . soaked with blood, drenched . . .

Christ was on the cross. Yet noble ones came hastening together there from far off. I saw it all. I was sorely troubled with cares, [I] bowed down . . .

wounded by arrows. They laid him down weary-limbed, stood at the head of his body; they looked there at . . .

I

II
5

III
10

IV

15

THE BRUSSELS
CROSS INSCRIPTION

Drahmal me worhte.

Rod is min nama.   Geo ic ricne cyning
bær byfigynde,   blode bestemed.

Þas rode het Æþlmær wyrican ond Aðelwold hys broþor,
Criste to lofe, for Ælfrices savle hyra broþor.

Drahmal made me.

Cross is my name. Once, shaking, I carried a powerful
king, soaked with blood.

Æthelmær and Athelwold his brother commanded this
cross to be made, in honor of Christ, for the soul of Ælfric
their brother.

ANDREAS

Hwæt we gefrunan   on fyrn-dagum
twelfe under tunglum   tir-eadige hæleð,
þeodnes þegnas!   No hira þrym alæg
camp-rædenne   þonne cumbol hneotan,
5   syððan hie gedældon   swa him Dryhten sylf,
heofona heah-cyning,   hlyt getæhte.
Þæt wæron mære   men ofer eorðan,
frome folc-togan   ond fyrd-hwate,
rofe rincas,   þonne rond ond hand
10   on here-felda   helm ealgodon,
on meotud-wange.
                Wæs hira Matheus sum,
se mid Iudeum ongan   god-spell ærest
wordum writan   wundor-cræfte.
Þam halig God   hlyt geteode
15   ut on þæt ig-land,   þær ænig þa git
ell-þeodigra   eðles ne mihte
blædes brucan;   oft him bonena hand
on here-felda   hearde gesceode.
Eal wæs þæt mearc-land   morðre bewunden,
20   feondes facne,   folc-stede gumena,
hæleða eðel.   Næs þær hlafes wist
werum on þam wonge,   ne wæteres drync
to bruconne,   ah hie blod ond fel,
fira flæsc-homan,   feorran-cumenra,

Much have we heard tell about twelve famous men under the heavens, disciples of the Lord, in days of old! When battle standards clashed their glory in warfare did not fail, after they had dispersed as the Lord himself, the high king of heaven, assigned them their lots. They were great men on earth, brave leaders of the people and valiant in war, strong warriors, when shields and hands defended helmets on the field of battle, on the fateful plain.

Matthew was one of them; he was the first among the Jews to write the gospel in words with wonderful skill. Holy God decreed that his lot would be out on that island, where no foreigner could as yet dwell and live; slayers' hands often fell heavily upon him on the battlefield. All that province, that dwelling place of men, that inhabited country, was enmeshed in evil, in devilish deceit. The people in that place had no bread to nourish them nor water to drink, but all that nation consumed blood and skin, the corpses of men,

25 ðegon geond þa þeode.　Swelc wæs þeaw hira
þæt hie æghwylcne　ellðeodigra
dydan him to mose　mete-þearfendum,
þara þe þæt ea-land　utan sohte;
swylc wæs þæs folces　freoðo-leas tacen,
30 unlædra eafoð,　þæt hie eagena gesihð,
hettend heoro-grimme,　heafod-gimmas
agetton gealg-mode　gara ordum.
Syððan him geblendan　bitere tosomne,
dryas þurh dwol-cræft,　drync unheorne,
35 se onwende gewit,　wera in-geþanc,
heortan on hreðre;　hyge wæs oncyrred,
þæt hie ne murndan　æfter man-dreame,
hæleþ heoro-grædige,　ac hie hig ond gærs
for mete-leaste　meðe gedrehte.
40 Þa wæs Matheus　to þære mæran byrig
cumen in þa ceastre.　Þær wæs cirm micel
geond Mermedonia,　manfulra hloð,
fordenera gedræg,　syþþan deofles þegn
geascodon　æðelinges sið.
45 Eodon him þa togenes,　garum gehyrsted,
lungre under linde;　nalas late wæron
eorre æsc-berend　to þam orlege.
Hie þam halgan þær　handa gebundon
ond fæstnodon　feondes cræfte,
50 hæleð hell-fuse,　ond his heafdes sigel
abreoton mid billes ecge.　Hwæðre he in breostum þa git
herede in heortan　heofon-rices weard,
þeah ðe he atres drync　atulne onfenge.

of people from afar. Such was their custom, that they took 25
as food for the hungry each of the foreigners who sought
out that island from outside; such was the hostile mark of
that people, the might of these accursed ones, that the sav- 30
age, bloody and fierce enemies destroyed the sight of eyes,
the jewels of heads, with the points of their spears. Then
sorcerers, with their heretical art, cruelly mixed together a
dreadful drink for them, which overturned men's wits and 35
thoughts and the hearts in their breasts; their minds were
altered, so that the fiercely ravenous men did not care for
human pleasures but, worn out from lack of food, hay and
grass tormented them.

Then Matthew came to that famous stronghold, into that 40
city. There was a great outcry throughout Mermedonia,
once the crowd of wicked men, the throng of the damned,
the devil's servants, found out about the noble man's jour-
ney. Armed with spears, protected by shields, they quickly 45
advanced against him; the angry spear bearers were not at all
slow to do battle. Those hell-bound men tied and fettered
the saint's hands there, with fiendish cunning, and destroyed 50
his head's suns with the sword's edge. Yet within his breast
he went on praising the guardian of heaven in his heart, even
though he had swallowed the horrible drink of poison.

Eadig ond onmod,   he mid elne forð
55   wyrðode wordum   wuldres Aldor,
heofon-rices weard,   halgan stefne,
of carcerne;   him wæs Cristes lof
on fyrhð-locan   fæste bewunden.
   He þa wepende   weregum tearum
60   his Sige-Dryhten   sargan reorde
grette, gumena brego,   geomran stefne,
weoruda wil-geofan,   ond þus wordum cwæð:
"Hu me elþeodige   inwit-wrasne,
searo-net seowað!   A ic symles wæs
65   on wega gehwam   willan þines
georn on mode;   nu ðurh geohða sceal
dæde fremman   swa þa dumban neat.
Þu ana canst   ealra gehygdo,
meotud man-cynnes,   mod in hreðre.
70   Gif þin willa sie,   wuldres Aldor,
þæt me wær-logan   wæpna ecgum,
sweordum aswebban,   ic beo sona gearu
to adreoganne   þæt ðu, Drihten min,
engla ead-gifa,   eðel-leasum,
75   dugeða dæd-fruma,   deman wille.
Forgif me to are,   ælmihtig God,
leoht on þissum life,   þy læs ic lungre scyle,
ablended in burgum   æfter bill-hete,
þurh hearm-cwide   heoru-grædigra,
80   laðra leod-sceaðena,   leng þrowian
edwit-spræce.   Ic to anum þe,
middan-geardes weard,   mod staþolige,
fæste fyrhð-lufan,   ond þe, Fæder engla,
beorht blæd-gifa,   biddan wille

Blessed and resolute, from his prison he courageously kept 55
on honoring with his words the Lord of glory, the guard-
ian of the heavenly kingdom, with his holy voice; praise of
Christ was firmly implanted in his breast.

Weeping miserable tears, with a sad voice, in sorrowful 60
speech he reverently addressed the ruler of men, the trium-
phant Lord, the gracious benefactor of the heavenly hosts,
and said these words: "How these foreign men weave chains
of evil and a web of treachery for me! I was always at all 65
times eager in my mind to do your will; now in my grief I
must act like the dumb beasts. You alone, creator of man-
kind, know everyone's intention, the minds in their breasts.
If it be your will, Lord of glory, that the evildoers put me to 70
death by the sword, with their weapons' blades, I am ready
to endure immediately whatever you, my Lord, who gives
happiness to the angels, ruler of hosts, may wish to decree 75
for me, far from my homeland. Almighty God, in your mercy
give me light in this life, lest I, sightless in the cities from
their sword hatred, may soon have to suffer for longer the 80
scornful talk of the people's hated enemies, the malicious
words of the bloodthirsty. Guardian of the world, I fix my
mind and the constant love of my spirit upon you alone,
and I entreat you, Father of the angels, radiant giver of

85 ðæt ðu me ne gescyrige   mid scyld-hetum,
werigum wroht-smiðum,   on þone wyrrestan,
dugoða demend,   deað ofer eorðan."
    Æfter þyssum wordum com   wuldres tacen
halig of heofenum,   swylce hadre sigel
90 to þam carcerne;   þær gecyðed wearð
þæt halig God   helpe gefremede.
Ða wearð gehyred   heofon-cyninges stefn
wrætlic under wolcnum,   word-hleoðres sweg
mæres þeodnes.   He his magu-þegne
95 under hearm-locan   hælo ond frofre
beadu-rofum abead   beorhtan stefne:
"Ic þe, Matheus,   mine sylle
sybbe under swegle.   Ne beo ðu on sefan to forht,
ne on mode ne murn;   ic þe mid wunige
100 ond þe alyse   of þyssum leoðu-bendum,
ond ealle þa menigo   þe þe mid wuniað
on nearo-nedum.   Þe is neorxna-wang,
blæda beorhtost,   bold-wela fægrost,
hama hyhtlicost,   halegum mihtum
105 torht ontyned,   þær ðu tyres most
to widan feore   willan brucan.
Geþola þeoda þrea!   Nis seo þrah micel
þæt þe wær-logan   wite-bendum,
synne ðurh searo-cræft,   swencan motan.
110 Ic þe Andreas   ædre onsende
to hleo ond to hroðre   in þas hæðenan burg;
he ðe alyseð   of þyssum leod-hete.
Is to þære tide   tæl-met hwile
emne mid soðe   seofon ond twentig

happiness, judge of hosts, that you do not ordain for me the   85
worst death upon earth among these wicked foes, these ac-
cursed evildoers."

After these words a holy sign of glory came from the
heavens into the prison, like the bright sun; there it was re-   90
vealed that holy God had provided his help. Then the won-
drous voice of the heavenly king was heard under the clouds,
the sound of the glorious ruler's voice. He proclaimed heal-   95
ing and comfort in a clear voice to his servant, brave and re-
nowned in battle, in his painful prison: "Matthew, I give you
my peace under the sky. Do not be afraid in your spirit or
fearful in your mind; I will remain with you and will rescue
you from your bonds, along with all the multitude who dwell   100
with you in dire hardship. By my holy powers the bright par-
adise will be opened for you, the most radiant of glories,
fairest of abodes, most joyful of homes, where, forever and   105
ever, you may partake of pleasure and glory. Endure the op-
pression of these people! These treacherous men with their
evil tricks will not be allowed to torment you in bonds of
torture for long. I will quickly send Andrew to you for your   110
protection and comfort in this heathen city; he will release
you from persecution by this people. It is a limited pe-
riod of time, exactly twenty-seven nights all told, truly,

115 niht-gerimes,   þæt ðu of nede most;
sorgum geswenced,   sigore gewyrðod,
hweorfest of henðum   in gehyld Godes."
    Gewat him þa se halga   helm æl-wihta,
engla scyppend,   to þam uplican
120 eðel-rice;   he is onriht cyning,
staðol-fæst styrend,   in stowa gehwam.

    Ða wæs Matheus   miclum onbryrded
niwan stefne.   Niht-helm toglad,
lungre leorde;   leoht æfter com,
125 dægred-woma.   Duguð samnade;
hæðne hild-frecan   heapum þrungon,
—guð-searo gullon,   garas hrysedon—
bolgen-mode   under bord-hreoðan.
Woldon cunnian   hwæðer cwice lifdon
130 þa þe on carcerne   clommum fæste
hleo-leasan wic   hwile wunedon,
hwylcne hie to æte   ærest mihton
æfter fyrst-mearce   feores berædan.
Hæfdon hie on rune   ond on rim-cræfte
135 awriten, wæl-grædige,   wera ende-stæf,
hwænne hie to mose   mete-þearfendum
on þære wer-þeode   weorðan sceoldon.
Cirmdon cald-heorte   —corðor oðrum getang;
reðe ræs-boran   rihtes ne gimdon,
140 meotudes mildse.   Oft hira mod onwod
under dim-scuan   deofles larum,
þonne hie unlædra   eaueðum gelyfdon.

until the hour when you may leave this hardship; oppressed 115
by sorrows, you will go from this humiliation into the keep-
ing of God, glorified by victory."

Then the holy protector of all creatures, the creator of
angels, departed to his homeland on high; he is the rightful 120
king, the steadfast ruler in every place.

Then Matthew was greatly inspired once again. The
shadow of night vanished, departed quickly; light came af-
ter it, the crack of dawn. The troop assembled; the heathen 125
warriors, enraged, thronged in crowds behind their shields
—their battle gear resounded, their spears rattled. They
wanted to find out whether those who had occupied for a
time that comfortless dwelling, fettered in prison, were still
alive, and which one they could first deprive of life, after 130
the appointed time, for eating. Those slaughter-greedy men
had written the men's appointed end in secret letters and
numbers, the time when they would have to become food 135
for those in need of sustenance among that nation. Cold-
hearted, they cried out—one armed troop crowded against
the other; the fierce leaders did not care about right or the 140
creator's mercy. Often their minds ranged beneath dark
shadows, at the devil's promptings, since they believed in
the might of the wicked.

Hie ða gemetton   modes glawne,
haligne hæle,   under heolstor-locan
145   bidan beadu-rofne   hwæs him beorht cyning,
engla Ord-Fruma,   unnan wolde.
Ða wæs first agan   frum-rædenne
þing-gemearces   butan þrim nihtum,
swa hit wæl-wulfas   awriten hæfdon
150   þæt hie ban-hringas   abrecan þohton,
lungre tolysan   lic ond sawle,
ond þonne todælan   duguðe ond geogoðe,
werum to wiste   ond to wil-þege,
fæges flæsc-homan.   Feorh ne bemurndan,
155   grædige guð-rincas,   hu þæs gastes sið
æfter swylt-cwale   geseted wurde.
Swa hie symble ymb þritig   þing gehedon
niht-gerimes;   wæs him neod micel
þæt hie tobrugdon   blodigum ceaflum
160   fira flæsc-homan   him to foddor-þege.
Þa wæs gemyndig,   se ðe middan-geard
gestaðelode   strangum mihtum,
hu he in ell-þeodigum   yrmðum wunode,
belocen leoðu-bendum,   þe oft his lufan adreg
165   for Ebreum   ond Israhelum;
swylce he Iudea   galdor-cræftum
wiðstod stranglice.   Þa sio stefn gewearð
gehered of heofenum,   þær se halga wer
in Achaia   Andreas wæs,
170   —leode lærde   on lifes weg—
þa him cine-baldum   cininga wuldor,
meotud man-cynnes,   mod-hord onleac,
weoruda Drihten,   ond þus wordum cwæð:

Then they found the holy man, wise in his mind, brave
and renowned in battle, waiting in his dark prison for what- 145
ever the radiant king, the Lord of angels, might wish for
him. By then the period of the original arrangement had
elapsed but for three days, that period of allotted time
which the slaughter wolves had written down, when they in- 150
tended to break apart his backbone, quickly separate body
and soul, and then share out the dead man's corpse to tried
and untried warriors, as a meal and as pleasant food for the
men. Those greedy warriors did not care about his life, 155
about what kind of journey might be ordained for his soul
after the pain of his death. They always held a council like
this after thirty days; they had a great longing to tear to
pieces the corpses of men with their bloody jaws, for their 160
food.

Then he who had established the world with his powerful
might was mindful of how he, who had often shown his love
for him in the presence of the Hebrews and the Israelites,
was dwelling in miseries among foreign people, confined in 165
bondage; he had also strongly opposed the Jews' occult arts.
Then in Achaia, where the holy man Andrew was—teach-
ing the people the path to life—a voice was heard from the 170
heavens, when the glorious king, the creator of mankind,
the Lord of hosts, unlocked the treasure of his mind to that

"Ðu scealt feran   ond frið lædan,

175 siðe gesecan,   þær sylf-ætan
eard weardigað,   eðel healdaþ
morðor-cræftum.   Swa is þære menigo þeaw
þæt hie uncuðra   ængum ne willað
on þam folc-stede   feores geunnan;

180 syþþan manfulle   on Mermedonia
onfindaþ fea-sceaftne,   þær sceall feorh-gedal,
earmlic ylda cwealm,   æfter wyrþan.
Ðær ic seomian wat   þinne sige-broðor
mid þam burg-warum   bendum fæstne.

185 Nu bið fore þreo niht   þæt he on þære þeode sceal
fore hæðenra   hand-gewinne
þurh gares gripe   gast onsendan,
ellor-fusne,   butan ðu ær cyme."

Ædre him Andreas   agef andsware:

190 "Hu mæg ic, Dryhten min,   ofer deop gelad
fore gefremman   on feorne weg
swa hrædlice,   heofona scyppend,
wuldres waldend,   swa ðu worde becwist?
Ðæt mæg engel þin   eað geferan,

195 halig of heofenum;   con him holma begang,
sealte sæ-streamas   ond swan-rade,
waroð-faruða gewinn   ond wæter-brogan,
wegas ofer wid-land.   Ne synt me winas cuðe,
eorlas elþeodige,   ne þær æniges wat

200 hæleða gehygdo,   ne me here-stræta
ofer cald wæter   cuðe sindon."

Him ða ondswarude   ece Dryhten:
"Eala Andreas,   þæt ðu a woldest
þæs sið-fætes   sæne weorþan!

very brave man and said these words: "You must go and risk your life, journey to a place where cannibals inhabit the country, guarding their homeland by murderous arts. Such is the custom of that multitude that they are not willing to grant life to any stranger in their dwelling place; as soon as the wicked men discover some miserable person in Mermedonia, after that there must be a severing from life, the wretched murder of men. I know that your glorious brother lies fastened in bonds among those townspeople. There will now be three days until the time when, as a result of the heathens' armed violence, the attack of their spears, he will have to yield up his spirit, ready for death, among that people, unless you arrive beforehand."

Andrew answered him quickly: "How can I, my Lord, creator of the heavens, ruler of glory, make the journey over the deep sea, over that great distance, as quickly as you declare? Your holy angel from the heavens can traverse that easily; he has knowledge of the expanse of the oceans, the salt sea-currents and the swan's road, the tumult of the eddying surf, the terror of the water, the paths over the wide land. The foreign warriors are not my familiar friends, nor do I know the thoughts of any of those men, nor are the sealanes over the cold water familiar to me."

The eternal Lord answered him: "O Andrew, that you would ever be reluctant about this journey! It is not difficult

205 Nis þæt uneaðe   eall-wealdan Gode
to gefremmanne   on fold-wege,
ðæt sio ceaster hider   on þas cneorisse
under swegles gang   aseted wyrðe,
breogo-stol breme,   mid þam burg-warum,
210 gif hit worde becwið   wuldres agend.
Ne meaht ðu þæs sið-fætes   sæne weorðan,
ne on gewitte to wac,   gif ðu wel þencest
wið þinne waldend   wære gehealdan,
treowe tacen.   Beo ðu on tid gearu;
215 ne mæg þæs ærendes   ylding wyrðan.
Ðu scealt þa fore geferan   ond þin feorh beran
in gramra gripe,   ðær þe guð-gewinn
þurh hæðenra   hilde-woman,
beorna beadu-cræft,   geboden wyrðeð.
220 Scealtu æninga   mid ær-dæge,
emne to morgene,   æt meres ende
ceol gestigan   ond on cald wæter
brecan ofer bæð-weg.   Hafa bletsunge
ofer middan-geard   mine þær ðu fere!"
225   Gewat him þa se halga   healdend ond wealdend,
up-engla fruma,   eðel secan,
middan-geardes weard,   þone mæran ham,
þær soð-fæstra   sawla moton
æfter lices hryre   lifes brucan.

230   Þa wæs ærende   æðelum cempan
aboden in burgum,   ne wæs him bleað hyge,
ah he wæs an-ræd   ellen-weorces,
heard ond hige-rof,   nalas hild-lata,
gearo, guðe fram,   to Godes campe.

for the omnipotent God to bring it about on earth that that city, the renowned principality, with its citizens, be set down here among this people, under the sky's expanse, if the Lord 210 of glory declares it. If you intend to keep your covenant fully with your ruler, your pledge of good faith, you cannot be reluctant about this journey, or weak minded. Be ready on time; there can be no delay on this mission. You must com- 215 plete this journey, risk your life in the grasp of enemies, where, in the terror of battle with the heathens, you will be threatened with the hardship of war, their warriors' strength in battle. You must at once, at daybreak this very morning, 220 board a ship at the ocean's edge and break open the ocean-way on the cold water. Have my blessing wherever you go throughout the world."

Then the holy defender and ruler, source of the heavenly 225 angels, guardian of the world, departed to seek out his own land, the glorious home where the souls of the righteous may enjoy life after the death of their bodies.

When this message was announced to the noble warrior 230 in the city, his mind was not cowardly, but he was resolved upon his courageous deed, bold and valiant, not at all slow to fight, but ready, strong in combat in God's battlefield.

235 Gewat him þa on uhtan   mid ær-dæge
ofer sand-hleoðu   to sæs faruðe,
þriste on geþance,   ond his þegnas mid,
gangan on greote;   gar-secg hlynede,
beoton brim-streamas.   Se beorn wæs on hyhte,
240 syðþan he on waruðe   wid-fæðme scip
modig gemette.   Þa com morgen-torht
beacna beorhtost   ofer breomo sneowan,
halig of heolstre.   Heofon-candel blac
ofer lago-flodas.   He ðær lid-weardas,
245 þrymlice þry   þegnas mette,
modiglice menn,   on mere-bate
sittan sið-frome,   swylce hie ofer sæ comon.
Þæt wæs Drihten sylf,   dugeða wealdend,
ece ælmihtig,   mid his englum twam.
250 Wæron hie on gescirplan   scip-ferendum,
eorlas onlice,   ea-liðendum,
þonne hie on flodes fæðm   ofer feorne weg
on cald wæter   ceolum lacað.
    Hie ða gegrette,   se ðe on greote stod,
255 fus on faroðe,   fægn reordade:
"Hwanon comon ge   ceolum liðan,
ma-cræftige menn,   on mere-þissan,
ane æg-flotan?   Hwanon eagor-stream
ofer yða gewealc   eowic brohte?"
260   Him ða ondswarode   ælmihti God,
swa þæt ne wiste,   se ðe þæs wordes bad,
hwæt se manna wæs   meðel-hegendra,
þe he þær on waroðe   wið þingode:
"We of Marmedonia   mægðe syndon

In the early morning, at daybreak, he went, firmly resolved, 235
over the sandy slopes to the sea's edge and his followers
walked with him over the shingle; the ocean roared, the sea
currents pounded. The brave warrior was joyful when he 240
found on the shore a ship with a large hold. Then the bright-
est of beacons, holy and radiant in the morning, came has-
tening over the sea, out of the darkness. The heavenly can-
dle blazed over the waters. There on the boat he found
seafarers, three magnificent noblemen, brave men, sitting 245
ready to go, as if they had just come over the sea. That was
the Lord himself, the ruler of hosts, the eternal almighty,
with his two angels. In their dress the men were like sailors 250
and seafarers, tossing in their ships on the cold water in the
sea's embrace, over a great distance.

Standing on the shingle, eager for the sea and rejoicing, 255
he greeted them then and spoke: "Where have you come
from, you men of mighty skill, journeying in a sea-speeder in
a solitary ocean-floater? Where did the flowing tide bring
you from over the rolling waves?"

Almighty God answered him then in such a way that the 260
man who was waiting for his words did not know with whom
he was conversing there on the shore: "We have been con-
veyed from far away, from the people of Mermedonia;

265 feorran geferede;   us mid flode bær
on hran-rade   heah-stefn naca,
snellic sæ-mearh,   sunde bewunden,
oð þæt we þissa leoda   land gesohton,
wære bewrecene,   swa us wind fordraf."
270 Him þa Andreas   eað-mod oncwæð:
"Wolde ic þe biddan,   þeh ic þe beaga lyt,
sinc-weorðunga,   syllan meahte,
þæt ðu us gebrohte   brante ceole,
hea horn-scipe,   ofer hwæles eðel
275 on þære mægðe;   bið ðe meorð wið God,
þæt ðu us on lade   liðe weorðe."
Eft him ondswarode   æðelinga helm
of yð-lide,   engla scippend:
"Ne magon þær gewunian   wid-ferende,
280 ne þær elþeodige   eardes brucað,
ah in þære ceastre   cwealm þrowiað,
þa ðe feorran þyder   feorh gelædaþ;
ond þu wilnast nu   ofer widne mere
þæt ðu on þa fægðe   þine feore spilde?"
285 Him þa Andreas   agef ondsware:
"Usic lust hweteð   on þa leod-mearce,
mycel modes hiht,   to þære mæran byrig,
þeoden leofesta,   gif ðu us þine wilt
on mere-faroðe   miltse gecyðan."
290 Him ondswarode   engla þeoden,
neregend fira,   of nacan stefne:
"We ðe estlice   mid us willað
ferigan freolice   ofer fisces bæð
efne to þam lande   þær þe lust myneð
295 to gesecanne,   syððan ge eowre

the high-prowed vessel, the swift sea horse, carried us with 265
the tide on the whale's road, surrounded by the sea, until we
reached this people's land, driven off course by the sea, as
the wind drove us on."

Humble, Andrew then replied: "Though I could give you 270
few treasures or costly gifts, I should like to entreat you to
bring us in your tall vessel, your high, beaked ship, over the
whale's homeland to that people; you will receive your re- 275
ward from God for being kind to us on this journey."

The protector of princes, the creator of angels, answered
him once more from his ship: "Travelers from far away can-
not live there nor do foreigners enjoy that country, but in- 280
stead those who risk their lives by journeying there from far
away suffer violent death in that city; and now you want to
go over the wide ocean to waste your life in that hostility?"

Then Andrew gave him an answer: "Desire and the great 285
hope of our minds urge us to go to that territory, to that fa-
mous city, dearest lord, if you will show kindness to us on
the ocean currents."

The Lord of angels, the savior of men, answered him 290
from the ship's prow: "We will gladly and willingly convey
you with us over the fishes' bath, right to that country which
you desire to visit, after you have made your payment, the 295

gaful-rædenne   agifen habbað,
sceattas gescrifene,   swa eow scip-weardas,
aras ofer yð-bord,   unnan willað."
    Him þa ofstlice   Andreas wið,
300   wine-þearfende,   wordum mælde:
"Næbbe ic fæted gold   ne feoh-gestreon,
welan ne wiste   ne wira gespann,
landes ne locenra beaga,   þæt ic þe mæge lust ahwettan,
willan in worulde,   swa ðu worde becwist."
305   Him þa beorna Breogo,   þær he on bolcan sæt,
ofer waroða geweorp   wið þingode:
"Hu gewearð þe þæs,   wine leofesta,
ðæt ðu sæ-beorgas   secan woldes,
mere-streama gemet,   maðmum bedæled,
310   ofer cald cleofu   ceoles neosan?
Nafast þe to frofre   on faroð-stræte
hlafes wiste   ne hlutterne
drync to dugoðe?   Is se drohtað strang
þam þe lago-lade   lange cunnaþ."
315   Ða him Andreas   ðurh ondsware,
wis on gewitte,   word-hord onleac:
"Ne gedafenað þe,   nu þe Dryhten geaf
welan ond wiste   ond woruld-spede,
ðæt ðu ondsware   mid ofer-hygdum
320   sece, sar-cwide;   selre bið æghwam
þæt he eað-medum   ellor-fusne
oncnawe cuðlice,   swa þæt Crist bebead,
þeoden þrym-fæst.   We his þegnas synd
gecoren to cempum.   He is cyning on riht,
325   wealdend ond wyrhta   wuldor-þrymmes,
an ece God   eallra gesceafta,

appointed price, which the crew, the attendants on the wave-traverser, shall decide for you."

Quickly, the friendless Andrew spoke these words to him: 300 "I have no adorned gold or treasure, wealth or food or orna- mented metalwork, no land or interlocked ornaments with which to whet your desire, your wish for worldly goods, as you declare in your speech."

The Lord of men, sitting on the deck, addressed him over 305 the surging surf: "How, dearest friend, did it come about that you intended, without any treasure, to seek out the sea mountains, the expanse of ocean currents, take ship over 310 the cold cliffs? Have you no bread to sustain and comfort you on a voyage nor the benefit of a pure drink? The plight of the man who explores the sea for a long time is hard."

Then Andrew, wise in his mind, unlocked his store of 315 words in answer: "It is not fitting in you, since the Lord has given you wealth and sustenance and worldly success, that you should try to answer arrogantly, with a bitter retort; it is 320 better for everyone to address humbly and kindly the man who is ready to depart, as Christ, the glorious ruler, com- manded. We are his followers, his chosen warriors. He is king by right, ruler and maker of glorious majesty, one eter- 325 nal God of all creatures who encompasses all things by his

swa he ealle befehð   anes cræfte,
hefon ond eorðan,   halgum mihtum,
sigora selost.   He ðæt sylfa cwæð,
330 Fæder folca gehwæs,   ond us feran het
geond ginne grund   gasta streonan:
'Farað nu geond ealle   eorðan sceatas
emne swa wide swa   wæter bebugeð,
oððe stede-wangas   stræte gelicgaþ.
335 Bodiað æfter burgum   beorhtne geleafan
ofer foldan fæðm;   ic eow freoðo healde.
Ne ðurfan ge on þa fore   frætwe lædan,
gold ne seolfor;   ic eow goda gehwæs
on eowerne agenne dom   est ahwette.'
340 Nu ðu seolfa miht   sið userne
gehyran hyge-þancol,   ic sceal hraðe cunnan
hwæt ðu us to duguðum   gedon wille."
    Him þa ondswarode   ece Dryhten:
"Gif ge syndon þegnas   þæs þe þrym ahof
345 ofer middangeard,   swa ge me secgaþ,
ond ge geheoldon   þæt eow se halga bead,
þonne ic eow mid gefean   ferian wille
ofer brim-streamas,   swa ge benan sint."
    Þa in ceol stigon   collen-fyrhðe,
350 ellen-rofe;   æghwylcum wearð
on mere-faroðe   mod geblissod.

    Ða ofer yða geswing   Andreas ongann
mere-liðendum   miltsa biddan
wuldres Aldor   ond þus wordum cwæð:
355 "Forgife þe Dryhten   dom-weorðunga,
willan in worulde   ond in wuldre blæd,

might alone, heaven and earth, by his holy powers, surpass-
ing in triumphs. He himself, the Father of every people, said
this and commanded us to travel throughout the broad   330
earth in order to gain souls: 'Go now to the earth's farthest
reaches, even as far as water surrounds them or as far as
roads lie upon the plains. Preach the glorious faith through-   335
out the cities, over the earth's compass; I shall protect you.
You will not need to take treasure, gold or silver, on that
journey; I shall provide you with a liberal supply of every
good thing according to your own desire.' Now, wise one,   340
that you have been able to hear about our journey for your-
self, I must know at once what you will do to help us."

The eternal Lord answered him: "If you are the followers
of him who raised up his might above the world, as you tell   345
me, and if you have held to what the holy one commanded
you, then I shall gladly convey you over the sea currents, as
you request."

Then they embarked, bold spirited and courageous; each   350
man's mind was gladdened on the seashore.

Then, on the tossing waves, Andrew began to pray to the
glorious Lord for compassion toward the seafarers and
spoke these words: "May the Lord, the creator of mankind,   355
give you honor, your desires in this world and the glory

meotud mann-cynnes,   swa ðu me hafast
on þyssum sið-fæte   sybbe gecyðed!"
   Gesæt him þa se halga   holm-wearde neah,
360 æðele be æðelum;   æfre ic ne hyrde
þon cymlicor   ceol gehladenne
heah-gestreonum.   Hæleð in sæton,
þeodnas þrymfulle,   þegnas wlitige.
Ða reordode   rice þeoden,
365 ece ælmihtig;   heht his engel gan,
mærne magu-þegn,   ond mete syllan,
frefran feasceafte   ofer flodes wylm,
þæt hie þe eað mihton   ofer yða geþring
drohtaþ adreogan.
         Þa gedrefed wearð,
370 onhrered hwæl-mere;   horn-fisc plegode,
glad geond garsecg,   ond se græga mæw
wæl-gifre wand.   Weder-candel swearc,
windas weoxon,   wægas grundon,
streamas styredon,   strengas gurron,
375 wædo gewætte;   wæter-egsa stod
þreata þryðum.   Þegnas wurdon
acol-mode;   ænig ne wende
þæt he lifgende   land begete,
þara þe mid Andreas   on eagor-stream
380 ceol gesohte.   Næs him cuð þa gyt
hwa þam sæ-flotan   sund wisode.
   Him þa se halga   on holm-wege
ofer ar-geblond,   Andreas þa git,
þegn Þeoden-hold,   þanc gesægde,

enjoyed by the blessed, for you have shown goodwill to me on this expedition!"

Then the saint seated himself next to the sea captain, one 360 noble man next to another; I never heard of a ship more finely laden with noble treasures. The men sat in it, glorious lords and fair followers. Then the powerful ruler, the eternal 365 almighty, spoke; he commanded his angel, his splendid attendant, to go over the surging sea and give food to comfort the wretched men, so that they could more easily endure their lot upon the tumultuous waves.

Then the mighty sea was disturbed and stirred up; the 370 whale leaped and glided through the ocean and the gray gull, greedy for carrion, circled round. The candle of the sky grew dark, the winds increased, the waves crashed, the sea was in uproar, the rigging and the drenched sails creaked; the terri- 375 ble water rose up with the strength of an army. His followers were frozen with fear; not one of those who had gone to the ship on the sea with Andrew thought that he would reach land alive. They did not yet know who was directing the sea- 380 floater's course.

Then the holy Andrew, a disciple true to his Lord, once more said thanks to him, his powerful leader, on the ocean,

385 ricum ræs-boran,   þa he gereordod wæs:
"Ðe þissa swæsenda   soð-fæst meotud,
lifes leoht-fruma,   lean forgilde,
weoruda waldend,   ond þe wist gife,
heofonlicne hlaf,   swa ðu hyldo wið me
390 ofer firigend-stream,   freode, gecyðdest!
Nu synt geþreade   þegnas mine,
geonge guð-rincas.   Garsecg hlymmeð,
geofon geotende;   grund is onhrered,
deope gedrefed.   Duguð is geswenced,
395 modigra mægen   myclum gebysgod."
    Him of holme oncwæð   hæleða scyppend:
"Læt nu geferian   flotan userne,
lid to lande   ofer lagu-fæsten,
ond þonne gebidan   beornas þine,
400 aras on earde,   hwænne ðu eft cyme."
    Edre him þa eorlas   agefan ondsware,
þegnas þroht-hearde,   þafigan ne woldon
ðæt hie forleton   æt lides stefnan
leofne lareow   ond him land curon:
405 "Hwider hweorfað we   hlaford-lease,
geomor-mode,   gode orfeorme,
synnum wunde,   gif we swicað þe?
We bioð laðe   on landa gehwam,
folcum fracoðe,   þonne fira bearn,
410 ellen-rofe,   æht besittaþ,
hwylc hira selost   symle gelæste
hlaforde æt hilde,   þonne hand ond rond
on beadu-wange   billum forgrunden
æt nið-plegan   nearu þrowedon."

over the sea's surge, when he had been fed: "May the righ-   385
teous creator, the author of life and light, ruler of hosts, re-
ward you for this meal and give you sustenance, heavenly
bread, just as you have shown kindness and friendship to   390
me on the ocean currents. Now my followers, the young
warriors, are distressed. The sea, the surging flood, is roar-
ing; the bottom of the sea is disturbed, stirred up from the
depths. The warriors, this troop of brave men, are distressed   395
and very anxious."

The creator of men answered him from where he was on
the sea: "Allow me now to direct the course of our ship over
the mighty sea to land, and then let the men, your atten-   400
dants, wait on land until you come back."

At once the men, followers who were strong in times of
hardship, answered him that they would not consent to for-
sake their beloved teacher at the ship's prow and choose
the land for themselves: "Where will we go, lordless, sad   405
at heart, destitute, wounded by sins, if we desert you? We
will be detested in every land, despised by people, when the
brave children of men deliberate about which of them al-   410
ways best supported his lord in battle, when hands and
shields suffered hardship in the fight, destroyed by swords
on the battlefield."

415 　　Þa reordade　　rice Þeoden,
　　　wær-fæst cining,　　word stunde ahof:
　　　"Gif ðu þegn sie　　þrym-sittendes,
　　　wuldor-cyninges,　　swa ðu worde becwist,
　　　rece þa gerynu,　　hu he reord-berend
420 　　lærde under lyfte.　　Lang is þes sið-fæt
　　　ofer fealuwne flod;　　frefra þine
　　　mæcgas on mode.　　Mycel is nu gena
　　　lad ofer lagu-stream,　　land swiðe feorr
　　　to gesecanne;　　sund is geblonden,
425 　　grund wið greote.　　God eaðe mæg
　　　heaðo-liðendum　　helpe gefremman."
　　　　Ongan þa gleawlice　　gingran sine,
　　　wuldor-spedige weras　　wordum trymman:
　　　"Ge þæt gehogodon,　　þa ge on holm stigon,
430 　　þæt ge on fara folc　　feorh gelæddon
　　　ond for Dryhtnes lufan　　dead þrowodon,
　　　on æl-myrcna　　eðel-rice
　　　sawle gesealdon.　　Ic þæt sylfa wat,
　　　þæt us gescyldeð　　scyppend engla,
435 　　weoruda Dryhten.　　Wæter-egesa sceal,
　　　geðyd ond geðreatod　　þurh þryð-cining,
　　　lagu lacende,　　liðra wyrðan.
　　　Swa gesælde iu,　　þæt we on sæ-bate
　　　ofer waruð-gewinn　　wæda cunnedan,
440 　　faroð-ridende.　　Frecne þuhton
　　　egle ea-lada.　　Eagor-streamas
　　　beoton bord-stæðu;　　brun oft oncwæð,
　　　yð oðerre.　　Hwilum upp astod
　　　of brimes bosme　　on bates fæðm
445 　　egesa ofer yð-lid.　　Ælmihtig þær,

Then at once the powerful Lord, the king true to his 415
pledge, spoke and uttered these words: "If you are a disciple
of him who dwells in majesty, the king of glory, as you de-
clare in your speech, explain the mysteries, tell us how he 420
taught speech-bearing men on earth. This journey over the
glinting sea is long; comfort the minds of your men. There is
still a great way to go over the ocean currents and the land
is very far off; the ocean, the bottom of the sea, is stirred
up against the shingle. God can easily help the seafaring 425
warriors."

Then, wisely, he proceeded to encourage his disciples,
those glorious men, with these words: "When you embarked
on the sea, you resolved to risk your lives among hostile peo- 430
ple and to suffer death for the love of the Lord, give up your
souls in the homeland of foreigners. I know myself that the
creator of angels, the Lord of hosts, will protect us. The ter- 435
rifying water, the leaping ocean, will become calmer, re-
strained and checked by the glorious king. That is what hap-
pened once, when we experienced the waves in a boat,
sailing through the sea over the tumultuous surf. The ter- 440
rible waterways seemed fierce. The flowing tides beat the
ship's sides; one dark wave constantly answered the other.
Sometimes, out of the sea's bosom, a terrifying one rose
violently up over the ship and into the hold. The radiant 445

meotud man-cynnes,   on mere-þyssan
beorht basnode.   Beornas wurdon
forhte on mode;   friðes wilnedon,
miltsa to mærum.   Þa seo menigo ongan
450 clypian on ceole,   cyning sona aras,
engla ead-gifa,   yðum stilde,
wæteres wælmum.   Windas þreade,
sæ sessade;   smylte wurdon
mere-streama gemeotu.   Ða ure mod ahloh
455 syððan we gesegon   under swegles gang
windas ond wægas   ond wæter-brogan
forhte gewordne   for Frean egesan.
Forþan ic eow to soðe   secgan wille,
þæt næfre forlæteð   lifgende God
460 eorl on eorðan,   gif his ellen deah."
    Swa hleoðrode   halig cempa,
ðeawum geþancul.   Þegnas lærde
eadig oreta,   eorlas trymede,
oð ðæt hie semninga   slæp ofereode,
465 meðe be mæste.   Mere sweoðerade;
yða ongin   eft oncyrde,
hreoh holm-þracu.   Þa þam halgan wearð
æfter gryre-hwile   gast geblissod.

    Ongan ða reordigan   rædum snottor,
470 wis on gewitte,   word-locan onspeonn:
"Næfre ic sæ-lidan   selran mette,
ma-cræftigran,   þæs ðe me þynceð,
rowend rofran,   ræd-snotterran,
wordes wisran.   Ic wille þe,
475 eorl unforcuð,   anre nu gena

almighty, the creator of mankind, waited there on the ocean-speeder. The men were frightened in their minds; they implored the glorious one for safekeeping and mercy. When that company cried out in the ship, the king, he who gives 450 happiness to the angels, arose at once and stilled the waves, the surging water. He subdued the winds, the sea subsided; the stretches of the ocean became calm. Then our minds exulted when we saw that, under the sky's expanse, the winds 455 and waves and the terrible waters had grown frightened, for fear of the Lord. Therefore I want to tell you truthfully that the living God will never forsake a man on earth, if his courage is good." 460

So spoke the holy soldier, wise in his way of life. The blessed warrior instructed his followers and encouraged his men until all at once, exhausted beside the mast, sleep overcame them. The sea became calm; the swell of the waves, 465 the rough tossing of the ocean, receded. Then the saint's spirit was gladdened after his time of terror.

The man prudent in counsel, learned in mind, proceeded to speak, unlocking his store of words: "It seems to me that 470 I have never met a better or more skillful seafarer or a more valiant sailor, anyone more prudent in counsel or wiser in words. I, a noble warrior, now wish to ask one more favor of 475

bene biddan,   þeah ic þe beaga lyt,
sinc-weorðunga,   syllan mihte,
fæted-sinces.   Wolde ic freondscipe,
þeoden þrym-fæst,   þinne, gif ic mehte,
480   begitan godne.   Þæs ðu gife hleotest,
haligne hyht   on heofon-þrymme,
gif ðu lid-werigum   larna þinra
este wyrðest.   Wolde ic anes to ðe,
cyne-rof hæleð,   cræftes neosan,
485   ðæt ðu me getæhte,   nu þe tir cyning
ond miht forgef,   manna scyppend,
hu ðu wæg-flotan   wære bestemdon,
sæ-hengeste,   sund wisige.
Ic wæs on gifene   iu ond nu þa
490   syxtyne siðum   on sæ-bate,
mere hrerendum   mundum freorig,
eagor-streamas   —is ðys ane ma—
swa ic æfre ne geseah   ænigne mann,
þryð-bearn hæleða,   þe gelicne,
495   steoran ofer stæfnan.   Stream-welm hwileð,
beateþ brim-stæðo.   Is þes bat ful scrid;
færeð famig-heals,   fugole gelicost
glideð on geofone.   Ic georne wat
þæt ic æfre ne geseah   ofer yð-lade
500   on sæ-leodan   syllicran cræft.
Is þon geliccost   swa he on land-sceare
stille stande,   þær hine storm ne mæg,
wind awecgan,   ne wæter-flodas
brecan brond-stæfne,   hwæðere on brim snoweð
505   snel under segle.   Ðu eart seolfa geong,
wigendra hleo,   nalas wintrum frod;

you, although I can give you no valuables or costly gifts or
ornamented treasure. If I could, I should like, glorious lord,
to win your good friendship. You will receive grace for that,   480
holy joy in the glory of heaven, if you are kind with your ad-
vice to us weary seafarers. O brave and noble man, since the
king, the creator of men, has given you renown and power,
I should like to find out about one skill from you, that you   485
should teach me how you guide the course of the drenched
wave-floater, your sea horse, on the ocean. I have been in a
boat on the sea sixteen times, in the past and now again,   490
freezing, stirring the sea, the ocean currents, with my hands
—this is one voyage more—without ever seeing any man
like you, any mighty son of heroes, steering upon the prow.   495
The ocean wave roars, beats the seashore. This boat is very
swift; the foamy-necked ship moves just like a bird, glides
along on the sea. I know for sure that I never saw more mar-
velous skill in a sailor on a voyage. It is exactly as if it were 500
standing still on a piece of land where storm and wind can-
not move it or waves break the high-prowed boat, yet it is
hurrying on the sea, swift under sail. You yourself, protec-   505
tor of warriors, are young, not advanced in years; yet, as you

hafast þeh on fyrhðe,   faroð-lacende,
eorles ondsware.   Æghwylces canst
worda for worulde   wislic andgit."

510   Him ondswarode   ece Dryhten:
"Oft þæt gesæleð   þæt we on sæ-lade,
scipum under scealcum,   þonne sceor cymeð,
brecað ofer bæð-weg,   brim-hengestum.
Hwilum us on yðum   earfoðlice
515   gesæleð on sæwe,   þeh we sið nesan,
frecne geferan.   Flod-wylm ne mæg
manna ænigne   ofer meotudes est
lungre gelettan;   ah him lifes geweald,
se ðe brimu bindeð,   brune yða
520   ðyð ond þreatað.   He þeodum sceal
racian mid rihte,   se ðe rodor ahof
ond gefæstnode   folmum sinum,
worhte ond wreðede,   wuldras fylde
beorhtne bold-welan,   swa gebledsod wearð
525   engla eðel   þurh his anes miht.
Forþan is gesyne,   soð orgete,
cuð oncnawen,   þæt ðu cyninges eart
þegen geþungen,   þrym-sittendes,
forþan þe sona   sæ-holm oncneow,
530   garsecges begang,   þæt ðu gife hæfdes
Haliges Gastes.   Hærn eft onwand,
ar-yða geblond;   egesa gestilde,
wid-fæðme wæg.   Wædu swæðorodon
seoðþan hie ongeton   þæt ðe God hæfde
535   wære bewunden,   se ðe wuldres blæd
gestaðolade   strangum mihtum."

sail the sea, your answers reflect a noble mind. You understand the true meaning of every man's words in the world."

The eternal Lord answered him: "It often happens that we are making our way over the waterway in our ships, our sea horses, manned by their crews, when a storm comes. Sometimes it goes hard with us on the waves on the sea, even though we survive the journey, pass through the danger. The surging sea cannot even hinder anyone against the creator's will; he who binds the waters, restrains and checks the dark waves, has power over life. He shall rule people by right, he who raised up the sky and secured it with his own hands, who created it and supported it, filled with glory that bright, rich dwelling, so that the land of angels was blessed through his power alone. The clear truth is visible, well known and acknowledged, that you are an excellent follower of the king, of him who dwells in glory, because the sea, the ocean's expanse, immediately acknowledged that you had the grace of the Holy Spirit. The ocean, the tumult of waves, returned to calm; that terrifying thing, the wide-reaching wave, grew still. The waves subsided when they perceived that God, who established the glory of heaven with his strong powers, had wrapped you in his protection."

Þa hleoðrade   halgan stefne
cempa collen-ferhð,   cyning wyrðude,
wuldres waldend,   ond þus wordum cwæð:
540 "Wes ðu gebledsod,   brego man-cynnes,
Dryhten hælend!   A þin dom lyfað,
ge neh ge feor;   is þin nama halig,
wuldre gewlitegad   ofer wer-þeoda,
miltsum gemærsod.   Nænig manna is
545 under heofon-hwealfe,   hæleða cynnes,
ðætte areccan mæg   oððe rim wite
hu ðrymlice,   þeoda Baldor,
gasta geocend,   þine gife dælest.
Huru is gesyne,   sawla nergend,
550 þæt ðu þissum hysse   hold gewurde,
ond hine geongne   geofum wyrðodest,
wison gewitte   ond word-cwidum;
ic æt efen-ealdum   æfre ne mette
on mod-sefan   maran snyttro."
555   Him ða of ceole oncwæð   cyninga wuldor,
frægn fromlice   fruma ond ende:
"Saga, þances gleaw   þegn, gif ðu cunne
hu ðæt gewurde   be werum tweonum,
þæt ða ar-leasan   inwid-þancum
560 Iudea cynn   wið Godes bearne
ahof hearm-cwide.   Hæleð unsælige
no ðær gelyfdon   in hira lif-fruman,
grome gealg-mode,   þæt he God wære;
þeah ðe he wundra feala   weorodum gecyðde,
565 sweotulra ond gesynra,   synnige ne mihton
oncnawan þæt cyne-bearn,   se ðe acenned wearð
to hleo ond to hroðre   hæleða cynne,

Then the bold-spirited warrior spoke in his holy voice, honoring the king, the ruler of glory, and spoke these words: "May you be blessed, ruler of mankind, Lord savior! Your 540 glory shall live forever, both far and near; your name is holy, adorned with glory throughout the nations, celebrated for mercy. There is no person under the vault of the sky, not 545 one of mankind, that may tell or recount how gloriously you dispense your grace, Lord of peoples, comforter of souls. Truly it is clear, savior of souls, that you have been gracious 550 to this youth and have honored him, young as he is, with your gifts, with wise understanding and speeches; I never met with more wisdom of mind in one of equal age."

The glory of kings replied to him from the ship, the be- 555 ginning and the end asked eagerly: "Tell me, if you, as a disciple who is prudent in thought, know how it came about among men that the impious, the Jewish people, with mali- 560 cious intent blasphemed against the son of God. Wretched men there, hostile and fierce, did not believe in the source of their lives, that he was God; although he performed many clear and manifest miracles for the multitudes, the sinful 565 ones could not recognize the royal son, who was born as a protector and a joy for mankind, for all who dwell on earth.

eallum eorð-warum.   Æþelinge weox
word ond wisdom,   ah he þara wundra a,
570   dom-agende,   dæl ænigne
frætre þeode   beforan cyðde?"
     Him ða Andreas   agef andsware:
"Hu mihte þæt gewyrðan   in wer-þeode
þæt ðu ne gehyrde   hælendes miht,
575   gumena leofost,   hu he his gif cyðde
geond woruld wide,   wealdendes Bearn?
Sealde he dumbum gesprec;   deafe gehyrdon;
healtum ond hreofum   hyge blissode,
ða þe lim-seoce   lange wæron,
580   werige, wan-hale,   witum gebundene;
æfter burh-stedum   blinde gesegon;
swa he on grund-wæge   gumena cynnes
manige missenlice   men of deaðe
worde awehte.   Swylce he eac wundra feala
585   cyne-rof cyðde   þurh his cræftes miht;
he gehalgode   for here-mægene
win of wætere   ond wendan het,
beornum to blisse,   on þa beteran gecynd.
Swylce he afedde   of fixum twam
590   ond of fif hlafum   fira cynnes
fif ðusendo.   Feðan sæton,
reonig-mode;   reste gefegon,
werige æfter waðe;   wiste þegon,
menn on moldan   swa him gemedost wæs.
595   Nu ðu miht gehyran,   hyse leofesta,
hu us wuldres weard   wordum ond dædum
lufode in life,   ond þurh lare speon
to þam fægeran gefean,   þær freo moton,

222

A good name and wisdom flourished in that prince; but did he ever, with his authority, make known any part of his miracles in the presence of that shameful people?"   570

Andrew answered him: "Dearest of men, how in the world could it happen that you have not heard of the savior's power, of how the ruler's Son manifested his grace far and   575 wide throughout the world? He gave speech to the dumb; the deaf heard; he delighted the minds of the lame and of lepers, whose limbs had been diseased for a long time, mis-   580 erable, sick, bound in torments; throughout the cities the blind received sight; in the same way by means of his word while he was on earth he raised from the dead many different people of the race of mankind. This man of royal bravery also performed many miracles through the might of his   585 power; he consecrated wine from water before the multitude and commanded it to change into that superior state to delight the people. Likewise he fed five thousand people with two fishes and five loaves. The troop sat, sad at heart;   590 tired after the journey, they rejoiced at the rest; the people on the ground partook of the food as was most pleasant for them. Now, dearest man, you can hear how the guardian of   595 glory loved us in his life, both in his words and deeds, and through his teaching drew us to that more beautiful place of

eadige mid englum, eard weardigan,
600 þa ðe æfter deaðe Dryhten secað."

 Ða gen weges weard word-hord onleac;
beorn ofer bolcan, beald reordade:
"Miht ðu me gesecgan, þæt ic soð wite,
hwæðer Wealdend þin wundor on eorðan,
605 þa he gefremede nalas feam siðum,
folcum to frofre beforan cyðde,
þær bisceopas ond boceras
ond ealdor-menn æht besæton,
mæðel-hægende? Me þæt þinceð,
610 ðæt hie for æfstum in-wit syredon
þurh deopne gedwolan. Deofles larum
hæleð hyn-fuse hyrdon to georne,
wraðum wær-logan. Hie seo wyrd beswac,
forleolc ond forlærde; nu hie lungre sceolon,
615 werige mid werigum, wræce þrowian,
biterne bryne on banan fæðme."
 Him ða Andreas agef ondsware:
"Secge ic ðe to soðe ðæt he swiðe oft
beforan fremede folces ræswum
620 wundor æfter wundre on wera gesiehðe;
swylce deogollice Dryhten gumena
folc-ræd fremede, swa he to friðe hogode."
 Him ondswarode æðelinga helm:
"Miht ðu, wis hæleð, wordum gesecgan,
625 maga mode rof, mægen þa he cyðde,
deor-mod on digle, ða mid Dryhten oft,
rodera rædend, rune besæton?"

joy where, free and blessed among the angels, they who after
their deaths go to the Lord may inhabit that homeland." 600

Once more the guardian of the waves unlocked his word-
hoard; the brave man on the deck spoke: "Can you tell me,
so that I may know the truth, whether your Lord openly
made known the miracles which he performed on earth on 605
many occasions as a comfort to the people, there where
bishops and scribes and the elders sat in council, deliberat-
ing? It seems to me that they plotted evil through profound 610
error, because of jealousy. Those doomed men listened all
too eagerly to the devil's teachings, to the hostile evildoer.
Destiny deluded, misled, and deceived them; now, they will
soon have to endure torment, fierce burning in the devil's
grasp, accursed among the accursed." 615

Andrew answered him: "I tell you truthfully that he very
often publicly performed miracle after miracle in the pres-
ence of the people's leaders, in full view of men; likewise the 620
Lord of men, who was resolved upon peace, secretly pro-
moted public good."

The protector of princes answered him: "Can you, a wise
man and a hero brave in mind, tell in words the miracles that 625
that bold-spirited man performed in secret when you often
sat deliberating with the Lord, the ruler of the heavens?"

Him þa Andreas ondsware agef:
"Hwæt frinest ðu me, frea leofesta,
630 wordum wrætlicum, ond þe wyrda gehwæs
þurh snyttra cræft soð oncnawest?"
    Ða git him wæges weard wið þingode:
"Ne frine ic ðe for tæle ne ðurh teon-cwide
on hran-rade, ac min hige blissað,
635 wynnum wridað, þurh þine word-læðe,
æðelum ecne. Ne eom ic ana ðæt,
ac manna gehwam mod bið on hyhte,
fyrhð afrefred, þam þe feor oððe neah
on mode geman hu se maga fremede,
640 God-Bearn on grundum. Gastas hweorfon,
sohton sið-frome swegles dreamas,
engla eðel, þurh þa æðelan miht."
    Edre him Andreas agef ondsware:
"Nu ic on þe sylfum soð oncnawe,
645 wisdomes gewit, wundor-cræfte,
sige-sped geseald —snyttrum bloweð,
beorhtre blisse, breost innanweard—
nu ic þe sylfum secgan wille
oor ond ende, swa ic þæs æðelinges
650 word ond wisdom on wera gemote
þurh his sylfes muð symle gehyrde.
Oft gesamnodon side herigeas,
folc unmæte, to Frean dome,
þær hie hyrcnodon haliges lare.
655 Ðonne eft gewat æðelinga helm,
beorht blæd-gifa, in bold oðer,
ðær him togenes, God herigende,
to ðam meðel-stede manige comon,

226

Andrew answered him: "Dearest lord, why are you questioning me in your elegant words, when, through the power   630
of your wisdom, you perceive the truth of every event?"

Still the guardian of the waves addressed him: "I am not
asking you in order to find fault with you or in rebuke, here
on the whale's road, but my mind rejoices, blossoms in de-   635
light because of your speech, endowed with nobility. I am
not alone in this but everyone's mind is hopeful, their spirits
comforted, everyone far and near who calls to mind how the
Son of God, the hero, acted on earth. Spirits eager for the   640
journey departed, sought out the joys of heaven, the home-
land of angels, by means of that noble power."

At once Andrew answered him: "Now that I perceive
truth and an understanding of wisdom in you, a triumphant   645
ability granted with marvelous skill—your breast within
blossoms with wisdom and sublime joy—I am willing to tell
you all, beginning and end, as I always heard the prince's
words and wisdom from his own mouth, where people were   650
assembled. Often large companies gathered together, count-
less people, at the Lord's command, when they listened to
the holy man's teaching. Then afterward the protector of   655
princes, the radiant giver of happiness, would go to another
dwelling, where, praising God, many wise hall counselors

snottre sele-rædend;   symble gefegon,
660   beornas blið-heorte,   burh-weardes cyme.
    "Swa gesælde iu   þæt se sige-dema
ferde, Frea mihtig.   Næs þær folces ma
on sið-fate   sinra leoda
nemne ellefne   orett-mæcgas,
665   geteled tir-eadige;   he wæs twelfta sylf.
Þa we becomon   to þam cyne-stole,
þær atimbred wæs   tempel Dryhtnes,
heah ond horn-geap,   hæleðum gefrege,
wuldre gewlitegod.   Husc-worde ongan
670   þurh inwit-ðanc   ealdor-sacerd
herme hyspan,   hord-locan onspeon;
wroht webbade.   He on gewitte oncneow
þæt we soð-fæstes   swaðe folgodon,
læston lar-cwide;   he lungre ahof
675   woðe wiðer-hydig   wean onblonden:
'Hwæt ge syndon earme   ofer ealle menn!
Wadað wid-lastas,   weorn geferað
earfoð-siða;   ell-þeodiges nu
butan leod-rihte   larum hyrað!
680   Eadiges orhlytte   æðeling cyðað;
secgað soðlice   þæt mid suna meotudes
drohtigen dæghwæmlice.   Þæt is duguðum cuð
hwanon þam ord-fruman   æðelu onwocon;
he wæs afeded   on þysse folc-sceare,
685   cild-geong acenned   mid his cneo-magum.
Þus syndon haten   ham-sittende,
fæder ond modur,   þæs we gefrægen habbað
þurh mod-gemynd,   Maria ond Ioseph.
Syndon him on æðelum   oðere twegen

came toward him, to the meeting place; the happy men always rejoiced at the coming of that guardian of cities. 660

"It happened once that the triumphant judge, the powerful Lord, was traveling. On that journey there were no more than eleven in number of his people and followers, re- 665 nowned warriors; he himself was the twelfth. Then we came to the royal city, where the Lord's temple had been built, high and wide-gabled, celebrated among men, beautifully adorned. The chief priest proceeded to mock us with hos- 670 tile intent and with evil in an insulting speech, unfastening the treasure chest of his thoughts; he wove an accusation. He knew in his mind that we followed in the footsteps of the righteous one, carried out his teaching; suddenly he shouted malevolently, corrupted by evil: 'How wretched you 675 are, more than all people! You wander far and wide, go on very many difficult journeys; you are obeying now the teachings of a foreigner without legitimate authority. You declare him a prince, though he is not endowed with wealth; you de- 680 clare truly that you live every day with the creator's son. It is known to the people of this kingdom where the nobility of that prince sprang from; he was brought up in this country, born as an infant among his kinsmen. His mother and fa- 685 ther, dwelling at home, are called Mary and Joseph, as we have learned from recollections. In his family there are two

690 beornas geborene,   broðor-sybbum,
suna Iosephes,   Simon ond Iacob.'
"Swa hleoðrodon   hæleða ræswan,
dugoð dom-georne;   dyrnan þohton
meotudes mihte.   Man eft gehwearf,
695 yfel ende-leas,   þær hit ær aras.

"Þa se þeoden gewat   þegna heape
fram þam meðel-stede   mihtum geswiðed,
dugeða Dryhten,   secan digol land.
He þurh wundra feala   on þam westenne
700 cræfta gecyðde   þæt he wæs cyning on riht
ofer middan-geard,   mægene geswiðed,
waldend ond wyrhta   wuldor-þrymmes,
an ece God   eallra gesceafta;
swylce he oðerra   unrim cyðde
705 wundor-worca   on wera gesyhðe.

"Syþþan eft gewat   oðre siðe
getrume mycle   þæt he in temple gestod,
wuldres Aldor.   Word-hleoðor astag
geond heah-ræced;   haliges lare
710 synnige ne swulgon,   þeah he soðra swa feala
tacna gecyðde,   þær hie to segon.
Swylce he wrætlice   wundor agræfene,
anlicnesse   engla sinra
geseh, sigora Frea,   on seles wage,
715 on twa healfe   torhte gefrætwed,
wlitige geworhte.   He worde cwæð:
'Ðis is anlicnes   engel-cynna
þæs bremestan   þe mid þam burg-warum
in þære ceastre is;   cheruphim et seraphim

other boys, Simon and James, born as brothers to him, sons 690
of Joseph.'

"So spoke the people's leaders, the troop eager for glory;
they intended to hide the creator's power. Their sin, their
endless evil, turned back upon themselves, where it had 695
originated.

"Then the prince, the Lord of hosts, with his company of
followers, strengthened by his powers, went from the meet-
ing place to seek out a remote land. Through many miracles
and manifestations of power in that desert, he revealed that 700
he was by right king over the world, strengthened by his
might, ruler and maker of heavenly glory, one eternal God of
all creatures; likewise he revealed countless other miracles 705
publicly.

"Afterward the glorious Lord went back a second time
with a great troop and stood up in the temple. The sound of
voices rose up throughout the tall building; the sinful did 710
not accept the holy man's teaching, even though he revealed
so many true signs in their sight. The Lord of victories
also saw marvelous objects wonderfully carved, images of
his angels, on the walls of the hall on two sides, splendidly 715
adorned, beautifully made. He spoke these words: 'This is
an image of the most illustrious order of angels among the
citizens in that city; they are called cherubim and seraphim

720 þa on swegel-dreamum   syndon nemned.
Fore onsyne   ecan Dryhtnes
standað stið-ferðe;   stefnum herigað,
halgum hleoðrum,   heofon-cyninges þrym,
meotudes mund-byrd.   Her amearcod is
725 haligra hiw,   þurh hand-mægen
awriten on wealle   wuldres þegnas.'
Þa gen worde cwæð   weoruda Dryhten,
heofon-halig gast,   fore þam here-mægene:
'Nu ic bebeode   beacen ætywan,
730 wundor geweorðan   on wera gemange,
ðæt þeos onlicnes   eorðan sece,
wlitig of wage,   ond word sprece,
secge soð-cwidum,   þy sceolon gelyfan
eorlas on cyððe   hwæt min æðelo sien.'
735   "Ne dorste þa forhylman   hælendes bebod
wundor fore weorodum,   ac of wealle ahleop,
frod fyrn-geweorc,   þæt he on foldan stod,
stan fram stane.   Stefn æfter cwom,
hlud þurh heardne;   hleoðor dynede,
740 wordum wemde.   Wrætlic þuhte
stið-hycgendum   stanes ongin.
Septe sacerdas   sweotolum tacnum;
witig werede   ond worde cwæð:
'Ge synd unlæde,   earmra geþohta
745 searowum beswicene,   oððe sel nyton,
mode gemyrde.   Ge mon cigað
Godes ece Bearn,   ond þone þe grund ond sund,
heofon ond eorðan   ond hreo wægas,
salte sæ-streamas   ond swegl uppe
750 amearcode   mundum sinum.

in the joy of heaven. Resolute, they stand before the face of 720
the eternal Lord; with their voices they praise in holy songs
the heavenly king's glory, the protection of the creator. Here
the form of the holy ones is depicted, the ministers of glory 725
drawn on the wall by skillful hand.' The Lord of hosts still
spoke these words, the heavenly and holy spirit, in front of
the mighty multitude: 'Now I command a sign to appear,
a miracle to happen among the people, that this beautiful 730
image should come down to the ground from the wall and
should speak words, tell in true speech what my lineage is,
so that the men in my native land will have to believe.'

"Then that wondrous thing did not dare to disregard the 735
savior's command in front of the crowd but jumped from
the wall, that worthy ancient work, stone from stone, so
that it stood on the ground. A loud voice came then out of
the hard stone; the voice resounded, uttering words. The 740
stone's behavior seemed remarkable to the stubborn peo-
ple. It instructed the priests with clear signs; having wis-
dom, it reprimanded them and spoke these words: 'You are
miserable, deluded by the snares of your own wretched 745
thoughts, and furthermore you know no better, your minds
confused. You call the eternal Son of God a human, he who
marked out with his own hands land and sea, heaven and
earth and the rough waves, the salt ocean currents and the 750

Þis is se ilca   eal-walda God,
ðone on fyrn-dagum   fæderas cuðon.
He Abrahame   ond Isace
ond Iocobe   gife bryttode,
welum weorðode;   wordum sægde
ærest Habrahame   æðeles geþingu,
þæt of his cynne   cenned sceolde
weorðan wuldres God.   Is seo wyrd mid eow
open, orgete;   magan eagum nu
geseon sigores God,   swegles Agend.'
    "Æfter þyssum wordum   weorud hlosnode
geond þæt side sel;   swigodon ealle.
Ða ða yldestan   eft ongunnon
secgan synfulle   —soð ne oncneowan—
þæt hit dry-cræftum   gedon wære,
scin-gelacum,   þæt se scyna stan
mælde for mannum.   Man wridode
geond beorna breost;   brand-hata nið
weoll on gewitte,   weorm blædum fag,
attor æl-fæle.   Þær wæs orcnawe
þurh teon-cwide   tweogende mod,
mæcga mis-gehygd   morðre bewunden.
    "Ða se Þeoden bebead   þryð-weorc faran,
stan on stræte   of stede-wange,
ond forð gan   fold-weg tredan,
grene grundas,   Godes ærendu
larum lædan   on þa leod-mearce
to Channaneum,   cyninges worde,
beodan Habrahame   mid his eaforum twæm
of eorð-scræfe   ærest fremman,
lætan land-reste,   leoðo gadrigean,

sky above. This is the same omnipotent God whom the patriarchs knew in days of old. He bestowed his favor on Abraham and Isaac and Jacob, honored them with riches; he 755
plainly told Abraham first of that noble man's fate, that the God of glory should be born of his people. How that event has come to pass is evident and obvious among you; with your own eyes you can now see the God of victory, the Lord 760
of heaven.'

"After these words the company listened astonished throughout that spacious hall; they were all silent. Then the sinful elders proceeded to say again—they did not acknowledge the truth—that it had been done by sorcery, by magi- 765
cal delusions, that the beautiful stone had spoken before the people. Sin flourished in people's hearts; a hatred hot as fire welled up in their minds, a serpent hostile to happiness, a deadly venom. Their doubting minds, the men's perverse 770
thoughts, enmeshed in deadly sins, were evident there in their blasphemous talk.

"Then the Lord commanded that mighty work, that stone, to go from that place onto the road and to go forth 775
to walk the earth, the green ground, to bring God's message, as it was taught by the king's words, to the country of the Canaanites, to command Abraham with his two descendants to arise from the grave, to leave behind their 780
sepulchers, bestir themselves, receive their spirits and their

ANDREAS

gaste onfon   ond geogoðhade,
ed-niwinga   andweard cuman,
frode fyrn-weotan,   folce gecyðan,
785 hwylcne hie God mihtum   ongiten hæfdon.
     "Gewat he þa feran,   swa him Frea mihtig,
scyppend wera,   gescrifen hæfde,
ofer mearc-paðu,   þæt he on Mambre becom
beorhte blican,   swa him bebead meotud,
790 þær þa lic-homan   lange þrage,
heah-fædera hra,   beheled wæron.
Het þa ofstlice   up astandan
Habraham ond Isaac,   æðeling þriddan
Iacob of greote   to Godes geþinge,
795 sneome of slæpe þæm fæstan;   het hie to þam siðe gyrwan,
faran to Frean dome.   Sceoldon hie þam folce gecyðan
hwa æt frumsceafte   furðum teode
eorðan eall-grene   ond up-heofon,
hwæt se wealdend wære   þe þæt weorc staðolade.
800 Ne dorston þa gelettan   leng owihte
wuldor-cyninges word;   geweotan ða ða witigan þry
modige mearc-land tredan.   Forlætan mold-ern wunigean
open eorð-scræfu;   woldon hie ædre gecyðan
frum-weorca Fæder.   Þa þæt folc gewearð
805 egesan geaclod,   þær þa æðelingas
wordum weorðodon   wuldres Aldor.
Hie ða ricene het   rices hyrde
to ead-welan   oþre siðe
secan mid sybbe   swegles dreamas,
810 ond þæs to widan feore   willum neotan.
     "Nu ðu miht gehyran,   hyse leofesta,
hu he wundra worn   wordum cyðde,

236

youth, to appear once more, those counselors, wise as they were of old, to reveal to the people what God they had perceived through his power. 785

"So it went making its way along the paths over that land, as the mighty Lord, the creator of men, had ordained, until it came to Mamre, glittering brightly, as the creator had commanded it, where the bodies, the patriarchs' corpses, had been buried for a long time. Quickly it commanded 790 Abraham and Isaac and Jacob, the third patriarch, to stand up at once from the grave, from that deep sleep, at God's 795 command; it commanded that they prepare themselves for the journey, to go in accordance with the Lord's decree. They would have to proclaim to the people who it was who, at the beginning of the world, first created the green earth and heaven above, who that ruler was who established that work. They did not dare to neglect the glorious king's word 800 any longer; then the three proud prophets went walking though that land. They left their sepulchers, their graves, remain open; they wished to acknowledge the Father of creation at once. Then the people were gripped by terror when 805 these princes honored the Lord of glory with their words. Then, to their delight, the shepherd of the heavenly kingdom quickly commanded them to seek out the joys of heaven in peace for a second time and to enjoy them forever 810 with delight.

"Now you can hear, dearest of men, how he revealed a multitude of miracles in his words, even though men, with

swa þeah ne gelyfdon   larum sinum
mod-blinde menn.   Ic wat manig nu gyt

815   mycel mære spell   ðe se Maga fremede,
rodera rædend,   ða ðu aræfnan ne miht,
hreðre behabban,   hyge-þances gleaw."
Þus Andreas   ondlangne dæg
herede hleoðor-cwidum   haliges lare,

820   oð ðæt hine semninga   slæp ofereode
on hron-rade   heofon-cyninge neh.

Ða gelædan het   lifes Brytta
ofer yða geþræc   englas sine,
fæðmum ferigean   on Fæder wære

825   leofne mid lissum   ofer lagu-fæsten,
oð ðæt slæp-werige   sæ ofereoden;
þurh lyft-gelac   on land becwom
to þære ceastre   þe him cining engla
. . .

Gewiton ða þa aras   eft siðigean,

830   eadige on upweg,   eðles neosan;
leton þone halgan   be here-stræte
swefan on sybbe   under swegles hleo,
bliðne bidan   burh-wealle neh,
his nið-hetum,   niht-langne fyrst,

835   oð þæt Dryhten forlet   dæg-candelle
scire scinan.   Sceadu sweðerodon,
wonn under wolcnum;   þa com wederes blæst,
hador heofon-leoma,   ofer hofu blican.
Onwoc þa wiges heard,   wang sceawode

840   fore burg-geatum.   Beorgas steape,
hleoðu hlifodon;   ymbe harne stan

their blinded minds, did not believe in his teachings. Now I know yet many a long and glorious tale of what the Son, the 815 ruler of the heavens, did, which you, wise in thought as you are, cannot bear, cannot comprehend in your breast." In this way, Andrew, the whole day through, praised the teaching of the holy one in his speeches until suddenly sleep overcame him on the sea, next to the king of heaven. 820

Then the generous Lord of life commanded his angels to carry the loved man kindly in their embrace over the tumul- 825 tuous waves, over the mighty ocean, in the Father's protection, until the tired sleepers should have crossed the sea; by means of flight through the air he came to the land, to the city which the king of angels . . .

Then the messengers, the blessed ones, departed to jour- 830 ney upward, to go to their homeland; they left the saint sleeping peacefully by the main road, under the shelter of the sky, happy to wait near the city wall, near to his fierce enemies, for the length of a night, until the Lord caused 835 the day's candle to shine brightly. Shadows, dark under the clouds, vanished; then came the torch of the sky, the bright heavenly radiance, shining over the houses.

The man, strong in battle, awoke then, surveyed the land in front of the city gates. Steep mountains and hillsides tow- 840 ered up; round the gray rock stood buildings with colored

tigel-fagan trafu,   torras stodon,
windige weallas.   Þa se wisa oncneow
þæt he Marmedonia   mægðe hæfde
845   siðe gesohte,   swa him sylf bebead,
þa he him fore gescraf,   Fæder man-cynnes.
Geseh he þa on greote   gingran sine,
beornas beadu-rofe,   biryhte him
swefan on slæpe.   He sona ongann
850   wigend weccean,   ond worde cwæð:
"Ic eow secgan mæg   soð orgete,
þæt us gystran-dæge   on geofones stream
ofer ar-welan   æðeling ferede.
In þam ceole wæs   cyninga wuldor,
855   waldend wer-ðeode.   Ic his word oncneow,
þeh he his mæg-wlite   bemiðen hæfde."
    Him þa æðelingas   ondsweorodon,
geonge gen-cwidum,   gast-gerynum:
"We ðe, Andreas,   eaðe gecyðað
860   sið userne,   þæt ðu sylfa miht
ongitan gleawlice   gast-gehygdum.
Us sæ-werige   slæp ofereode.
Þa comon earnas   ofer yða wylm
on flyhte faran,   feðerum hremige;
865   us of slæpendum   sawle abrugdon,
mid gefean feredon   flyhte on lyfte,
brehtmum bliðe,   beorhte ond liðe.
Lissum lufodon   ond in lofe wunedon,
þær wæs singal sang   ond swegles gong,
870   wlitig weoroda heap   ond wuldres þreat.
Utan ymbe æðelne   englas stodon,
þegnas ymb þeoden,   þusend-mælum;

tiles, towers and windswept walls. Then that wise man realized that he had reached the people of Mermedonia on his expedition, as the Father of mankind himself had commanded him, when he allotted the journey to him. Then he saw his followers on the ground, the warriors brave and renowned in battle, resting close by him asleep. He immediately woke the warriors and spoke these words: "I can tell you an obvious truth, that yesterday a prince conveyed us over the expanse of waters on the ocean current. The glory of kings was in the ship, the ruler of the people. I recognized his words, even though he had concealed his face."

The young noblemen, in their replies, answered him with spiritual mysteries: "We will willingly reveal our experience to you, Andrew, so that you yourself can clearly understand it in your thoughts. Sleep overpowered us, sea-weary as we were. Then eagles came flying over the surging of the waves, exulting in their wings; they snatched our souls out of us as were sleeping, joyfully carried them into the air in flight, happy in their singing, radiant and gracious. They treated us lovingly and kindly and continued in praise, there where there was continual singing throughout the expanse of heaven, the fair assembly of hosts and the glorious multitude. Angels stood in thousands around the noble one,

845

850

855

860

865

870

heredon on hehðo   halgan stefne
dryhtna Dryhten.   Dream wæs on hyhte.
875   "We ðær heah-fæderas   halige oncneowon
ond martyra   mægen unlytel;
sungon sige-dryhtne   soð-fæstlic lof,
dugoð dom-georne.   Þær wæs Dauid mid,
eadig oretta,   Essages sunu,
880   for Crist cumen,   cining Israhela.
Swylce we gesegon   for suna meotudes,
æðelum ecne,   eowic standan,
twelfe getealde,   tir-eadige hæleð;
eow þegnodon   þrym-sittende,
885   halige heah-englas.   Ðam bið hæleða well
þe þara blissa   brucan moton!
Þær wæs wuldres wynn,   wigendra þrym,
æðelic onginn;   næs þær ænigum gewinn.
Þam bið wræc-sið witod,   wite geopenad,
890   þe þara gefeana sceal   fremde weorðan,
hean hwearfian,   þonne heonon gangaþ."
    Þa wæs mod-sefa   myclum geblissod
haliges on hreðre,   syðþan hleoðor-cwide
gingran gehyrdon,   þæt hie God wolde
895   onmunan swa mycles   ofer menn ealle,
ond þæt word gecwæð   wigendra hleo:
"Nu ic, God Dryhten,   ongiten hæbbe
þæt ðu on faroð-stræte   feor ne wære,
cyninga wuldur,   þa ic on ceol gestah,
900   ðeh ic on yð-fare,   engla þeoden,
gasta geocend,   ongitan ne cuðe.
Weorð me nu milde,   meotud ælmihtig,
bliðe, beorht cyning!   Ic on brim-streame

followers around their Lord; with holy voice they praised
him in heaven, the Lord of lords. Joyful was that music.

"There we recognized the holy patriarchs and no small   875
troop of martyrs; a host eager for glory, they sang true praise
to the triumphant Lord. David was there with them, the
blessed warrior, Jesse's son, king of the Israelites, come into
the presence of Christ. In front of the creator's son, en-   880
dowed with noble virtues, we also saw you standing, glorious
heroes, twelve in number; holy archangels, dwelling in maj-
esty, served you. It will be well for those men who may en-   885
joy those delights! There was glorious joy, the majesty of
warriors, noble behavior; there was no conflict with anyone
there. Exile will be ordained, torment opened up for those   890
who will have to become estranged from these pleasures,
will have to depart miserable when they go from there."

Then the saint's mind was greatly gladdened in his breast,
after the disciples had heard the song, because God wished
to honor them so much above other people, and the protec-   895
tor of warriors spoke these words: "Now, Lord God, glory of
kings, I have understood that you were not far away on our
voyage, when I embarked in the ship, although I did not   900
know how to understand that on the ocean, prince of an-
gels, comforter of souls. Be merciful and kind to me now,
almighty creator, radiant king! On the ocean current I spoke

spræc worda worn;   wat æfter nu
905   hwa me wyrð-myndum   on wudu-bate
ferede ofer flodas.   Þæt is frofre gast
hæleða cynne.   Þær is help gearu,
milts æt mærum,   manna gehwylcum,
sigor-sped geseald,   þam þe seceð to him."
910   Ða him fore eagum   onsyne wearð
æðeling oðywed   in þa ilcan tid,
cining cwicera gehwæs,   þurh cnihtes had.
Þa he worde cwæð,   wuldres Aldor:
"Wes ðu, Andreas, hal,   mid þas will-gedryht,
915   ferð-gefeonde!   Ic þe friðe healde,
þæt þe ne moton   man-geniðlan,
grame gryn-smiðas,   gaste gesceððan."
     Feoll þa to foldan,   frioðo wilnode
wordum wis hæleð,   Wine-Dryhten frægn:
920   "Hu geworhte ic þæt,   waldend fira,
synnig wið seolfne,   sawla nergend,
þæt ic þe swa godne   ongitan ne meahte
on wæg-fære,   þær ic worda gespræc
minra for meotude   ma þonne ic sceolde?"
925   Him andswarode   eal-walda God:
"No ðu swa swiðe   synne gefremedest
swa ðu in Achaia   ondsæc dydest,
ðæt ðu on feor-wegas   feran ne cuðe
ne in þa ceastre   becuman mehte,
930   þing gehegan   þreora nihta
fyrst-gemearces,   swa ic þe feran het
ofer wega gewinn.   Wast nu þe gearwor
þæt ic eaðe mæg   anra gehwylcne
fremman ond fyrþran   freonda minra

a great many words; I now know who it was who graciously 905
conveyed me in the wooden boat over the water. That is
the spirit who comforts mankind. Help and mercy are ready
there from the glorious one, triumphant success given to ev-
ery person who seeks it from him."

Then at the same time the prince, the king of every living 910
thing, became visible, revealed before his eyes in the form of
a young man. Then the Lord of glory spoke these words:
"Hail to you, Andrew, with this glorious company, rejoicing 915
in heart! I shall protect you so that evil enemies, those angry
men who cause nothing but grief, may not harm your soul."

Then the wise man fell to the ground, implored for pro-
tection, asked his friendly Lord in these words: "Ruler of 920
men, savior of souls, what did I do, sinning against you, that
I was not able to recognize you, you who are so good, on the
sea journey when I said more than I should have in the pres-
ence of the creator?"

The all-ruling God answered him: "You did not sin as 925
much as when you protested in Achaia that you did not
know how to travel to distant parts and that you could not
enter the city and carry out that task in the space of three 930
days, when I commanded you to travel over the billow-
ing waves. Now you know more clearly that I can easily
advance and further each and every one of my friends

935   on landa gehwylc,   þær me leofost bið.
Aris nu hrædlice,   ræd ædre ongit,
beorn gebledsod,   swa þe beorht Fæder
geweorðað wuldor-gifum   to widan aldre,
cræfte ond mihte.   Ðu in þa ceastre gong
940   under burg-locan,   þær þin broðor is.
Wat ic Matheus   þurh mænra hand
hrinen heoru-dolgum,   heafod-magan
searo-nettum beseted.   Þu hine secan scealt,
leofne alysan   of laðra hete,
945   ond eal þæt man-cynn   þe him mid wunige,
elþeodigra   inwit-wrasnum,
bealuwe gebundene;   him sceal bot hraðe
weorþan in worulde   ond in wuldre lean,
swa ic him sylfum ær   secgende wæs.

950   "Nu ðu, Andreas, scealt   edre geneðan
in gramra gripe.   Is þe guð weotod,
heardum heoru-swengum;   scel þin hra dæled
wundum weorðan,   wættre geliccost
faran flode blod.   Hie þin feorh ne magon
955   deaðe gedælan,   þeh ðu drype ðolie,
synnigra slege.   Ðu þæt sar aber;
ne læt þe ahweorfan   hæðenra þrym,
grim gar-gewinn,   þæt ðu Gode swice,
Dryhtne þinum.   Wes a domes georn;
960   læt ðe on gemyndum,   hu þæt manegum wearð
fira gefrege   geond feala landa,
þæt me bysmredon   bennum fæstne
weras wan-sælige.   Wordum tyrgdon,

in every country, wherever it pleases me most. Arise quickly 935
now, grasp my purpose at once, blessed man, so that the ra-
diant Father will honor you with glorious gifts, with power
and might forever. Go into the city, down into the strong- 940
hold where your brother is. I know that your kinsman Mat-
thew has been wounded by swords at the hands of the
wicked, enmeshed in nets of treachery. You must seek him
out, rescue the beloved man from the persecution of his en-
emies, along with all the people who are with him there, 945
bound in torment in the cruel chains of the foreigners; de-
liverance will quickly come to him in this world and a reward
in heaven, as I myself said to him earlier.

"Now, Andrew, you must venture at once into the enemy's 950
clutches. A battle is ordained for you; your body must be
dealt hard blows and wounds, your blood must run in a
stream just like water. They will not be able to consign your
life to death, although you may suffer the blows and the 955
strokes of sinful men. Endure that pain; do not allow the
heathens' might, the fierce spear battle, to turn you away
so that you desert God, your Lord. Always be eager for
glory; keep in mind how widely known it was among men 960
throughout many countries that evil men mocked me when
I was held fast in fetters. They insulted me with their words,

slogon ond swungon;   synnige ne mihton
965   þurh sar-cwide   soð gecyðan,
þa ic mid Iudeum   gealgan þehte.
Rod wæs aræred;   þær rinca sum
of minre sidan   swat ut forlet,
dreor to foldan.   Ic adreah feala
970   yrmþa ofer eorðan;   wolde ic eow on ðon
þurh bliðne hige   bysne onstellan,
swa on ell-þeode   ywed wyrðeð.
Manige syndon   in þysse mæran byrig
þara þe ðu gehweorfest   to heofon-leohte
975   þurh minne naman,   þeah hie morðres feala
in fyrn-dagum   gefremed habban."
    Gewat him þa se halga   heofonas secan,
eallra cyninga cining,   þone clænan ham,
eað-medum upp,   þær is ar gelang
980   fira gehwylcum,   þam þe hie findan cann.
    Ða wæs gemyndig   mod-geþyldig,
beorn beaduwe heard;   eode in burh hraðe,
an-ræd oretta,   elne gefyrðred,
maga mode rof,   meotude getreowe.
985   Stop on stræte   —stig wisode—
swa hine nænig gumena   ongitan ne mihte,
synfulra geseon.   Hæfde sigora weard
on þam wang-stede   wære betolden
leofne leod-fruman   mid lofe sinum.
990   Hæfde þa se æðeling   in geþrungen,
Cristes cempa,   carcerne neh;
geseh he hæðenra   hloð ætgædere
fore hlin-dura,   hyrdas standan,
seofone ætsomne.   Ealle swylt fornam;

struck and scourged me; the sinful men with their bit- 965
ter speech could not acknowledge the truth, when I was
stretched out on the gallows among the Jews. The cross was
raised up; there one of the men shed blood from my side,
blood on to the ground. I suffered many torments on earth; 970
in this I wished, kindly, to set you an example of what will be
made manifest in this foreign land. There are many in this
famous city whom you will convert to the light of heaven in 975
my name, although in former days they may have commit-
ted many deadly sins."

Then the holy one, the king of all kings, in his humility,
departed to go up to heaven, his pure home, where grace can
be obtained by all who know how to find it. 980

Then the battle-bold man was thoughtful, his mind pa-
tient; the resolute warrior quickly went into the city, sus-
tained by his courage, the hero brave in his mind, faithful to
his creator. He walked along the street—the path guided 985
him—so that none of the sinful men could perceive or see
him. The guardian of victories had surrounded the people's
beloved leader with his protection, his favor in that place.
Then the noble man, Christ's warrior, hurried on near the 990
prison; he saw a band of heathens, the guards, seven in all,
standing together in front of the grated door. Destruction
carried them all off; the inglorious ones perished. Death's

ANDREAS

995   druron dom-lease.   Deað-ræs forfeng
hæleð heoro-dreorige.   Ða se halga gebæd
bilwytne Fæder;   breost-gehygdum
herede on hehðo   heofon-cyninges þrym,
Godes dryhtendom.   Duru sona onarn
1000   þurh hand-hrine   haliges gastes,
ond þær in eode,   elnes gemyndig,
hæle hilde-deor.   Hæðene swæfon,
dreore druncne;   deað-wang rudon.
Geseh he Matheus   in þam morðor-cofan,
1005   hæleð hige-rofne   under heolstor-locan,
secgan Dryhtne lof,   dom-weorðinga
engla ðeodne;   he ðær ana sæt
geohðum geomor   in þam gnorn-hofe.
Geseh þa under swegle   swæsne geferan,
1010   halig haligne;   hyht wæs geniwad.
Aras þa togenes,   Gode þancade
þæs ðe hie onsunde   æfre moston
geseon under sunnan;   syb wæs gemæne
bam þam gebroðrum,   blis edniwe.
1015   Æghwæðer oðerne   earme beþehte;
cyston hie ond clypton.   Criste wæron begen
leofe on mode.   Hie leoht ymbscan
halig ond heofon-torht;   hreðor innan wæs
wynnum awelled.
Þa worde ongan
1020   ærest Andreas   æðelne geferan
on clustor-cleofan   mid cwide sinum
gretan god-fyrhtne;   sæde him guð-geðingu,

onslaught seized the blood-drenched men. Then the saint   995
prayed to the merciful Father; in his innermost thoughts he
praised to the skies the heavenly king's glory, God's majesty.
The door gave way immediately at the touch of the holy visi-
tor's hand and he went in there, mindful of courage, the   1000
hero brave in battle. The heathens slept, drunk with blood;
they reddened the field of death.

He saw Matthew in the chamber of evil, the valiant man,   1005
in the dark prison, praising and honoring the Lord, the
prince of angels; he was sitting alone there in the dismal
building, mournful in his sorrows. Then under the heavens
one saint saw the other saint, his beloved companion; hope   1010
was renewed. He rose to meet him, thanking God that they
were able to see each other unharmed under the sun; the
love between the two brothers was mutual, their joy re-
newed. Each of them clasped the other in his arms; they   1015
kissed and embraced. Both were dear to Christ's heart. A
light shone around them, holy and heaven-bright. Their
breasts within were surging with joy.

Then Andrew greeted his noble, God-fearing companion   1020
in the prison cell first with this speech; he told him about

feohtan fara monna: "Nu is þin folc on luste,
hæleð hyder on   . . .

1025   . . . gewyrht   eardes neosan."
Æfter þyssum wordum   wuldres þegnas,
begen þa gebroðor,   to gebede hyldon;
sendon hira bene   fore Bearn Godes.
Swylce se halga   in þam hearm-locan

1030   his God grette   ond him geoce bæd,
hælend helpe,   ær þan hra crunge
fore hæðenra   hilde-þrymme;
ond þa gelædde   of leoðo-bendum
fram þam fæstenne   on frið Dryhtnes

1035   tu hundteontig   geteled rime,
swylce feowertig,
generede fram niðe   —þær he nænigne forlet
under burg-locan   bennum fæstne—
ond þær wifa þa gyt,   weorodes to eacan,

1040   anes wana þe fiftig
forhte gefreoðode.   Fægen wæron siðes,
lungre leordan;   nalas leng bidon
in þam gnorn-hofe   guð-geþingo.
    Gewat þa Matheus   menigo lædan

1045   on gehyld Godes,   swa him se halga bebead;
weorod on wil-sið   wolcnum beþehte,
þe læs him scyld-hatan   scyððan comon
mid earh-fare,   eald-geniðlan.
Þær þa modigan mid him   mæðel gehedan,

1050   treow-geþoftan,   ær hie on tu hweorfan.
Ægðer þara eorla   oðrum trymede
heofon-rices hyht;   helle witu
wordum werede.   Swa ða wigend mid him,

battles, about their enemies' fights: "Now your people are eager, the men toward this place . . . deed, to go home."   1025

After these words, the glorious disciples, the two brothers, bowed down in prayer; they sent their prayer into the presence of the Son of God. Likewise the saint in his evil prison prayed to God and asked the savior for aid, for help,   1030 before his body should die violently by the armed might of the heathens; and then he led out of their bondage, out from that prison, two hundred and forty men reckoned by num-   1035 ber into the Lord's safekeeping, released from affliction— there he left no one behind in the stronghold, held fast in fetters—and also, in addition to that multitude, he set free   1040 forty-nine frightened women there. Rejoicing in their departure, they left at once; they did not wait any longer in the dismal building for the battle.

Matthew departed then, leading the multitude with God's protection, as the saint had asked him to; he covered   1045 the group with clouds on that happy journey, lest the evil foes, the old enemies, should come to harm them with a flight of arrows. There the brave men, the faithful companions, held council between themselves, before they went   1050 their separate ways. Each of the warriors strengthened the other's hope of the heavenly kingdom; with his words he warded off the torments of hell. So together the warriors,

hæleð hige-rofe,   halgum stefnum,
1055   cempan coste,   cyning weorðadon,
wyrda waldend,   þæs wuldres ne bið
æfre mid eldum   ende befangen.

    Gewat him þa Andreas   inn on ceastre
glæd-mod gangan,   to þæs ðe he gramra gemot,
1060   fara folc-mægen,   gefrægen hæfde,
oð ðæt he gemette   be mearc-paðe,
standan stræte neah,   stapul ærenne.
Gesæt him þa be healfe.   Hæfde hluttre lufan,
ece up-gemynd   engla blisse;
1065   þanon basnode   under burh-locan
hwæt him guð-weorca   gifeðe wurde.
Þa gesamnedon   side herigeas,
folces frum-garas.   To þam fæstenne
wær-leasra werod   wæpnum comon,
1070   hæðne hild-frecan,   to þæs þa hæftas ær
under hlin-scuwan   hearm þrowedon.
Wendan ond woldon   wiðer-hycgende
þæt hie on elþeodigum   æt geworhton,
weotude wiste;   him seo wen geleah,
1075   syððan mid corðre   carcernes duru
eorre æsc-berend   opene fundon,
onhliden hamera geweorc,   hyrdas deade.
Hie þa unhyðige   eft gecyrdon,
luste belorene,   lað-spell beran;
1080   sægdon þam folce   þæt ðær feorr-cundra,
ell-reordigra,   ænigne to lafe
in carcerne   cwicne ne gemetten,
ah þær heoro-dreorige   hyrdas lagan,

the valiant men, the tried soldiers, with holy voices honored   1055
the king, the ruler of destiny, whose glory among men will
never end.

Then Andrew walked joyfully into the city, to the place
where he had learned of an assembly of angry ones, a power-   1060
ful host of foes, until he came upon a brass column next to
the path, standing close to the street. He sat down beside it.
He felt pure love and had a perpetual awareness of the bliss
of angels above; there he waited for whatever exploits in war   1065
might be granted to him within the city walls. Then large
crowds gathered, the leaders of the people. A troop of faith-
less men with weapons, fierce heathen warriors, came to the
prison, to the place where the captives had previously en-   1070
dured grief in the confined darkness. With hostile inten-
tions, they expected and wished that they might make their
meal on the foreigners, their appointed feast; their expecta-
tion proved false, when the angry spear bearers with their   1075
armed band found the prison door open, the hammered
work undone, the guards dead. They turned back then,
empty handed, deprived of what they desired, to bear the
bad news; they told the people that they had found none of   1080
the strangers, the foreigners, alive, but there the guards lay

gæsne on greote,   gaste berofene,
1085 fægra flæsc-haman.   Þa wearð forht manig
for þam fær-spelle   folces ræswa,
hean, hyge-geomor,   hungres on wenum,
blates beod-gastes.   Nyston beteran ræd,
þonne hie þa belidenan   him to lifnere
1090 gefeormedon.   ...
...   Duru-þegnum wearð
in ane tid   eallum ætsomne
þurh heard gelac   hilde-bedd styred.
Ða ic lungre gefrægn   leode tosomne
burg-wara bannan.   Beornas comon,
1095 wiggendra þreat,   wicgum gengan,
on mearum modige,   mæðel-hegende,
æscum dealle.   Þa wæs eall geador
to þam þing-stede   þeod gesamnod.
Leton him þa betweonum   taan wisian
1100 hwylcne hira ærest   oðrum sceolde
to foddur-þege   feores ongyldan;
hluton hell-cræftum,   hæðen-gildum
teledon betwinum.   Ða se tan gehwearf
efne ofer ænne   eald-gesiða,
1105 se wæs uð-weota   eorla dugoðe,
heriges on ore;   hraðe siððan wearð
fetor-wrasnum fæst,   feores orwena.
Cleopode þa collen-ferhð   cearegan reorde,
cwæð he his sylfes sunu   syllan wolde
1110 on æht-geweald,   eaforan geongne,
lifes to lisse;   hie ða lac hraðe
þegon to þance.

dead on the ground, drenched in blood, deprived of their spirits, the corpses of the doomed. Then, because of that 1085 unexpected news, many of the people's leaders became afraid, downcast, sad at heart, anticipating hunger, a pale guest at their table. They knew no better plan than to feast upon the departed for their sustenance. . . . Within an hour 1090 the violent deathbed of all the doorkeepers was disturbed by harsh battle.

I have heard that the people, the citizens, were quickly summoned together then. The men came, a multitude of 1095 warriors, riding on horses, proud on their steeds, deliberating together, resplendent with their spears. Then the entire people was assembled together at the meeting place. They allowed themselves be directed by a divining stick as to who 1100 among them would first have to pay for the others' food with his life; they cast lots and calculated among themselves with their hellish arts, their idolatry. Then the stick moved just over one of the old retainers, who was the leader of a body of nobles, in the front of the army; after that he was 1105 at once held fast in fetters, despairing of his life. Then the proud-spirited man called out in a voice full of anxiety, said that, in order to save his life, he would give his own son, his young child, into their power in exchange. They thankfully 1110 received this offering at once.

Þeod wæs oflysted,
metes mod-geomre;   næs him to maðme wynn,
hyht to hord-gestreonum.   Hungre wæron
1115   þearle geþreatod,   swa se ðeod-sceaða
reow ricsode.   Þa wæs rinc manig,
guð-frec guma,   ymb þæs geongan feorh
breostum onbryrded   to þam beadu-lace.
Wæs þæt wea-tacen   wide gefrege,
1120   geond þa burh bodad   beorne manegum,
þæt hie þæs cnihtes cwealm   corðre gesohton,
duguðe ond eogoðe;   dæl onfengon
lifes to leofne.   Hie lungre to þæs,
hæðene herig-weardas,   here samnodan
1125   ceastre-warena;   cyrm upp astah.
Ða se geonga ongann   geomran stefne,
gehæfted for herige,   hearm-leoð galan,
freonda fea-sceaft,   friðes wilnian.
Ne mihte earm-sceapen   are findan,
1130   freoðe æt þam folce,   þe him feores wolde,
ealdres geunnan.   Hæfdon æglæcan
sæcce gesohte;   sceolde sweordes ecg,
scerp ond scur-heard,   of sceaðan folme,
fyr-mælum fag,   feorh acsigan.
1135   Ða þæt Andrea   earmlic þuhte,
þeod-bealo þearlic   to geðolianne,
þæt he swa unscyldig   ealdre sceolde
lungre linnan.   Wæs se leod-hete
þrist ond þroht-heard.   Þrymman sceocan,
1140   modige magu-þegnas,   morðres on luste;
woldon æninga,   ellen-rofe,
on þam hyse-beorðre   heafolan gescenan,

The people, sorrowful in their minds, were filled with desire for food; they took no pleasure in precious things, no joy in hoarded treasure. They were greatly harassed by hunger, for that savage enemy of the people reigned. Then there was many a warrior, many a man greedy for the fight, excited in his breast about the youth's life, excited for the battle. This signal of woe was widely reported, announced throughout the city to many a man, that with an armed band, with old and young warriors, they were seeking the boy's death; they would each receive a share to sustain their lives. The heathen guardians of the temple quickly assembled the multitude of citizens for that; the shouting rose up. Then the youth, bound fast in front of the multitude, proceeded to sing a song of grief with a sad voice, friendless, begging for protection. The unfortunate young man could not obtain mercy, protection from the people, anyone who would grant him life and existence. The ferocious fighters had looked for a fight; the sword's blade, sharp and hardened in the storm of battle, gleaming with marks burned into it by fire, would have to demand his life from the hands of the enemy.

Then that seemed wretched to Andrew, a cruel and great evil to suffer that he, so innocent, would have to lose his life suddenly. The people's hostility was shameless and persistent. The proud warriors rushed in crowds, eager for that violent deed; the strong men wished to break open the boy's

1115
1120
1125
1130
1135
1140

garum agetan.　Hine God forstod,
halig of hehðo,　hæðenum folce.
1145　Het wæpen wera　wexe gelicost
on þam orlege　eall formeltan,
þy læs scyld-hatan　sceððan mihton,
egle ondsacan,　ecga þryðum.
Swa wearð alysed　of leod-hete,
1150　geong of gyrne.　Gode ealles þanc,
dryhtna Dryhtne,　þæs ðe he dom gifeð
gumena gehwylcum　þara þe geoce to him
seceð mid snytrum.　Þær bið symle gearu
freod unhwilen　þam þe hie findan cann.

1155　Þa wæs wop hæfen　in wera burgum,
hlud heriges cyrm.　Hreopon friccan,
mændon mete-leaste,　meðe stodon,
hungre gehæftc.　Horn-salu wunedon,
weste win-ræced.　Welan ne benohton
1160　beornas to brucanne　on þa bitran tid;
gesæton searu-þancle　sundor to rune,
ermðu eahtigan.　Næs him to eðle wynn!
Fregn þa gelome　freca oðerne:
"Ne hele se ðe hæbbe　holde lare,
1165　on sefan snyttro!　Nu is sæl cumen,
þrea ormæte;　is nu þearf mycel
þæt we wis-fæstra　wordum hyran."
Þa for þære dugoðe　deoful ætywde,
wann ond wlite-leas;　hæfde weriges hiw.
1170　Ongan þa meldigan　morþres brytta,
helle hinca,　þone halgan wer
wiðer-hycgende,　ond þæt word gecwæð:

head immediately, to strike him down with spears. God, the holy one on high, protected him from the heathen people; he commanded the men's weapons to melt away completely in the battle, just like wax, lest the evil foes, the loathsome opponents, might have been able to harm him with the power of their sword blades. So the young man was rescued from the persecution of that people, from that affliction. Thanks be to God for everything, the Lord of lords, for he grants just judgment to every man who wisely seeks help from him. There eternal peace is always at hand for anyone who knows how to find it.

Then the cries of lamentation rose up in their cities, the loud shrieking of the multitude. The heralds shouted, bewailed the lack of food, stood exhausted, bound by hunger. The gabled dwellings, the wine halls, remained deserted. It was not enjoyment of their riches that the men needed at that bitter time; wise in thought, they sat apart in counsel, considering their miseries. They took no pleasure in the land of their birth! Then one warrior frequently asked another: "Let him who has true advice and wisdom in his mind not conceal it! A time of boundless calamity is upon us now; the need to hear the words of the wise is now great."

Then a devil appeared in front of the people, dark and ugly; he had the appearance of a criminal. This perpetrator of deadly evil, this cripple from hell, with his hostile intentions, proceeded to announce who the holy man was and

"Her is gefered   ofer feorne weg
æðelinga sum   innan ceastre,
1175   ell-þeodigra,   þone ic Andreas
nemnan herde.   He eow neon gesceod
ða he aferede   of fæstenne
mann-cynnes ma   þonne gemet wære.
Nu ge magon eaðe   oncyð-dæda
1180   wrecan on gewyrhtum.   Lætað wæpnes spor
iren ecg-heard,   ealdor-geard sceoran,
fæges feorh-hord.   Gað fromlice
þæt ge wiðer-feohtend   wiges gehnægan!"
     Him þa Andreas   agef ondsware:
1185   "Hwæt ðu þristlice   þeode lærest,
bældest to beadowe!   Wast þe bæles cwealm,
hatne in helle,   ond þu here fysest,
feðan to gefeohte;   eart ðu fag wið God,
dugoða demend.   Hwæt ðu, deofles stræl,
1190   icest þine yrmðo!   Ðe se almihtiga
heanne gehnægde,   ond on heolstor besceaf,
þær þe cyninga cining   clamme belegde;
ond þe syððan a   Satan nemdon,
ða ðe Dryhtnes a   deman cuðon."
1195   Ða gyt se wiðer-meda   wordum lærde
folc to gefeohte,   feondes cræfte:
"Nu ge gehyrað   hæleða gewinnan,
se ðyssum herige mæst   hearma gefremede;
ðæt is Andreas,   se me on fliteð
1200   wordum wrætlicum   for wera menigo."
     Ða wæs beacen boden   burh-sittendum;
ahleopon hild-frome   heriges brehtme
ond to weall-geatum   wigend þrungon,

spoke these words: "A certain foreign lord, whom I heard called by the name of Andrew, has been conveyed here within the city, over a great distance. He injured you here 1175 when he took away more of mankind than was fitting from the prison. Now you can easily avenge these harmful deeds on their perpetrators. Let the weapon's mark, the hard- 1180 edged iron, cut the life enclosure, the life treasure of the doomed man. Go bravely to subdue your opponent in battle!"

Then Andrew answered him: "How boldly you instruct 1185 this people, urge them to battle! You know for yourself the hot punishment of the hell flames, and you are inciting this multitude, this company, to a fight; you are hostile to God, judge of hosts. How you are adding to your miseries, you 1190 devil's arrow! The almighty vanquished you, you miserable being, and thrust you into darkness, where the king of kings fettered you; and since then those who knew how to value the Lord's law have always called you Satan."

Still his opponent with his words urged on the people to 1195 the fight, with the devil's cunning: "Now you are listening to the enemy of the people, who has done the utmost harm to this multitude; this is Andrew, who is accusing me in ornate 1200 words in front of this throng of people."

Then a signal was given to the citizens; men bold in battle leaped up, to the clamor of the crowd, and warriors, valiant

cene under cumblum,　corðre mycle
1205　to ðam orlege,　ordum ond bordum.
　　Þa worde cwæð　weoroda Dryhten;
meotud mihtum swið　sægde his magoþegne:
"Scealt ðu, Andreas,　ellen fremman;
ne mið ðu for menigo,　ah þinne mod-sefan
1210　staðola wið strangum!　Nis seo stund latu
þæt þe wæl-reowe　witum belecgaþ,
cealdan clommum.　Cyð þe sylfne,
herd hige þinne,　heortan staðola,
þæt hie min on ðe　mægen oncnawan.
1215　Ne magon hie ond ne moton　ofer mine est
þinne lic-homan,　lehtrum scyldige,
deaðe gedælan,　ðeah ðu drype þolige,
mirce man-slaga;　ic þe mid wunige."
　　Æfter þam wordum com　werod unmæte,
1220　lyswe lar-smeoðas,　mid lind-gecrode,
bolgen-mode;　bæron ut hræðe
ond þam halgan þær　handa gebundon.
Siþþan geypped wæs　æðelinga wynn
ond hie andweardne　eagum meahton
1225　gesion sige-rofne,　þær wæs secg manig
on þam wel-wange　wiges oflysted
leoda duguðe.　Lyt sorgodon
hwylc him þæt edlean　æfter wurde.
　　Heton þa lædan　ofer land-sceare,
1230　ðrag-mælum teon,　torn-geniðlan,
swa hie hit frecnost　findan meahton;
drogon deormode　æfter dun-scræfum,
ymb stan-hleoðo,　stærced-ferþþe,

in arms, thronged to the gates in the city walls, in an armed
band to the battle, with spears and shields.   1205

Then the Lord of the heavenly hosts spoke these words;
the creator, mighty in his powers, said to his servant:
"Andrew, you must perform courageous deeds; do not hide
yourself from the multitude, but strengthen your mind
against violent men! The time is approaching when savage   1210
men will fetter you in cold torments. Reveal yourself, for-
tify your mind, strengthen your heart, so that they may per-
ceive my power in you. Guilty of wickedness, they cannot   1215
and may not give your body over to death against my will,
although you will endure assaults, cruel wicked blows; I shall
remain with you."

After these words an immense throng came, their minds
swollen with rage, corrupt counselors, along with a troop   1220
bearing shields; they rushed out in force and bound the
saint's hands there. When the delight of princes was re-
vealed and they could see the triumphant one present be-   1225
fore their eyes, many a man among the company of people
there on the field of slaughter was possessed by the desire
for battle. They cared little what their reward would be af-
terward!

Then they commanded that their bitter enemy be led
across the country, dragged at times wherever they could   1230
find it to be most dangerous for him; the savage, hard-
hearted men dragged him through mountain gorges, round

265

efne swa wide swa   wegas to lagon,
1235   enta ær-geweorc,   innan burgum,
stræte stan-fage.   Storm upp aras
æfter ceaster-hofum,   cirm unlytel
hæðnes heriges.   Wæs þæs halgan lic
sar-bennum soden,   swate bestemed,
1240   ban-hus abrocen;   blod yðum weoll,
haton heolfre.   Hæfde him on innan
ellen untweonde;   wæs þæt æðele mod
asundrad fram synnum,   þeah he sares swa feala
deopum dolg-slegum   dreogan sceolde.
1245   Swa wæs ealne dæg   oð ðæt æfen com
sigel-torht swungen;   sar eft gewod
ymb þæs beornes breost,   oð þæt beorht gewat
sunne swegel-torht   to sete glidan.
Læddan þa leode   laðne gewinnan
1250   to carcerne.   He wæs Criste swa þeah
leof on mode;   him wæs leoht sefa
halig, heortan neh,   hige untyddre.

Þa se halga wæs   under heolstor-scuwan,
eorl ellen-heard,   ondlange niht
1255   searo-þancum beseted.   Snaw eorðan band
winter-geworpum.   Weder coledon
heardum hægel-scurum;   swylce hrim ond forst,
hare hild-stapan,   hæleða eðel
lucon, leoda gesetu.   Land wæron freorig;
1260   cealdum cyle-gicelum   clang wæteres þrym.
Ofer ea-streamas   is brycgade
blæce brim-rade.   Blið-heort wunode
eorl unforcuð,   elnes gemyndig,

rocky slopes, as far and wide as the roads extended, the an-   1235
cient work of giants, within the cities, the streets paved
with stones. A storm, not a little outcry, rose up through-
out the city houses, from the heathen multitude. The saint's
body was subjected to painful wounds, wet with blood, his   1240
bone house broken apart; blood flowed in hot, gory waves.
He had unwavering courage within himself; that noble mind
was untouched by sins, although he had to endure so much
pain from blows that wounded him deeply. So all day until   1245
evening came, this man, bright as the sun, was beaten; pain
penetrated through the warrior's breast once more, until
the bright sun shining in the sky went down. Then the peo-
ple led their hated enemy to prison. Nevertheless, he was   1250
dear to Christ in his mind; his holy spirit felt light, near to
his heart, his mind unwavering.

Then the saint, the warrior firm in courage, was im-
mersed in wise thoughts under the shadow of darkness the   1255
whole night through. Snow bound the earth in winter snow-
drifts. The skies grew cold with fierce hail showers; likewise
frozen mist and frost, stalking gray warriors, locked the
homeland of men, the dwellings of peoples. Lands were fro-
zen; the mighty water clung together in cold icicles; the ice   1260
formed a bridge over the rivers, the dark surging water. Joy-
ful in heart, the noble warrior, mindful of courage, bold and

þrist ond þroht-heard,   in þrea-nedum
1265 winter-cealdan niht.   No on gewitte blon,
acol for þy egesan,   þæs þe he ær ongann,
þæt he a domlicost   Dryhten herede,
weorðade wordum,   oð ðæt wuldres gim
heofon-torht onhlad.

                        Ða com hæleða þreat
1270 to ðære dimman ding,   duguð unlytel,
wadan wæl-gifre   weorodes brehtme.
Heton ut hræðe   æðeling lædan
in wraðra geweald,   wær-fæstne hæleð.
Ða wæs eft swa ær   ondlangne dæg
1275 swungen sar-slegum.   Swat yðum weoll
þurh ban-cofan;   blod lifrum swealg,
hatan heolfre.   Hra weorces ne sann,
wundum werig.

                        Þa cwom wopes hring
þurh þæs beornes breost,   blat ut faran;
1280 weoll waðuman stream   ond he worde cwæð:
"Geseoh nu, Dryhten God,   drohtað minne,
weoruda will-geofa!   Þu wast ond const
anra gehwylces   earfeð-siðas.
Ic gelyfe to ðe,   min lif-fruma,
1285 þæt ðu mild-heort me   for þinum mægen-spedum,
nerigend fira,   næfre wille,
ece ælmihtig,   anforlætan,
swa ic þæt gefremme,   þenden feorh leofað,
min on moldan,   þæt ic, meotud, þinum
1290 larum leof-wendum   lyt geswice.
Þu eart gescyldend   wið sceaðan wæpnum,
ece ead-fruma,   eallum þinum;

strong in endurance, spent the winter-cold night in great 1265
affliction. In the face of terror, he did not waver mentally
from what he had begun earlier, so that he kept on praising
the Lord most gloriously, honoring him in his words, until
the jewel of glory appeared, shining in the sky.

Then a troop of men, a great company, came to the dark 1270
dungeon, advancing eager for slaughter, to the clamor of the
crowd. At once they ordered that the prince, the faithful
man, be led out into the control of his enemies. Then again
as before he was beaten the whole day through with pain- 1275
ful blows. Blood flowed in waves over his body; the blood
poured out in thick streams, in hot gore. His body had no
respite from pain, exhausted from its wounds.

Then came an outpouring of pale tears over the man's
breast, running out; the water welled up in floods and he 1280
spoke these words: "See now, Lord God, my plight, gracious
benefactor of the heavenly hosts! You know and understand
the misfortunes of each and every person. I trust in you, my
source of life, that you, the merciful savior of men, the eter- 1285
nal almighty, because of your abundant powers, will never
forsake me if I, for the duration of my life here on earth,
may contrive never to be false to your gracious teachings, 1290
my creator. Eternal author of happiness, you are the protec-
tor against the enemies' weapons for all of your people; do

ne læt nu bysmrian   banan mann-cynnes,
facnes frum-bearn,   þurh feondes cræft
1295 leahtrum belecgan   þa þin lof berað."
  Ða ðær ætywde   se atola gast,
wrað wær-loga;   wigend lærde
for þam here-mægene   helle dioful
awerged in witum,   ond þæt word gecwæð:
1300 "Sleað synnigne   ofer seolfes muð,
folces gewinnan;   nu to feala reordaþ."
  Þa wæs orlege   eft onhrered,
niwan stefne;   nið upp aras
oþ ðæt sunne gewat   to sete glidan
1305 under niflan næs.   Niht helmade,
brun-wann oferbræd   beorgas steape,
ond se halga wæs   to hofe læded,
deor ond dom-georn,   in þæt dimme ræced;
sceal þonne in nead-cofan   niht-langne fyrst
1310 wær-fæst wunian   wic unsyfre.
  Þa com seofona sum   to sele geongan
atol æglæca,   yfela gemyndig,
morðres man-frea   myrce gescyrded,
deoful deað-reow   duguðum bereafod.
1315 Ongan þa þam halgan   hosp-word sprecan:
"Hwæt hogodest ðu, Andreas,   hider-cyme þinne
on wraðra geweald?   Hwær is wuldor þin,
þe ðu ofer-higdum   upp arærdest,
þa ðu goda ussa   gilp gehnægdest?
1320 Hafast nu þe anum   eall getihhad
land ond leode,   swa dyde lareow þin.
Cyne-þrym ahof,   þam wæs Crist nama,

not now allow the slayer of mankind, the firstborn of iniq-
uity, to insult those who spread praise of you, to vilify them   1295
with the devil's cunning."

Then the terrible spirit, the hostile traitor, appeared
there; the devil from hell, cursed in torments, urged the
warriors in front of the multitude and spoke these words:
"Hit that sinful man, that enemy of the people, on the   1300
mouth; he is talking too much now."

Then war was stirred up once again; the hostility
mounted until the sun departed, set beneath the dark hori-   1305
zon. The night helmeted, spread over the steep mountains,
burnished dark, and the saint, bold and eager for renown,
was brought to the building, into that dark hall; the faithful
man had to occupy the foul prison dwelling for the space of   1310
the entire night.

Then with seven others the terrible enemy came advanc-
ing into the hall, intent on evil, the lord of wickedness and
crime, shrouded in darkness, the murderously cruel devil,
deprived of good. He proceeded to speak these insulting   1315
words to the saint: "What was the purpose of your journey
here, Andrew, into the power of your enemies? Where is
your glory, which in your arrogance you elevated when you
brought down the pride of our gods? Now you have claimed   1320
for yourself alone all this land and people, as your teacher
did. He whose name was Christ puffed up his kingly glory

ofer middan-geard,   þynden hit meahte swa.
Þone Herodes   ealdre besnyðede,
1325 forcom æt campe   cyning Iudea,
rices berædde,   ond hine rode befealg,
þæt he on gealgan   his gast onsende.
Swa ic nu bebeode   bearnum minum,
þegnum þryðfullum,   ðæt hie ðe hnægen,
1330 gingran æt guðe.   Lætað gares ord,
earh attre gemæl,   in gedufan
in fæges ferð;   gað fromlice,
ðæt ge guð-frecan   gylp forbegan!"
    Hie wæron reowe,   ræsdon on sona
1335 gifrum grapum.   Hine God forstod,
staðul-fæst steorend,   þurh his strangan miht.
Syððan hie oncneowon   Cristes rode
on his mæg-wlite,   mære tacen,
wurdon hie ða acle   on þam onfenge,
1340 forhte, afærde,   ond on fleam numen.
Ongan eft swa ær   eald-geniðla,
helle hæftling,   hearm-leoð galan:
"Hwæt wearð eow swa rofum,   rincas mine,
lind-gesteallan,   þæt eow swa lyt gespeow?"
1345 Him þa earm-sceapen   agef ondsware,
fah fyrn-sceaþa,   ond his fæder oncwæð:
"Ne magan we him lungre   lað ætfæstan,
swilt þurh searwe.   Ga þe sylfa to!
Þær þu gegninga   guðe findest,
1350 frecne feohtan,   gif ðu furður dearst
to þam an-hagan   aldre geneðan.

throughout the world, as long as he was able to do so. Herod, the king of the Jews, deprived him of life, overcame him in battle, dispossessed him of his kingdom and consigned him to the cross, so that he gave up his spirit on the gallows. So now I command my children, my powerful warriors, followers in battle, to bring you down. Let spear points, arrows stained with poison, pierce the life of the doomed man; go boldly, that you may humble the pride of this warrior."

They were savage, rushed at him immediately with greedy clutches. God, the steadfast ruler, defended him with his strong power. When, in the act of seizing him, they perceived Christ's cross, that glorious sign, on his face, they became afraid, fearful, frightened, and were put to flight. Once again, as before, the archenemy, hell's captive, proceeded to sing a song of sorrow: "What happened to you, such brave men, my warriors, my comrades in battle, that you have been so unsuccessful?" A vile creature, a hostile ancient enemy, answered him and replied to his father: "Suddenly we are unable to inflict harm on him, death by treachery. Go to him yourself! There you will find a contest at once, a dangerous fight, if you dare to risk your life further against that solitary man.

"We ðe magon eaðe,   eorla leofost,
æt þam secg-plegan   selre gelæran
ær ðu gegninga   guðe fremme,
1355   wiges woman,   weald hu ðe sæle
æt þam gegn-slege.   Utan gangan eft,
þæt we bysmrigen   bendum fæstne,
oðwitan him his wræc-sið;   habbað word gearu
wið þam æglæcan   eall getrahtod!"
1360   Þa hleoðrade   hludan stefne,
witum bewæled,   ond þæt word gecwæð:
"Þu þe, Andreas,   aclæc-cræftum
lange feredes!   Hwæt ðu leoda feala
forleolce ond forlærdest!   Nu leng ne miht
1365   gewealdan þy weorce.   Þe synd witu þæs grim
weotud be gewyrhtum.   Þu scealt werig-mod,
hean, hroðra leas,   hearm þrowigan,
sare swylt-cwale.   Secgas mine
to þam guð-plegan   gearwe sindon,
1370   þa þe æninga   ellen-weorcum
unfyrn faca   feorh ætþringan.
Hwylc is þæs mihtig   ofer middan-geard
þæt he þe alyse   of leoðu-bendum
manna cynnes   ofer mine est?"
1375   Him þa Andreas   agef ondsware:
"Hwæt me eaðe   ælmihtig God,
niða neregend,   se ðe in niedum iu
gefæstnode   fyrnum clommum!
Þær ðu syððan a,   susle gebunden,
1380   in wræc wunne,   wuldres blunne,
syððan ðu forhogedes   heofon-cyninges word.
Þær wæs yfles or;   ende næfre

"We can easily, dearest of warriors, give you better advice in this swordplay, rather than your waging war, the tumult 1355 of battle, immediately, however you may succeed in the exchange of blows. Let us go back so that we may insult him, held fast in his fetters, taunt him about his wretchedness; we have words ready, all prepared, against the ferocious fighter!"

Then, oppressed by torments, he spoke in a loud voice 1360 and said these words: "Andrew, you have long dealt in evil arts! How you have misled and deceived many people! Now you will not be able to direct this work any longer. Harsh 1365 punishments are deservedly appointed for you. Dejected, miserable, comfortless, you will have to suffer injury, the painful torments of death. My men, who will certainly drive 1370 the life out of you with their courageous deeds very soon, are ready for the battle-play. What man in the world is so powerful that he may rescue you from chains against my will?"

Then Andrew answered him: "How easily almighty God, 1375 savior of men, may rescue me, he who long ago fettered you in suffering, in burning bonds! Ever since, bound in torment, you have suffered exile there, having forfeited heav- 1380 enly glory, since you scorned the word of the heavenly king.

þines wræces weorðeð.   Ðu scealt widan feorh
ecan þine yrmðu;   þe bið a symble
1385   of dæge on dæg   drohtaþ strengra."
    Ða wearð on fleame   se ðe ða fæhðo iu
wið God geara   grimme gefremede.
Com þa on uhtan   mid ær-dæge
hæðenra hloð   haliges neosan
1390   leoda weorude.   Heton lædan ut
þroht-heardne þegn   þriddan siðe;
woldon aninga   ellen-rofes
mod gemyltan.   Hit ne mihte swa.
Þa wæs niowinga   nið onhrered,
1395   heard ond hete-grim;   wæs se halga wer
sare geswungen,   searwum gebunden,
dolg-bennum þurhdrifen,   ðendon dæg lihte.
    Ongan þa geomor-mod   to Gode cleopian,
heard of hæfte,   halgan stefne;
1400   weop werig-ferð,   ond þæt word gecwæð:
"Næfre ic geferde   mid Frean willan
under heofon-hwealfe   heardran drohtnoð,
þær ic Dryhtnes æ   deman sceolde.
Sint me leoðu tolocen,   lic sare gebrocen,
1405   ban-hus blod-fag;   benne weallað,
seono-dolg swatige.   Hwæt ðu sigora weard,
Dryhten hælend,   on dæges tide
mid Iudeum   geomor wurde
ða ðu of gealgan,   God lifigende,
1410   fyrn-weorca Frea,   to Fæder cleopodest,
cininga wuldor,   ond cwæde ðus:
'Ic ðe, Fæder engla,   frignan wille,
lifes leoht-fruma: hwæt forlætest ðu me?'

276

That was the origin of evil; there will never be an end to your exile. You will have to add to your miseries for evermore; your plight will be harder from day to day, eternally." 1385

Then he fled, he who had once long ago waged a violent feud against God. Then, in the early morning, at daybreak, a band of heathens came with a troop of the people to seek out the saint. They commanded that the warrior, strong in 1390 times of hardship, be brought out for the third time; they wished to subdue the brave man's mind straightaway. This could not happen. Then cruel and fierce hatred was stirred up once more; the holy man was painfully beaten, bound 1395 cunningly, pierced through with wounds, while there was daylight.

Then, sad of mind, resolute, he called to God with his holy voice from his captivity; weary hearted, he wept and 1400 spoke these words: "I never experienced, by the Lord's will, a more painful plight under the vault of heaven, wherever I had to proclaim the law of God. My limbs are pulled apart, my body broken by pain, my bone house bloodstained; the 1405 wounds cut into my sinews flow with blood. How sorrowful you became, guardian of victories, Lord savior, in the space of one day among the Jews when you, the living God, the 1410 Lord of creation, the glory of kings, called from the gallows to your Father and spoke thus: 'Father of angels, author of life and light, I want to ask you: why do you forsake me?'

277

Ond ic nu þry dagas   þolian sceolde
1415 wæl-grim witu.   Bidde ic, weoroda God,
þæt ic gast minne   agifan mote,
sawla symbel-gifa,   on þines sylfes hand.
Ðu ðæt gehete   þurh þin halig word,
þa ðu us twelfe   trymman ongunne,
1420 þæt us hete-rofra   hild ne gesceode,
ne lices dæl   lungre oððeoded,
ne synu ne ban   on swaðe lagon,
ne loc of heafde   to forlore wurde,
gif we þine lare   læstan woldon.
1425 Nu sint sionwe toslopen,   is min swat adropen,
licgað æfter lande   loccas todrifene,
fex on foldan.   Is me feorh-gedal
leofre mycle   þonne þeos lif-cearo."
Him þa stefn oncwæð,   stið-hycgendum,
1430 wuldor-cyninges;   word hleoðrode:
"Ne wep þone wræc-sið,   wine leofesta,
nis þe to frecne.   Ic þe friðe healde,
minre mund-byrde   mægene besette.
Me is miht ofer eall,   . . .
1435 sigor-sped geseald.   Soð þæt gecyðeð
mænig æt meðle   on þam myclan dæge,
þæt ðæt geweorðeð,   þæt ðeos wlitige gesceaft,
heofon ond eorðe,   hreosaþ togadore,
ær awæged sie   worda ænig
1440 þe ic þurh minne muð   meðlan onginne.
Geseoh nu seolfes swæðe,   swa þin swat aget
þurh ban-gebrec   blodige stige,
lices lælan;   no þe laðes ma

And now for three days I have had to suffer murderously 1415
cruel torments. I pray, God of heavenly hosts, feast-giver to
the souls in heaven, that I may give up my spirit into your
hands. You promised by your holy word, when you were
comforting us twelve, that the fighting of fierce enemies 1420
would not harm us, nor would any part of our bodies be sud-
denly severed, nor would our sinews and bones lie on the
ground in our wake, nor would a lock of our hair perish if we
were willing to follow your teaching. Now my sinews are 1425
torn apart, my blood has been shed, my locks lie scattered
over the land, my hair is on the ground. I would prefer death
to this life of sorrow."

Then the voice of the king of glory answered the resolute 1430
man; the words resounded: "Do not weep over your wretch-
edness, dearest friend, it is not dangerous for you. I am
keeping you safe from harm, surrounding you with the
power of my protection. Power, triumphant success, over
everything . . . is given to me. Many a person assembled on 1435
that great day will declare the truth, that it will come about
that this beautiful creation, heaven and earth, will pass away
together before any word which I speak from my mouth 1440
may be nullified. Now, see your own trail, wherever your
blood has shed a gory track through the breaking of your
bones and the bruising of your body; those who have done

þurh daroða gedrep   gedon motan,

1445   þa þe heardra mæst   hearma gefremedan."

Þa on last beseah   leoflic cempa

æfter word-cwidum   wuldor-cyninges;

geseh he geblowene   bearwas standan

blædum gehrodene,   swa he ær his blod aget.

1450   Ða worde cwæð   wigendra hleo:

"Sie ðe ðanc ond lof,   þeoda waldend,

to widan feore   wuldor on heofonum,

ðæs ðu me on sare,   sige-dryhten min,

ell-þeodigne,   an ne forlæte."

1455   Swa se dæd-fruma   Dryhten herede

halgan stefne   oð ðæt hador sigel

wuldor-torht gewat   under wadu scriðan.

Þa þa folc-togan   feorðan siðe,

egle ondsacan,   æðeling læddon

1460   to þam carcerne;   woldon cræfta gehygd,

mago-rædendes   mod oncyrran

on þære deorcan niht.   Þa com Dryhten God

in þæt hlin-ræced,   hæleða wuldor,

ond þa wine synne   wordum grette

1465   ond frofre gecwæð,   Fæder mann-cynnes,

lifes lareow.   Heht his lic-homan

hales brucan: "Ne scealt ðu in henðum a leng

searo-hæbbendra   sar þrowian."

Aras þa mægene rof;   sægde meotude þanc,

1470   hal of hæfte   heardra wita.

Næs him gewemmed wlite,   ne wloh of hrægle

lungre alysed,   ne loc of heafde,

ne ban gebrocen,   ne blodig wund

lice gelenge,   ne laðes dæl

you the most cruel harm will not be allowed to do you any 1445
more injury by attacking you with spears."

Then, after the glorious king's speech, the beloved war-
rior looked behind him; he saw flowering groves standing
adorned with fruit, where he had poured out his blood.
Then the protector of warriors spoke these words: "Thanks 1450
and praise be to you forever, ruler of peoples, glory in the
heavens, because you, my triumphant Lord, did not forsake
me, a stranger, in my pain." So the leader praised the Lord 1455
with his holy voice until the clear, gloriously bright sun
glided under the sea.

Then, for the fourth time, the leaders of the people, the
loathsome enemies, led the prince to the prison; they 1460
wanted to alter the mighty thoughts, the mind of that coun-
selor of men, in the dark night. Then the Lord God, the
glory of men, came into that prison and the Father of man-
kind, the teacher of life, greeted his friend and spoke con- 1465
solingly to him. He commanded him to have the use of his
unharmed body: "You will not have to endure the humiliat-
ing torment of these armed men any longer."

Then, brave and mighty, he arose; unharmed by those 1470
cruel torments, in his prison he said thanks to his creator.
His appearance was not disfigured nor was even the hem
torn off his garment nor a lock torn from his head, nor was a
bone broken nor a bloody wound on his body nor was any

1475 þurh dolg-slege   dreore bestemed,
ac wæs eft swa ær   þurh þa æðelan miht
lof lædende   ond on his lice trum.

   Hwæt ic hwile nu   haliges lare,
leoð-giddinga,   lof þæs þe worhte,
1480 wordum wemde,   wyrd undyrne!
Ofer min gemet   mycel is to secganne,
langsum leornung,   þæt he in life adreag,
eall æfter orde.   Þæt scell æ-glæwra
mann on moldan   þonne ic me tælige
1485 findan on ferðe,   þæt fram fruman cunne
eall þa earfeðo   þe he mid elne adreah,
grimra guða.   Hwæðre git sceolon
lytlum sticcum   leoð-worda dæl
furður reccan;   þæt is fyrn-sægen,
1490 hu he weorna feala   wita geðolode,
heardra hilda,   in þære hæðenan byrig.

   He be wealle geseah   wundrum fæste
under sæl-wage   sweras unlytle,
stapulas standan,   storme bedrifene,
1495 eald enta geweorc.   He wið anne þæra,
mihtig ond mod-rof,   mæðel gehede,
wis, wundrum gleaw;   word stunde ahof:
"Geher ðu, marman-stan,   meotudes rædum,
fore þæs onsyne   ealle gesceafte
1500 forhte geweorðað,   þonne hie fæder geseoð
heofonas ond eorðan   herigea mæste
on middan-geard   man-cynn secan.
Læt nu of þinum staþole   streamas weallan,
ea inflede,   nu ðe ælmihtig

282

kind of injury drenched with blood from a wounding blow, 1475
but through that noble power he was again as he had been,
giving praise and whole in his body.

How I have been proclaiming for some time now the
saint's story in my words, in poetry, praise of what he accom- 1480
plished, the well-known events! It is much beyond my abil-
ity, a protracted study, to relate what he endured in his life,
from start to finish. A man on earth more learned in scrip-
ture than I consider myself to be will have to find in his 1485
mind knowledge of all the hardships of fierce combats
which he endured with courage from the start. Neverthe-
less we must narrate still more poetry in short sections; it is
an ancient tradition, how he suffered very many torments, 1490
cruel battles, in that heathen city.

By a wall in the building he saw large pillars standing,
marvelously solid, beaten by storms, the ancient work of
giants. Powerful and brave minded, wise, marvelously pru- 1495
dent, he addressed one of them; he raised up his voice at
once: "Obey, marble, the creator's commands, before whose
face all creatures will be fearful, when they see the Father of 1500
heaven and earth coming into the world, coming to man-
kind with the greatest of armies. Let water flow now from
your base, a river full of water, now that the almighty,

1505 hateð, heofona cyning,   þæt ðu hrædlice
on þis fræte folc   forð onsende
wæter wid-rynig   to wera cwealme,
geofon geotende.   Hwæt ðu golde eart,
sinc-gife, sylla!   On ðe sylf cyning
1510 wrat, wuldres God;   wordum cyðde
recene geryno,   ond ryhte æ
getacnode   on tyn wordum,
meotud mihtum swið.   Moyse sealde,
swa hit soð-fæste   syðþan heoldon,
1515 modige mago-þegnas,   magas sine,
God-fyrhte guman,   Iosua ond Tobias.
Nu ðu miht gecnawan   þæt þe cyning engla
gefrætwode   furður mycle
giofum gear-dagum   þonne eall gimma cynn.
1520 Þurh his halige hæs   þu scealt hræðe cyðan
gif ðu his ondgitan   ænige hæbbe."
    Næs þa word-latu   wihte þon mare
þæt se stan togan.   Stream ut aweoll,
fleow ofer foldan.   Famige walcan
1525 mid ær-dæge   eorðan þehton;
myclade mere-flod.   Meodu-scerwen wearð
æfter symbel-dæge;   slæpe tobrugdon
searu-hæbbende.   Sund grunde onfeng,
deope gedrefed;   duguð wearð afyrhted
1530 þurh þæs flodes fær.   Fæge swulton;
geonge on geofene   guð-ræs fornam,
þurh sealtne weg.   Þæt wæs sorg-byrþen,
biter beor-þegu.   Byrlas ne gældon,
ombeht-þegnas.   Þær wæs ælcum genog

the king of heaven, commands you to pour out water to flow 1505
far and wide onto this shameful people at once, a surging
flood to kill men. How much better you are than gold or a
rich gift! On you the king himself, the God of glory, wrote; 1510
the creator strong in might revealed in words the awful mys-
teries and expressed the true law in ten sentences. He gave
them to Moses, just as the righteous men, the brave war- 1515
riors, his kinsmen, the God-fearing Joshua and Tobias, kept
them afterward. Now you can recognize that the king of an-
gels adorned you in days of old with gifts much greater than
the whole family of gems. At his holy command you must at 1520
once reveal if you have any understanding of him."

There was no more delay at all in answering before the
stone split open. A stream welled out, flowed over the
ground. Foamy billows covered the earth at daybreak; the 1525
deluge was increasing. After the day of feasting there was a
dispensing of mead; the armed men started from sleep. The
water, stirred up from the depths, took possession of the
land. The people were frightened by the sudden danger of 1530
the deluge. The doomed died; the battle rush, by means of
the salt wave, carried the young men off into the flood. That
was a sorrowful brew, a bitter beer-drinking. The cupbear-
ers, the servingmen, did not delay. From the dawn of day,

1535   fram dæges orde   drync sona gearu.
    Weox wæteres þrym.   Weras cwanedon,
    ealde æsc-berend.   Wæs him ut myne
    fleon fealone stream;   woldon feore beorgan,
    to dun-scræfum   drohtað secan,
1540   eorðan ondwist.   Him þæt engel forstod,
    se ða burh oferbrægd   blacan lige,
    hatan heaðo-wælme;   hreoh wæs þær inne
    beatende brim.   Ne mihte beorna hloð
    of þam fæstenne   fleame spowan.
1545   Wægas weoxon,   wadu hlynsodon,
    flugon fyr-gnastas,   flod yðum weoll.
    Ðær wæs yð-fynde   innan burgum
    geomor-gidd wrecen,   gehðo mænan
    forht-ferð manig,   fus-leoð galen.
1550   Egeslic æled   eag-syne wearð,
    heardlic here-team,   hleoðor gryrelic.
    Þurh lyft-gelac   leges blæstas
    weallas ymbwurpon;   wæter mycladon.
        Þær wæs wop wera   wide gehyred,
1555   earmlic ylda gedræg.   Þa þær an ongann,
    fea-sceaft hæleð,   folc gadorigean;
    hean, hyge-geomor,   heofende spræc:
    "Nu ge magon sylfe   soð gecnawan,
    þæt we mid unrihte   ell-þeodigne
1560   on carcerne   clommum belegdon,
    wite-bendum.   Us seo wyrd scyðeð,
    heard ond hete-grim;   þæt is her swa cuð!
    Is hit mycle selre,   þæs þe ic soð talige,
    þæt we hine alysan   of leoðo-bendum,
1565   ealle an-mode   —ofost is selost—

286

enough drink for everyone was ready immediately. The   1535
force of the water grew. Men, old spear-bearers, lamented.
They desired to flee away from the gleaming flood; they
wanted to save their lives, to seek a new way of life in the
mountain caves, a refuge in the earth. An angel, who envel-   1540
oped the city with bright flames, hot fierce billows, pre-
vented them doing that; in there the pounding sea was wild.
The throng of men could not succeed in escaping from
the stronghold. The waves increased, the floods resounded,   1545
sparks of fire flew, the water surged up in waves. There
within the city it was easy to find a song of sorrow uttered,
many a man, terrified at heart, lamenting his sorrow, chant-
ing a song of death. The terrifying fire was plainly visible,   1550
the devastation dreadful, the noise terrible. With the turbu-
lent winds the fire's blaze surrounded the walls; the waters
rose.

There the people's weeping was heard far and wide, the   1555
miserable commotion of men. Then one wretched man
there proceeded to assemble the people; disconsolate, sad
at heart, lamenting, he spoke: "Now you can discern the
truth for yourselves, that we unjustly fettered the stranger
in prison, in cruel bonds. Fate, cruel and fierce, is harming   1560
us; that is evident here! It is much better, in my truthful
opinion, that we release him from bondage, all of us unani-
mously—speed is best—and entreat the holy man for help,   1565

287

ANDREAS

ond us þone halgan   helpe biddan,
geoce ond frofre.   Us bið gearu sona
sybb æfter sorge,   gif we secaþ to him."
        Þa þær Andrea   orgete wearð
1570 on fyrhð-locan   folces gebæro,
þær wæs modigra   mægen forbeged,
wigendra þrym.   Wæter fæðmedon,
fleow firgend-stream;   flod wæs on luste,
oþ þæt breost oferstag,   brim weallende,
1575 eorlum oð exle.   Þa se æðeling het
stream-fare stillan,   stormas restan
ymbe stan-hleoðu.   Stop ut hræðe
cene collen-ferð;   carcern ageaf,
gleaw-mod, Gode leof.   Him wearð gearu sona
1580 þurh stream-ræce   stræt gerymed.
Smeolt wæs se sige-wang;   symble wæs dryge
folde fram flode,   swa his fot gestop.
        Wurdon burg-ware   bliðe on mode,
ferhð-gefeonde.   Þa wæs forð cumen
1585 geoc æfter gyrne.   Geofon swaðrode
þurh haliges hæs;   hlyst yst forgeaf,
brim-rad gebad.   Þa se beorg tohlad,
eorð-scræf egeslic,   ond þær in forlet
flod fæðmian,   fealewe wægas;
1590 geotende gegrind   grund eall forswealg.
Nalas he þær yðe   ane bisencte,
ach þæs weorodes eac   ða wyrrestan,
faa folc-sceaðan,   feowertyne
gewiton mid þy wæge   in forwyrd sceacan
1595 under eorþan grund.   Þa wearð acol-mod,
forht-ferð manig   folces on laste;

aid and comfort for ourselves. Peace after sorrow will be available at once if we look for it from him."

Then the people's attitude became clear there to Andrew in his heart, that the power of the arrogant, the strength of the warriors, was humbled. The waters were spreading, the torrent flowing; the flood was gluttonous until the surging waters rose up over the men's breasts, up to their shoulders. Then the noble man commanded the flow of water to stop, the storms to be still around the rocky slopes. Bold and brave, he walked out at once; he left the prison, a man of discerning mind, dear to God. At once a road was cleared and ready for him through the watercourse. The place of his victory was tranquil; wherever his foot stepped, the ground was dry from flooding.

The citizens were happy in their minds, rejoicing in spirit, since help had been forthcoming after their grief. The ocean became calm at the saint's command; the storm obeyed, the surging water remained still. Then the mountain split open, a terrifying chasm, and it allowed the flood, the dark waves, to spread in there; an abyss swallowed up all the gushing tumult. He not only caused the waves to sink into the earth, but also the worst of the company, fourteen of those hostile enemies, hastened to destruction with the wave, under the depths of the earth. Then many of those left behind became frozen with fright, terrified at heart;

1570

1575

1580

1585

1590

1595

wendan hie wifa   ond wera cwealmes,
þearlra geþinga   ðrage hnagran,
syððan mane faa,   morðor-scyldige,
1600 guð-gelacan   under grund hruron.
Hie ða an-mode   ealle cwædon:
"Nu is gesyne   ðæt þe soð meotud,
cyning eall-wihta,   cræftum wealdeð,
se ðisne ar hider   ær onsende
1605 þeodum to helpe;   is nu þearf mycel
þæt we gum-cystum   georne hyran."

Þa se halga ongann   hæleð blissigean,
wigendra þreat   wordum retan:
"Ne beoð ge to forhte,   þeh þe fell curen
1610 synnigra cynn;   swylt þrowode,
witu be gewyrhtum.   Eow is wuldres leoht
torht ontyned,   gif ge teala hycgað."
Sende þa his bene   fore Bearn Godes;
bæd haligne   helpe gefremman
1615 gumena geogoðe,   þe on geofene ær
þurh flodes fæðm   feorh gesealdon,
ðæt þa gastas,   Gode orfeorme,
in wita forwyrd,   wuldre bescyrede,
in feonda geweald   gefered ne wurdan.
1620 Þa ðæt ærende   eal-wealdan Gode
æfter hleoðor-cwidum   haliges gastes
wæs on þanc sprecen,   ðeoda ræswan,
het þa onsunde   ealle arisan,
geonge of greote,   þa ær geofon cwealde.
1625 Þa þær ofostlice   upp astodon
manige on meðle,   mine gefrege,

they were expecting the violent death of women and men, an even worse time of harsh consequences, after the warriors, stained with wickedness, guilty of deadly evil, sank under the ground. Unanimously, they all said: "Now it is evident that the true creator, the king of all creatures, governs with power, he who has sent this messenger here to help this people; it is necessary for us now to obey this virtuous man eagerly." 1600

1605

Then the saint proceeded to make the men, the multitude of warriors, happy, to cheer them with these words: "Do not be so afraid even though that race of sinners has chosen ruin; they deservedly suffered death and punishment. The radiant light of heaven will be revealed to you, if you think rightly." 1610

Then he sent his prayer to the Son of God; he asked the holy one to help the young men, who had earlier given up their lives in the deluge, in the flood's clutches, so that their souls, devoid of goodness, should not be led into the torment of damnation, into the power of fiends, cut off from heaven. When this petition, the speech of the saintly visitor, had been pleasingly uttered to the all-ruling God, the leader of peoples, then he commanded all the young men whom the flood had killed to rise up unharmed from the ground. Then, as I have heard say, many young men rose up instantly 1615

1620

1625

eaforan unweaxne,　ða wæs eall eador
leoðolic ond gastlic,　þeah hie lungre ær
þurh flodes fær　feorh aleton.

1630 Onfengon fulwihte　ond freoðu-wære,
wuldres wedde　witum aspedde,
mund-byrd meotudes.

　　　　　　　　Þa se modiga het,
Cyninges cræftiga,　ciricean getimbran,
gerwan Godes tempel,　þær sio geogoð aras

1635 þurh Fæder fulwiht　ond se flod onsprang.
Þa gesamnodon　secga þreate
weras geond þa win-burg　wide ond side,
eorlas an-mode,　ond hira idesa mid;
cwædon holdlice　hyran woldon,

1640 onfon fromlice　fullwihtes bæð
Dryhtne to willan,　ond diofol-gild,
ealde eolh-stedas,　anforlætan.
Þa wæs mid þy folce　fulwiht hæfen,
æðele mid eorlum,　ond æ Godes

1645 riht aræred,　ræd on lande
mid þam ceaster-warum,　cirice gehalgod.
Þær se ar Godes　anne gesette,
wis-fæstne wer,　wordes gleawne,
in þære beorhtan byrig　bisceop þam leodum,

1650 ond gehalgode　fore þam here-mægene
þurh apostolhad,　Platan nemned,
þeodum on þearfe;　ond þriste bebead
þæt hie his lare　læston georne,
feorh-ræd fremedon.　Sægde his fusne hige,

1655 þæt he þa gold-burg　ofgifan wolde,
secga sele-dream　ond sinc-gestreon,

292

in the assembly, when body and spirit were all united, although they had given up their lives just before in the sudden danger of the flood. Released from their torments, they $_{1630}$ received baptism and a covenant, a pledge of heavenly glory, the creator's protection.

Then the brave craftsman of the King commanded them to build a church, to make a temple of God, in that place where the young people had arisen through the Father's $_{1635}$ baptism and where the flood had burst out. Then men along with their women gathered together in a throng of people throughout the joyful city, from far and wide, all of one mind; they said that they wished to obey faithfully, eagerly $_{1640}$ receive the bath of baptism at the Lord's will and give up idolatry, their old heathen temples. Then among that multitude, among the men, holy baptism was instituted and God's just law established, his decree in that country among the citizens, the church consecrated. There God's messen- $_{1645}$ ger appointed one wise man, skilled in words, as bishop to the people in that beautiful city and, through his apostolic office, he consecrated a man named Plato in front of the $_{1650}$ mighty multitude, for the people in their need; and he firmly commanded them that they should eagerly follow his teaching, that they should encourage salvation. He said that his $_{1655}$ mind was eager to depart from this world, that he wished to leave that city rich in gold, men's joy in the hall and precious

beorht beag-selu,   ond him brim-þisan
æt sæs faroðe   secan wolde.

 Þæt wæs þam weorode   weorc to geþoligenne,
1660 þæt hie se leod-fruma   leng ne wolde
wihte gewunian.   Þa him wuldres God
on þam sið-fæte   sylfum ætywde,
ond þæt word gecwæð   weoruda Dryhten:
. . .

"folc of firenum.   Is him fus hyge;
1665 gað geomriende,   geohðo mænað
weras wif samod.   Hira wop becom,
murnende mod,   fore me sneowan.
Ne scealt ðu þæt eowde   anforlætan
1670 on swa niowan gefean,   ah him naman minne
on ferð-locan   fæste getimbre.
Wuna in þære win-byrig,   wigendra hleo,
salu sinc-hroden,   seofon nihta fyrst;
syððan ðu mid mildse   minre ferest."

1675 Þa eft gewat   oðre siðe
modig, mægene rof,   Marmedonia
ceastre secan.   Cristenra weox
word ond wisdom,   syððan wuldres þegn,
Æþel-Cyninges ar,   eagum sawon.
1680 Lærde þa þa leode   on geleafan weg,
trymede torhtlice,   tir-eadigra
wenede to wuldre   weorod unmæte,
to þam halgan ham   heofona rices,
þær Fæder ond Sunu   ond frofre Gast
1685 in Þrinnesse   þrymme wealdeð
in woruld worulda   wuldor-gestealda.
Swylce se halga   herigeas þreade,

valuables, the bright treasure-hall, and that he wished to go to an ocean-speeder at the sea's edge.

That was distressing for the multitude to endure, that 1660 their leader did not wish to remain with them any longer. Then the God of glory appeared to him on the journey, and the Lord of hosts spoke these words: ". . . the people from their sins. Their minds are eager to depart from this world; they go about sighing, lamenting their sorrow, both men and 1665 women. Their weeping, their mourning minds, came hastening before me. You must not abandon that flock in such a 1670 new state of spiritual joy, but establish my name securely in their breasts. Remain, protector of warriors, in that joyful city, in those richly adorned halls, for seven days. After that you will set out with my blessing."

Then, brave and strong in his power, he went back to go 1675 to the city of Mermedonia for the second time; the fame and the wisdom of the Christians flourished after they had seen with their own eyes the glorious disciple, the noble King's messenger. Then he taught the people the way of 1680 faith, strengthened them splendidly; he prepared an immense company of the glorious for heaven, for the holy home of the heavenly kingdom, where the Father and the Son and the comforting Spirit, in the majesty of the Trinity, rule the glorious dwellings for all eternity. The saint also at- 1685 tacked heathen temples, destroyed idolatry and suppressed

deoful-gild todraf   ond gedwolan fylde;
þæt wæs Satane   sar to geþolienne,
1690   mycel modes sorg,   þæt he ða menigeo geseah
hweorfan hige-bliðe   fram hell-trafum
þurh Andreas   este lare
to fægeran gefean,   þær næfre feondes ne bið,
gastes gram-hydiges,   gang on lande.
1695   Þa wæron gefylde   æfter frean dome
dagas on rime,   swa him Dryhten bebead,
þæt he þa weder-burg   wunian sceolde.
Ongan hine þa fysan   ond to flote gyrwan,
blissum hremig;   wolde on brim-þisan
1700   Achaie   oðre siðe
sylfa gesecan,   þær he sawul-gedal,
beadu-cwealm gebad.   Þæt þam banan ne wearð
hleahtre behworfen,   ah in helle ceafl
sið asette,   ond syððan no,
1705   fah, freonda leas,   frofre benohte.
    Ða ic lædan gefrægn   leoda weorode
leofne lareow   to lides stefnan,
mæcgas mod-geomre;   þær manegum wæs
hat æt heortan   hyge weallende.
1710   Hie ða gebrohton   æt brimes næsse
on wæg-þele   wigan unslawne.
Stodon him ða on ofre   æfter reotan
þendon hie on yðum   æðelinga wunn
ofer seolh-paðu   geseon mihton,
1715   ond þa weorðedon   wuldres agend,
cleopodon on corðre,   ond cwædon þus:

heresy; that was a painful thing for Satan to endure, a great 1690
sorrow in his mind, when he saw the multitude, through An-
drew's gracious teaching, turning, joyful in heart, from the
hellish temples to a delightful happiness, in the land where
there shall never be an attack by the fiend, the hostile spirit.

Then the number of days that he had to remain in the 1695
pleasant city, in obedience to the ruler's decree, was com-
pleted, as the Lord had commanded him. He proceeded to
make himself ready and to prepare himself for the sea, bliss-
fully jubilant; he himself wanted to go by ocean-speeder for 1700
a second time to Achaia, where he endured the separation of
soul and body, death in battle. That was no laughing matter
for his slayer, but he journeyed into the jaws of hell and af- 1705
terwards, as a friendless enemy, enjoyed no respite.

Then I have heard that sad-minded men, along with a
throng of people, conducted the beloved teacher to the
ship's prow; many people's minds there were seething with
hot emotions in their hearts. Then they brought the eager 1710
warrior to the wave plank at the headland by the sea. Then
they stood wailing after him on the shore, as long as they
could see the delight of princes on the waves over the seal's
path, and then they worshipped the Lord of glory, crying 1715
out in unison as a group and saying: "There is one eternal

"An is ece God   eallra gesceafta!
Is his miht ond his æht   ofer middan-geard
breme gebledsod,   ond his blæd ofer eall
1720   in heofon-þrymme   halgum scineð,
wlitige on wuldre   to widan ealdre,
ece mid englum;   þæt is æðele Cyning!"

God of all created things! His might and his rule are glori-
ously blessed throughout the world and his splendor shines   1720
above all in heavenly majesty upon the saints, radiantly in
heavenly glory, forever and ever, eternally among the angels;
that is a noble King!"

CHRIST AND SATAN

Þæt wearð underne   eorð-buendum,
þæt meotod hæfde   miht and strengðo
ða he gefestnade   foldan sceatas.
Seolfa he gesette   sunnan and monan,
5   stanas and eorðan,   stream ut on sæ,
wæter and wolcn,   ðurh his wundra miht.
Cleowne ymb lyfte   clene ymbhaldeð
meotod on mihtum,   and alne middan-geard.
He selfa mæg   sæ geondwlitan,
10   grundas in heofene,   Godes agen bearn,
and he ariman mæg   rægnas scuran,
dropena gehwelcne.   Daga ende-rim
seolua he gesette   þurh his soðan miht.
Swa se wyrhta   þurh his wuldres gast
15   serede and sette   on six dagum
eorðan dæles,   up on heofonum,
heanne holm.   Hwa is þæt ðe cunne
orðonc clene   nymðe ece God?
Dreamas he gedelde   duguðe and geþeode:
20   Adam ærest   and þæt æðele cyn,
engla ord-fruman,   þæt þe eft forwarð.
Ðuhte him on mode   þæt hit mihte swa,
þæt hie weron seolfe   swegles brytan,
wuldres waldend.   Him ðær wirse gelamp,

It was not concealed from the inhabitants of the world that the creator had power and strength when he firmly established the surfaces of the earth. He himself made the sun and the moon, the stones and earth, the current out at sea, water and clouds, by his wonderful power. The creator in his power entirely supports the sphere around the air, and all the world. He himself, God's own son, can survey the sea, the foundations in heaven, and he can count the showers of rain, every drop. He himself, through his true power, decreed the finite number of days. In this way the maker, through his glorious spirit, designed and made in six days, up in the heavens, the regions of the earth, the high sea. Who but eternal God is able to understand his ingenious work completely?

He distributed joys to the host and to the people: Adam originally and that glorious race, the princes of angels, which subsequently came to ruin. It seemed to them in their own minds that it could be possible that they themselves might be the lords of the sky, the rulers of heaven. That turned out

25 ða heo in helle   ham staðeledon,
    an æfter oðrum,   in þæt atole scref,
    þær heo bryne-welme   bidan sceolden
    saran sorge,   nales swegles leoht
    habban in heofnum   heah-getimbrad,
30 ac gedufan sceolun   in ðone deopan wælm
    niðær under nessas   in ðone neowlan grund,
    gredige and gifre.   God ana wat
    hu he þæt scyldige werud   forscrifen hefde!
        Cleopað ðonne se alda   ut of helle,
35 wriceð word-cwedas   weregan reorde,
    eisegan stefne: "Hwær com engla ðrym,
    þe we on heofnum   habban sceoldan?
    Þis is ðeostræ ham,   ðearle gebunden
    fæstum fyr-clommum;   flor is on welme
40 attre onæled.   Nis nu ende feor
    þæt we sceolun ætsomne   susel þrowian,
    wean and wergu,   nalles wuldres blæd
    habban in heofnum,   heh-selda wyn.
    Hwæt we for Dryhtene iu   dreamas hefdon,
45 song on swegle   selrum tidum,
    þær nu ymb ðone ecan   æðele stondað,
    heleð ymb heh-seld,   herigað Drihten
    wordum and wercum,   and ic in wite sceal
    bidan in bendum,   and me bættran ham
50 for ofer-hygdum   æfre ne wene."
        Ða him andsweradan   atole gastas,
    swarte and synfulle,   susle begnornende:
    "Þu us gelærdæst   ðurh lyge ðinne
    þæt we helende   heran ne scealdon.
55 Ðuhte þe anum   þæt ðu ahtest alles gewald,

the worse for them there when they set up home in hell, one   25
by one, in that horrible cavern, where they would have to
endure painful sorrow in the surging flame, have no celestial
light at all in the lofty heavens, but they had to plunge into   30
that deep surging flame, down under the ground, into that
profound abyss, greedy and covetous. God alone knows how
he condemned that guilty troop!

Then the old one cries out from hell, and, with an evil   35
voice and with a dreadful noise, utters these words: "Where
has the glory of angels gone, which we were destined to have
in the heavens? This is a dark home, tightly bound by firmly
fastened fiery chains; the abyss is surging and burning with   40
venom. The end is not a long time off now, when we will
have to suffer torment together, woe and misery, and have
no splendor of glory in the heavens, no joy in its high halls.
How much joy did we once have in the presence of the Lord,
singing in heaven in better times, where now the noble   45
stand around the eternal one, warriors around the throne,
praising the Lord in words and deeds, while I must remain
bound in punishment and never expect a better home for
myself because of my pride."   50

Then the horrible spirits answered him, dark and sinful,
lamenting over their torment: "You with your lying taught
us that we did not have to obey the savior. It seemed to you   55
alone that you possessed power over everything, heaven and

heofnes and eorþan, wære halig God,
scypend seolfa. Nu earttu earm sceaða,
in fyr-locan feste gebunden.
Wendes ðu ðurh wuldor ðæt þu woruld ahtest,
60 alra onwald, and we englas mid ðec.
Atol is þin onseon! Habbað we alle swa
for ðinum leasungum lyðre gefered.
Segdest us to soðe þæt ðin sunu wære
meotod mon-cynnes; hafustu nu mare susel!"
65 Swa firenfulle facnum wordum
heora aldor-ðægn on reordadon,
on cearum cwidum. Crist heo afirde,
dreamum bedelde. Hæfdan Dryhtnes liht
for ofer-hygdum ufan forleton,
70 hæfdon hym to hyhte helle floras,
beornende bealo. Blace hworfon
scinnan forscepene; sceaðan hwearfedon,
earme æglecan, geond þæt atole scref,
for ðam an-medlan þe hie ær drugon.

II
75 Eft reordade oðre siðe
feonda aldor. Wæs þa forworht agen,
seoððan he ðes wites worn gefelde.
He spearcade ðonne he spreocan ongan,
fyre and atre; ne bið swelc fæger dream
80 ðonne he in witum wordum indraf:
"Ic wæs iu in heofnum halig ængel,
Dryhtene deore; hefde me dream mid Gode,
micelne for meotode, and ðeos menego swa some.

earth, that you were holy God, the creator himself. Now you are a wretched evildoer, bound fast in a fiery prison. In your glory you believed, and we angels with you, that you possessed the world, power over everything. Your appearance is hideous! We have all fared just as miserably because of your lies. You declared to us as a fact that the creator of mankind was your son; now you are tormented all the more!"

So the sinful amid their sorrows spoke with treacherous words and speeches to their leader. Christ had expelled them, cut them off from joy. They had lost the light of the Lord above because of their pride and had the depths of hell, burning pain, as their only expectation. The dark deformed demons wandered about; the evildoers, miserable warriors, roamed throughout that terrible pit because of the arrogance with which they had formerly acted.

II

The lord of fiends spoke again, for a second time. He was accursed once more when he had felt the multitude of torments. He emitted sparks whenever he spoke, fire and poison; this is no pleasant melody whenever he forced out words in his torments:

"Once I was a holy angel in heaven, dear to the Lord; I had great joy with God, in the presence of the creator, and

60

65

70

75

80

Þa ic in mode   minum hogade
85 þæt ic wolde towerpan   wuldres leoman,
Bearn helendes,   agan me burga gewald
eall to æhte,   and ðeos earme heap
þe ic hebbe to helle   ham geledde.
Wene þæt tacen sutol   þa ic aseald wes on wærgðu,
90 niðer under nessas   in ðone neowlan grund.
Nu ic eow hebbe to hæftum   ham gefærde
alle of earde.   Nis her eadiges tir,
wloncra win-sele,   ne worulde dream,
ne ængla ðreat,   ne we up-heofon
95 agan moten.   Is ðes atola ham
fyre onæled.   Ic eom fah wið God.
Æce æt helle duru   dracan eardigað,
hate on reðre;   heo us helpan ne magon.
Is ðæs walica ham   wites afylled;
100 nagan we ðæs heolstres   þæt we us gehydan mægon
in ðissum neowlan genipe.   Hær is nedran swæg,
wyrmas gewunade.   Is ðis wites clom
feste gebunden.   Feond seondon reðe,
dimme and deorce.   Ne her dæg lyhteð
105 for scedes sciman,   sceppendes leoht.
Iu ahte ic gewald   ealles wuldres,
ær ic moste in ðeossum atolan   æðele gebidan
hwæt me Drihten God   deman wille,
fagum on flora.   Nu ic feran com
110 deofla menego   to ðissum dimman ham,
ac ic sceal on flyge   and on flyhte ðragum
earda neosan,   and eower ma,
þe ðes ofer-hydes   ord onstaldon.

this multitude likewise. Then I resolved in my mind that I 85
and this wretched band which I have led home to hell would
overthrow the radiance of glory, the Son of the healer, and
obtain for myself total power and control over the cities. I
think that was a clear sign when I was banished into damna-
tion, down under the ground into that profound abyss. Now 90
I have led you all home out of your native land as captives.
There is no glory of the blessed one here, no wine halls of
the great, or worldly joy, or troop of angels, nor may we ob-
tain possession of heaven above. This horrible home is 95
burning with fire. I am God's enemy. Dragons dwell eter-
nally at hell's door, flaming inside their breasts; they can-
not help us. This woeful home is filled with torment; in this 100
deep obscurity we have no darkness in which to hide our-
selves. Here, where serpents dwell, there is the sound of
snakes. The prison of this torment is firmly locked. The
fiends are fierce, dark, and evil. Day, the light of the creator,
does not illuminate this place, because of the gloom of the 105
darkness. Once I had power over all heaven, before I had to
wait in this terrible home, to see what the Lord God might
wish to decree for me, God's enemy in the abyss. Now I have
come making my way with a throng of devils to this dark 110
home, but I will have to take to flight, and, in flying, at times
will have to seek out dwelling places, along with more of
you, who were the source of this pride.

Ne ðurfon we ðes wenan   þæt us wuldor-cyning
115   æfre wille   eard alefan,
æðel to æhte,   swa he ær dyde,
ece onwald;   ah him alles gewald,
wuldres and wita,   waldendes sunu.
Forðon ic sceal hean and earm   hweorfan ðy widor,
120   wadan wræc-lastas,   wuldre benemed,
duguðum bedeled,   nænigne dream agan
uppe mid ænglum,   þes ðe ic ær gecwæð
þæt ic wære seolfa   swægles brytta,
wihta wealdend."   Ac hit him wyrse gelomp!

III
125   Swa se werega gast   wordum sæde
his earfoðo   ealle ætsomne,
fah in fyrnum,   fyr-leoma stod
geond þæt atole scræf   attre geblonden.
"Ic eom lim-wæstmum   þæt ic gelutian ne mæg
130   on þyssum sidan sele,   synnum forwundod.
Hwæt her hat and ceald   hwilum mencgað!
Hwilum ic gehere   helle-scealcas,
gnornende cynn,   grundas mænan,
niðer under næssum;   hwilum nacode men
135   winnað ymb wyrmas.   Is þes windiga sele
eall inneweard   atole gefylled.
Ne mot ic hihtlicran   hames brucan,
burga ne bolda,   ne on þa beorhtan gescæft
ne mot ic æfre ma   eagum starian.
140   Is me nu wyrsa   þæt ic wuldres leoht
uppe mid englum   æfre cuðe,
song on swegle,   þær sunu meotodes
habbað eadige bearn   ealle ymbfangen

We need not expect that the king of glory will ever be 115
willing to grant us a dwelling place, a homeland to possess,
as he did before, power everlasting; the ruler's Son has com-
mand over everything, over glory and punishment. There-
fore, downcast and wretched, I must wander all the further,
travel the paths of exile, cut off from heaven, deprived of 120
blessings, possessing no joy on high among the angels, be-
cause I said once that I myself was the lord of heaven, the
ruler of all beings." But it turned out worse for him!

III
As the accursed spirit, hostile and sinful, related all his 125
hardships at once, a fiery light, mixed with venom, flashed
out throughout that terrible cavern.

"I am so large of limb that I cannot hide in this vast hall, 130
sorely wounded by my sins. How both heat and cold are
mixed here at times! Sometimes I hear the subjects of hell,
the lamenting tribe, complaining of the abyss, down under-
neath the ground; at other times naked people fight among 135
serpents. Within, all this windswept hall is filled with hor-
ror. I shall never be allowed to possess a more pleasant
home, citadel or hall, nor shall I ever be allowed to look with
my own eyes on the bright creation again. It is now worse 140
for me that I ever knew the light of celestial glory on high
with the angels, their song in heaven, where all his blessed
children have surrounded the Son of the creator with song.

seolfa mid sange.   Ne ic þam sawlum ne mot
145   ænigum sceððan,
bûtan þam anum   þe he âgan nyle;
þa ic mot to hæftum   ham geferian,
bringan to bolde   in þone biteran grund.
Ealle we syndon   ungelice
150   þonne þe we iu in heofonum   hæfdon ærror
wlite and weorð-mynt.   Ful oft wuldres sweg
brohton to bearme   bearn hælendes,
þær we ymb hine utan   ealle hofan,
leomu ymb leofne,   lof-songa word,
155   Drihtne sædon.   Nu ic eom dædum fah,
gewundod mid wommum;   sceal nu þysne wites clom
beoran beornende   in bæce minum,
hat on helle,   hyht-willan leas."
    Þa gyt feola cwiðde   firna herde,
160   atol æglæca,   ut of helle,
witum werig.   Word spearcum fleah
attre gelicost,   þonne he ut þorhdraf:
    "Eala Drihtenes þrym!   Eala duguða helm!
Eala meotodes miht!   Eala middan-eard!
165   Eala dæg leohta!   Eala dream Godes!
Eala engla þreat!   Eala upheofen!
Eala þæt ic eam ealles leas   ecan dreames,
þæt ic mid handum ne mæg   heofon geræcan,
ne mid eagum ne mot   up locian,
170   ne huru mid earum ne sceal   æfre geheran
þære byrhtestan   beman stefne!
Ðæs ic wolde of selde   sunu meotodes,
Drihten adrifan,   and agan me þæs dreames gewald,
wuldres and wynne,   me þær wyrse gelamp

I may not harm any of those souls except for those alone 145
whom he does not wish to have; I may lead those home as
captives and bring them to my dwelling in the bitter abyss.
All of us are different from what we were when we formerly, 150
long ago in heaven, had beauty and honor. Very often the
children of the savior brought glorious song to his bosom,
there where we all, limbs about the beloved one, round
about him raised up and uttered songs of praise to the Lord. 155
Now I am stained by my deeds, wounded by sins; now I
must bear these burning bonds of punishment on my back,
fiercely hot in hell, without hope of any joy."

Then the lord of sin, that terrible enemy, weary of his 160
torments, lamented much more from his place in hell. His
words flew in sparks, most like poison, whenever he forced
them out:

"O the majesty of the Lord! O the Lord of hosts! O the
might of the creator! O world! O the bright day! O the joy of 165
God! O the troop of angels! O the heavens above! O that
I am entirely deprived of eternal joy, that I cannot reach to
heaven with my hands, nor may I look up with my eyes nor 170
indeed shall I ever hear with my ears the sound of the clear-
est trumpet! Because I wished to drive the son of the cre-
ator, the Lord, from his throne and have for myself power
over that joy, glory and delight, it turned out worse for me

175 þonne ic to hihte   agan moste.
Nu ic eom asceaden   fram þære sciran driht,
alæded fram leohte   in þone laðan ham.
Ne mæg ic þæt gehicgan   hu ic in ðæm becwom,
in þis neowle genip,   nið-synnum fah,
180 aworpen of worulde.   Wat ic nu þa
þæt bið alles leas   ecan dreamas
se ðe heofen-cyninge   heran ne þenceð,
meotode cweman.   Ic þæt morðer sceal,
wean and witu   and wrace dreogan,
185 goda bedæled,   iu-dædum fah,
þæs ðe ic geþohte adrifan   Drihten of selde,
weoroda waldend;   sceal nu wrec-lastas
settan sorhg-cearig,   siðas wide."

[IV]
    Hwearf þa to helle   þa he gehened wæs,
190 Godes andsaca;   dydon his gingran swa,
gifre and grædige,   þa hig God bedraf
in þæt hate hof   þam is hel nama.
Forþan sceal gehycgan   hæleða æghwylc
þæt he ne abælige   Bearn waldendes.
195 Læte him to bysne   hu þa blacan feond
for ofer-hygdum   ealle forwurdon.
Neoman us to wynne   weoroda Drihten,
uppe ecne gefean,   engla waldend.
He þæt gecydde   þæt he mægen-cræft hæfde,
200 mihta miccle,   þa he þa mænego adraf,
hæftas of ðæm hean selde.   Gemunan we þone halgan
                                                            Drihten,
ecne alra gescefta;   ceosan us eard in wuldre
mid ealra cyninga cyninge,   se is Crist genemned;

there than I might have hoped. Now I am cut off from that 175
radiant host, led away from the light into this loathsome
home. I cannot understand how I came here, into this deep
darkness, stained with evil sins, expelled from the world. I 180
know now that he who does not desire to obey the heavenly
king, to please the creator, will be devoid of all eternal joy.
I will have to suffer this deadly torment, grief and punish-
ment and banishment, deprived of everything good, stained 185
by my former deeds, because I resolved to drive the Lord
from his throne, the ruler of hosts; now with sorrowful care
I must travel the paths of exile, journeying far and wide."

[IV]

Then, when he had been overthrown, he departed to
hell, God's enemy; so too did his followers, rapacious and 190
greedy, when God drove them into that fiery dwelling whose
name is hell. Therefore every man must resolve not to pro-
voke the Son of the ruler to anger. Let it be an example to 195
him how the black fiends all perished on account of their
pride. Let us take as our delight the Lord of hosts, the eter-
nal joy on high, the ruler of angels. He showed that he had
mighty strength, great powers, when he drove that multi- 200
tude, his captives, away from his high throne. Let us be
mindful of the eternal holy Lord of all creatures; let us
choose for ourselves a dwelling in glory with the king of
all kings who is called Christ; let us bear in our breasts

beoran on breostum   bliðe geþohtas,
205 sibbe and snytero;   gemunan soð and riht
þonne we to heh-selde   hnigan þencað,
and þone anwaldan   ara biddan.
      Þonne behofað   se ðe her wunað
weorulde wynnum   þæt him wlite scine
210 þonne he oðer lif   eft geseceð,
fægere land   þonne þeos folde seo;
is þær wlitig and wynsum;   wæstmas scinað,
beorhte ofer burgum.   Þær is brade lond,
hyhtlicra ham   in heofon-rice,
215 Criste gecwemra.   Uta cerran þider
þær he sylfa sit,   sigora waldend,
Drihten hælend,   in ðæm deoran ham,
and ymb þæt heh-setl   hwite standað
engla feðan   and eadigra;
220 halige heofen-þreatas   herigað Drihten
wordum and weorcum.   Heora wlite scineð
geond ealra worulda woruld   mid wuldor-cyninge.

v   Ða get ic furðor gefregen   feond ondetan;
wæs him eall ful strang
225 wom and witu.   Hæfdon wuldor-cyning
for ofer-higdum   anforlæten;
cwædon eft hraðe   oðre worde:
      "Nu is gesene   þæt we syngodon
uppe on earde.   Sceolon nu æfre þæs
230 dreogan dom-lease gewinn   Drihtnes mihtum.
Hwæt we in wuldres wlite   wunian moston
þær we halgan Gode   heran woldon,
and him sang ymb seld   secgan sceoldon

joyful thoughts, love and wisdom; let us be mindful of truth   205
and justice when we are about to bow down to the high
throne and ask the ruler for mercy.

He who lives here in the delights of this world will need
to shine in beauty when, later, he seeks that other life, a   210
fairer land than this earth is; it is beautiful and joyful there
and magnificent fruits shine throughout the cities. That is
a spacious land, a more pleasant home in the kingdom of
heaven, the home of those agreeable to Christ. Let us go to   215
where he himself, the ruler of victories, the savior Lord, sits
in that dear home and around that high throne stand radiant
bands of angels and of the blessed; the holy heavenly bands   220
praise the Lord in their words and deeds. Their beauty
shines with the king of glory, world without end.

v

Then I learned that the devils admitted still more; their
defilement and punishment were all very hard for them.   225
They had forsaken the king of glory because of their pride;
straightaway they spoke again in other words:

"Now it is obvious that we sinned in our home on high.
Because of that we will now have to conduct forever an in-   230
glorious struggle against the powers of the Lord. How hap-
pily we were allowed to live in the beauty of heaven while we
were willing to obey holy God and were accustomed to sing

þusend-mælum!   Þa we þær wæron,
235 wunodon on wynnum,   geherdon wuldres sweg,
beman stefne.   Byrht word aras,
engla ord-fruma,   and to þæm æþelan
hnigan him sanctas;   sige-torht aras
ece Drihten,   ofer us gestod
240 and gebletsode   bile-witne heap
dogra gehwilcne,   and his se deora Sunu,
gasta scyppend.   God seolfa wæs
eallum andfeng   þe ðær up becom,
and hine on eorðan   ær gelefde."

245   "Þa ðæs ofþuhte   þæt se þeoden wæs
strang and stið-mod.   Ongan ic þa steppan forð
ana wið englum,   and to him eallum spræc:
'Ic can eow læran   langsumne ræd,
gif ge willað minre   mihte gelefan.
250 Uta oferhycgan   Helm þone micclan,
weroda waldend,   agan us þis wuldres leoht,
eall to æhte.   Þis is idel gylp
þæt we ær drugon   ealle hwile.'

VI
        "Ða gewearð usic   þæt we woldon swa
255 Drihten adrifan   of þam deoran ham,
cyning of cestre.   Cuð is wide
þæt wrec-lastas   wunian moton,
grimme grundas.   God seolfa him
rice haldeð.   He is ana cyning,
260 þe us eorre gewearð,   ece Drihten,
meotod mihtum swið.   Sceal nu þeos menego her
licgan on leahtrum,   sume on lyft scacan,
fleogan ofer foldan;   fyr bið ymbutan

songs to him around his throne in our thousands! When
we were there we dwelt in joy, listening to the music of   235
heaven, the sound of the trumpet. The radiant word arose,
the source of angels, and the saints bowed to that noble one;
splendid in victory, the eternal Lord arose, with his beloved
Son, creator of souls, and stood above us, blessing the pure   240
host every day. God himself received all who came up there
and who had believed in him on earth."

"Then it caused resentment that the prince was severe   245
and stern. I came forward alone, confronting the angels and
spoke to all of them:

'I can teach you something which will be to your lasting
advantage if you are willing to believe in my power. Let us   250
scorn this great Lord, the ruler of hosts, and obtain all this
light of heaven for ourselves. What we have experienced all
this time is empty ostentation.'

"Then we agreed to drive the Lord out of that dear home,   VI
the king out of his city. It is widely known that we must live   255
in the paths of exile, the terrible depths. God himself
keeps the kingdom for himself. He alone is king, the eternal   260
Lord, the creator strong in his powers, who became angry
with us. Now this multitude here must remain subject to
sin, some speeding through the air, flying over the earth; fire

on æghwylcum   þæh he uppe seo.
265 Ne mot he þam sawlum   þe ðær secað up
eadige of eorþan   æfre gehrinan,
ah ic be hondum mot   hæþenre sceale
gripan to grunde,   Godes andsacan.
Sume sceolon hweorfan   geond hæleða land
270 and unsibbe   oft onstyrian
monna mægðum   geond middan-eard.
Ic her geþolian sceal   þinga æghwylces,
bitres niðæs   beala gnornian,
sic and sorhful,   þæs ic seolfa weold
275 þonne ic on heofonum   ham staðelode.
Hwæðer us se eca   æfre wille
on heofona rice   ham alefan,
eðel to æhte,   swa he ær dyde?"
        Swa gnornedon   Godes andsacan,
280 hate on helle.   Him wæs hælend God
wrað geworden   for wom-cwidum.
Forþon mæg gehycgan   se ðe his heorte deah
þæt he him afirre   frecne geþohtas,
laðe leahtras,   lifigendra gehwylc.
285 Gemunan symle on mode   meotodes strengðo;
gearwian us togenes   grene stræte
up to englum,   þær is se ælmihtiga God.
And us befæðman wile   Freo-Bearn Godes
gif we þæt on eorðan   ær geþencað
290 and us to þam halgan   helpe gelefað.
Þonne he us no forlæteð,   ah lif syleð
uppe mid englum,   eadigne dream.
Tæceð us se torhta   trumlicne ham,
beorhte burh-weallas.   Beorhte scinað

surrounds each one even if he be up in the air. He is never 265
allowed to touch those blessed souls who strive to go up-
ward there from the earth, but with my hands I am allowed
to seize and carry God's enemies off into the abyss, the
throng of heathens. Some are obliged to wander all over the
lands of men and often to stir up dissension among people 270
throughout the world. Here, sick and sorrowful, I must suf-
fer the loss of everything which I myself possessed when I 275
set up home in heaven, lament over the torment of my bit-
ter oppression. Will the eternal one ever be willing to grant
us a home in the kingdom of heaven, a land to possess, as he
did before?"

So the opponents of God lamented, burning in hell. God 280
the savior had become angry with them, because of their
sinful words. Therefore every living person whose heart is
worthy has good cause for resolving to expel dangerous
thoughts, hateful vices, from himself. Let us always be mind- 285
ful in our hearts of the strength of the creator; let us prepare
for ourselves a green path up to meet the angels, where al-
mighty God is. And the true Son of God will be willing
to embrace us if we have previously set our minds on that
while we were on earth and have trusted in his holy help. 290
Then he will never desert us, but he will give us life on high
with the angels, blessed joy. The radiant Lord will direct
us to a strong home and bright city walls. The blessed souls

295 gesælige sawle,   sorgum bedælde,
þær heo æfre forð   wunian moten
cestre and cyne-stol.   Uton cyþan þæt!
Deman we on eorðan,   ærror lifigend,
onlucan mid listum   locen waldendes,
300 ongeotan gastlice!   Us ongean cumað
þusend engla,   gif þider moton
and þæt on eorðan   ær gewyrcað.
    Forþon se bið eadig   se ðe æfre wile
man oferhycgen,   meotode cweman,
305 synne adwæscan.   Swa he sylfa cwæð:
"Soð-fæste men,   sunnan gelice,
fægre gefrætewod,   in heora fæder rice
scinað in sceld-byrig."   Þær sceppend seolf
heo befæðmeð,   Fæder man-cynnes,
310 ahefeð holdlice   in heofones leoht,
þær heo mid wuldor-cyninge   wunian moton
awa to aldre,
agan dreama dream   mid Drihtne Gode,
a to worulde   a buton ende.

[VII]
315   Eala, hwæt se awyrgda   wraðe geþohte
þæt he heofen-cyninge   heran ne wolde,
Fæder frefergendum!   Flor attre weol,
hat under hæftum;   hreopan deofla,
wide geond wind-sele   wean cwanedon,
320 man and morður.   Wæs seo menego þær
swylce onæled;   wæs þæt eall full strong!
Þonne wæs heora aldor,   þe ðær ærest com
forð on feþan,   fæste gebunden
fyre and lige;   þæt wæs fæstlic þreat!

will shine brightly there, freed from sorrows, where they 295
may for evermore occupy the city and the royal seat. Let us
proclaim that! Let us take thought beforehand, while we are
living on earth, to unlock the ruler's locks skillfully, to un- 300
derstand spiritually! A thousand angels will come to meet us,
if we are permitted to go there and if we will have deserved
it while we were on earth.

Therefore he who is always willing to scorn wickedness,
to please the creator and to put an end to sin, will be blessed. 305
As he himself said: "The righteous, beautifully adorned, will
shine like the sun in their father's kingdom, in the city of
refuge." There the creator himself, the Father of mankind,
will embrace them and will graciously raise them into the 310
light of heaven, where they may dwell to eternity with the
king of glory, possessing the joy of joys with the Lord God
forever, world without end, forever and ever.

[VII]
O, how evilly that cursed being resolved not to obey the 315
heavenly king, the consoling Father! The abyss seethed with
poison, fiery hot beneath the captives; devils cried out far
and wide throughout the windy hall, lamented their miser-
ies, their sin and wickedness. This was how the multitude 320
there was burned; that was all very hard! Then their prince,
who had been the first in the troop to arrive there, was
firmly bound in fire and flame; that was an immutable

325 Ec sceoldon his þegnas   þær gewunian
atolan eðles,   nalles up þanon
geheran in heofonum   haligne dream,
þær heo oft fægerne   folgað hæfdon
uppe mid englum.   Wæron þa alles þæs
330 goda lease,   ah nymþe gryndes ad
wunian ne moten   and þone werigan sele,
þær is wom and wop   wide gehered,
and grist-bitunge   and gnornunge mecga:
"Nabbað we to hyhte   nymþe cyle and fyr,
335 wean and witu   and wyrma þreat,
dracan and næddran   and þone dimman ham."
Forðon mihte geheran   se ðe æt hylle wæs
twelf milum neh   þæt ðær wæs toða geheaw,
hlude and geomre.   Godes andsacan
340 hweorfan geond helle   hate onæled
ufan and utan   —him wæs æghwær wa—
witum werige,   wuldres bescyrede,
dreamum bedælde.   Heofon deop gehygd,
þa heo on heofonum   ham staðelodon,
345 þæt hie woldon benæman   nergendne Crist
rodera rices,   ah he on riht geheold
hired heofona   and þæt halige seld.
      Nis nænig swa snotor   ne swa cræftig
ne þæs swa gleaw,   nymþe God seolfa,
350 þæt asecgan mæge   swegles leoman,
hu scima þær   scineð ymbutan
meotodes mihte,   geond þæt mære cynn,
þær habbað englas   eadigne dream,
sanctas singað   —þæt is se seolfa God!
355 Þonne beoð þa eadigan   þe of eorðan cumað,

punishment! His followers also had to live there in that ter- 325
rible home, not hearing at all the holy joy in the heavens
above where they had often happily served on high among
the angels. Then they were bereft of all good things, and 330
they were not permitted to live anywhere except in the fire
of the pit and in the accursed hall, where wailing and weep-
ing and the gnashing of teeth and the lamentations of men
are heard far and wide: "We can expect nothing but cold and
fire, grief and torments and swarming serpents, dragons and 335
snakes and this dark home." Because of that anyone who
was within twelve miles of hell could hear that there was a
loud, mournful gnashing of teeth. God's enemies wandered 340
throughout hell, burned up by heat from above and from
without—there was misery for them everywhere—ex-
hausted by their torments, cut off from heaven, bereft of
joys. They lamented the heinous thought by which, after
they had set up their home in the heavens, they had in- 345
tended to deprive the saving Christ of his kingdom in the
skies, but he rightfully kept possession of the court of
heaven and that holy throne.

There is no one so wise or so learned or so discerning, ex-
cept for God himself, who could describe the radiance of 350
heaven, how light shines all over that splendid race, by the
power of the creator, where the angels have blessed joy and
the saints sing—that is God himself! Then they will be the 355

bringað to bearme   blostman stences,
wyrte wynsume   —þæt synd word Godes—
þonne hie befæðmeð   Fæder man-cynnes,
and hie gesegnað   mid his swiðran hond,
360   lædeð to lihte,   þær hi lif agon
a to aldre,   uplicne ham,
byrhtne burh-styde.   Blæd bið æghwæm
þæm ðe hælende   heran þenceð,
and wel is þam   ðe þæt wyrcan mot.

[VIII]
365   Wæs þæt encgel-cyn   ær genemned
Lucifer haten,   leoht-berende,
on gear-dagum   in Godes rice.
Þa he in wuldre   wrohte onstalde,
þæt he ofer-hyda   agan wolde;
370   Satanus   swearte geþohte
þæt he wolde on heofonum   heh-seld wyrcan
uppe mid þam ecan.   Þæt wæs ealdor heora,
yfeles ord-fruma.   Him þæt eft gehreaw,
þa he to helle   hnigan sceolde,
375   and his hired mid hine,   in hynðo geglidan,
nergendes nið,   and no seoððan
þæt hi mosten in þone ecan   andwlitan seon
buton ende.   Þa him egsa becom,
dyne for deman,   þa he duru in helle
380   bræc and begde.   Blis wearð monnum
þa hi hælendes   heafod gesawon.
Þonne wæs þam atolan   þe we ær nemdon
. . .
Þa wæron mid egsan   ealle afyrhte,
wide geond wind-sele   wordum mændon:

blessed ones who come from this world, bringing into his possession the fragrance of flowers, delightful plants— those are the words of God—when the Father of mankind embraces them, blesses them with his right hand, leads 360 them into the light where they will receive life forever and ever, a home on high, a bright city. Glory awaits everyone who desires to obey the savior, and well is it for him who may attain it.

[VIII]

That angelic being had been named and was called Luci- 365 fer, light-bearer, in days of old in God's kingdom. Then, because he was willing to be possessed by pride, he instigated a dispute in heaven; Satan evilly resolved to make a throne in 370 heaven, on high with the eternal one. He was their lord, the prince of evil. He repented of that subsequently, when he was forced to sink down to hell and his followers with him, 375 to fall into disgrace, into enmity with the savior, and never afterward might they look upon the face of the eternal one, forever without end. Then a terrifying thing approached them, a din that the judge made, when he broke and bent the doors in hell. People were happy when they saw the head 380 of the savior. Then for that terrible one whom we named before, it was

. . .

Then they were all frightened by that terrifying thing, far and wide throughout that windy hall they lamented in these

385 "Þis is stronglic, nu þes storm becom,
þegen mid þreate, þeoden engla.
Him beforan fereð fægere leoht
þonne we æfre ær eagum gesawon,
buton þa we mid englum uppe wæron.
390 Wile nu ure witu þurh his wuldres cræft
eall toweorpan. Nu ðes egsa com,
dyne for Drihtne, sceal þes dreorga heap
ungeara nu atol þrowian.
Hit is se seolfa sunu waldendes,
395 engla Drihten. Wile uppe heonan
sawla lædan, and we seoððan a
þæs yrre-weorces henðo geþoliað."
    Hwearf þa to helle hæleða bearnum,
meotod þurh mihte; wolde manna rim,
400 fela þusenda, forð gelædan
up to eðle. Þa com engla sweg,
dyne on dægred; hæfde Drihten seolf
feond oferfohten. Wæs seo fæhðe þa gyt
open on uhtan, þa se egsa becom.
405 Let þa up faran eadige sawle,
Adames cyn, and ne moste Efe þa gyt
wlitan in wuldre ær heo wordum cwæð:
    "Ic þe æne abealh, ece Drihten,
þa wit Adam twa eaples þigdon
410 þurh næddran nið, swa wit na ne sceoldon.
Gelærde unc se atola, se ðe æfre nu
beorneð on bendum, þæt wit blæd ahton,
haligne ham, heofon to gewalde.
Þa wit ðæs awærgdan wordum gelyfdon,

words: "This is very hard to bear, now that this violent at- 385
tack has come, the warrior with his troop, the prince of an-
gels. In front of him goes a light more beautiful than our
eyes have ever seen, except when we were on high among
the angels. Now, by the power of his glory, he will put an end 390
entirely to the torments we inflict. Now that this terrifying
thing has come, this din made by the Lord, soon now this
sad band will have to endure horror. It is the son of the ruler
himself, the Lord of angels. He intends to lead the souls up 395
and away from here, and forever after we will suffer the hu-
miliation of that act of anger."

Then the creator, by means of his power, went to hell,
to the sons of men; he intended to lead out many thousands 400
of people, up to their homeland. Then came the sound of
angels, the din at dawn; the Lord himself had conquered
the fiend. The hostility was still evident in the hour before
dawn when that terrifying thing came. Then he allowed the 405
blessed souls ascend, Adam's kin, but Eve was still not per-
mitted to see heaven until she spoke these words:

"I once angered you, eternal Lord, when we two, Adam
and I, ate of an apple because of the serpent's enmity, as 410
we should never have done. The terrible one, who will now
burn in fetters forever, persuaded us two that we would
possess glory and a holy home, power over heaven. Then
the two of us believed the words of that accursed being,

415 namon mid handum   on þam halgan treo
beorhte blæda;   unc þæs bitere forgeald
þa wit in þis hate scræf   hweorfan sceoldon,
and wintra rim   wunian seoððan,
þusenda feolo,   þearle onæled.

420   Nu ic þe halsige,   heofen-rices weard,
for þan hirede   þe ðu hider læddest,
engla þreatas,   þæt ic up heonon
mæge and mote   mid minre mægðe.
And ymb þreo niht com   þegen hælendes

425 ham to helle;   is nu hæftum strong,
witum werig,   swylce him wuldor-cyning
for onmædlan   eorre geworden.
Segde us to soðe   þætte seolfa God
wolde hel-warum   ham gelihtan.

430 Aras þa anra gehwylc,   and wið earm gesæt,
hleonade wið handa.   Þeah hylle gryre
egeslic þuhte,   wæron ealle þæs
fægen in firnum   þæt heora Freo-Drihten
wolde him to helpe   helle gesecan."

435   Ræhte þa mid handum   to heofen-cyninge,
bæd meotod miltse   þurh Marian had:
    "Hwæt þu fram minre dohtor,   Drihten, onwoce
in middan-geard   mannum to helpe!
Nu is gesene   þæt ðu eart sylfa God

440 and ece ord-fruma   ealra gesceafta."
[IX]
    Let þa up faran   ece Drihten;
wuldre hæfde   wites clomma
feondum oðfæsted,   and heo furðor sceaf
in þæt neowle genip,   nearwe gebeged,

took with our hands the bright fruit on that holy tree; we 415
paid bitterly for that when we had to go into this burning pit
and then remain here for many thousands of years, cruelly
burned.

Now I beseech you, guardian of the heavenly kingdom, 420
before the host which you have led here, the bands of an-
gels, that I may be able and may be permitted to ascend
from here with my descendants. And three days ago a fol-
lower of the savior came home to hell; he is now fast in fet- 425
ters, exhausted by torments, because the king of glory be-
came angry with him for his presumption. He said to us
truly that God himself intended to give light to the home of
those in hell. Then each one of them rose and sat up, sup- 430
porting himself on his arm, leaning on his hands. Although
the horror of hell appeared terrifying, they were all glad in
the midst of their suffering that their noble Lord was willing
to seek out hell in order to help them."

She reached out her hands to the king of heaven, en- 435
treated the creator for mercy through the person of Mary:

"Lord, you were born into this world from my daughter
to help people! Now it is plain to see that you are God him-
self and the eternal origin of all created things." 440
[IX]

Then the eternal Lord let them ascend; he had gloriously
inflicted bonds of punishment on the devils, and thrust
them, forcibly humbled, further into that profound darkness,

445 þær nu Satanus   swearte þingað,
     earm aglæca,   and þa atolan mid him,
     witum werige.   Nalles wuldres leoht
     habban moton,   ah in helle grund,
     ne hi edcerres   æfre moton
450 wenan seoððan.   Him wæs Drihten God
     wrað geworden,   sealde him wites clom,
     atole to æhte,   and egsan gryre,
     dimne and deorcne   deaðes scuwan,
     hatne helle grund,   hinsið-gryre.
455   Þæt, la, wæs fæger   þæt se feða com
     up to earde   and se eca mid him,
     meotod man-cynnes,   in þa mæran burh!
     Hof hie mid handum   halige witigan
     up to eðle,   Abrahames cynn.
460 Hæfde þa Drihten seolf   dead oferwunnen,
     feond geflemed;   þæt in fyrn-dagum
     witegan sædon   þæt he swa wolde.
     Þis wæs on uhtan   eall geworden,
     ær dæg-rede,   þæt se dyne becom,
465 hlud of heofonum,   þa he helle duru
     forbræc and forbegde;   ban weornodon
     þa hie swa leohtne   leoman gesawon.
         Gesæt þa mid þære fyrde   frum-bearn Godes,
     sæde soð-cwidum: "Snotre gastas,
470 ic eow þurh mine   mihte geworhte,
     Adam ærest   and þæt æðele wif.
     Þa hie begeton   on Godes willan
     feowertig bearna   þæt forð þonon

where Satan, that miserable enemy, and the horrible crea- 445
tures with him, now dismally plead, exhausted by torments.
They may not have the light of heaven at all, but rather the
abyss in hell, nor may they expect to return ever afterward. 450
The Lord God had become angry with them, had, in horror,
given them bonds of torment and that dreadful terror as
their possessions, the gloomy and dark shadow of death, the
fiery abyss of hell, the terror of death.

O that was splendid when that band arrived up to their 455
home and the eternal one with them, the creator of man-
kind, into that celebrated city! He raised them by their
hands, the holy prophets, the kin of Abraham, up to his
homeland. The Lord himself had conquered death, put the 460
devil to flight; in days of old, the prophets had said that he
would do so. This all happened in the hour before dawn, be-
fore daybreak, that that din came, loud from the heavens, 465
when he demolished and cast down the doors of hell; their
bones lost their strength when they saw such a bright light.

Then the firstborn son of God sat with that vast com-
pany and announced in true words: "Wise spirits, by my 470
power I made you, first Adam and the noble woman. Then,
by the will of God, they begot forty children so that from

on middan-geard menio onwocon
475 and wintra feola wunian moston,
eorlas on eðle, oð ðæt eft gelamp
þæt hie afyrde eft
feond in firenum; fah is æghwær.
 "Ic on neorxna-wonge niwe asette
480 treow mid telgum, þæt ða tanas up
æpla bæron, and git æton þa
beorhtan blæda, swa inc se balewa het,
hand-þegen helle. Hæfdon forþon hatne grund,
þæs git ofergymdon hælendes word,
485 æten þa egsan. Wæs se atola beforan
se inc bam forgeaf balewe geþohtas.
 "Þa me gehreaw þæt min hand-geweorc
þæs carcernes clom ðrowade.
Næs ða monna gemet, ne mægen engla,
490 ne witegena weorc, ne wera snytero,
þæt eow mihte helpan, nimðe hælend God,
se þæt wite ær to wrece gesette.
Ferde to foldan þurh fæmnan had
ufan from eðle, and on eorþan gebad
495 tintregan fela and teonan micelne.
Me seredon ymb secgas monige
dæges and nihtes, hu heo me deaðes cwealm,
rices ræd-boran, hrefnan mihten.
Þa wæs þæs mæles mearc agangen
500 þæt on worulde wæs wintra gerimes
þreo and þritig geara ær ic þrowode.
Gemunde ic ðæs mænego on þam minnan ham
lange þæs ðe ic of hæftum ham gelædde
up to earde, þæt heo agan sceolon

then on multitudes were born in the world and were permit-   475
ted to live for many years, men in their home, until it hap-
pened later that the devil in his wickedness caused their ex-
ile in turn; he is hostile in every way.

"I had planted a tree with boughs in the newly created   480
paradise, whose branches bore apples up high, and the two
of you ate the bright fruit just as that evil being, the ser-
vant of hell, directed you both. That is why you experienced
the fiery abyss, because you disregarded the savior's word,
ate that terrible thing. The horrible being who caused evil   485
thoughts in both of you was present there.

"Then I regretted that the work of my own hands was en-
during these prison bonds. There was no human ability, no
might of angels, no actions of the prophets, no wisdom of   490
men that could help you then, except for God the savior,
who had decreed that punishment in vengeance. He came
to earth from his home above through the person of a vir-
gin, and on earth he endured many torments and terrible vi-   495
olence. Day and night many men plotted against me, as to
how they, the pillars of that state, could carry out the pen-
alty of death on me. Then the period of the appointed time
had elapsed so that I had been in the world for thirty-three   500
years all told, before my passion. I was mindful that the mul-
titude in that wretched home was longing that I should lead
them home from their captivity, up to my native land to

505 Drihtnes domas   and duguðe þrym;
wuniað in wynnum,   habbað wuldres blæd
þusend-mælum.   Ic eow þingade
þa me on beame   beornas sticedon,
garum on galgum.   Heow se giunga þær,
510 and ic eft up becom   ece dreamas
to haligum Drihtne."

[x]
      Swa wuldres weard   wordum sæde,
meotod mon-cynnes,   ær on morgen
þæs þe Drihten God   of deaðe aras.
515 Næs nan þæs stronglic   stan gefæstnod,
þeah he wære mid irne   eall ymbfangen,
þæt mihte þam miclan   mægne wiðhabban,
ah he ut eode,   engla Drihten,
on þæm fæstenne,   and gefatian het
520 englas eall-beorhte   andleofan gingran,
and huru secgan het   Simon Petre
þæt he moste in Galileam   God sceawian,
ecne and trumne,   swa he ær dyde.
      Þa ic gongan gefregn   gingran ætsomne
525 ealle to Galileam;   hæfdon Gastes bled,
ongeton haligne   Godes Sunu
swa heo gesegon   hwær Sunu meotodes
þa on upp gestod,   ece Drihten,
God in Galileam.   To ðæs gingran þider
530 ealle urnon   þær se eca wæs.
Feollon on foldan,   and to fotum hnigon;
þanceden þeodne   þæt hit þus gelomp
þæt hi sceawodon   scyppend engla.

obtain the glory of the Lord and the splendor of the heav- 505
enly host; they will dwell in delights and possess the glory of
heaven in their thousands. I interceded for you when men
pierced me with spears on the tree, on the gallows. The
young man cut me open there and I attained eternal joys on 510
high again, at the hands of the holy Lord."

[x]

So spoke the Guardian of glory, the creator of mankind,
early in the morning on which the Lord God arose from
death. There was no stone so firmly fixed, even if it had been 515
all enclosed in iron, that could withstand that great power,
but the Lord of angels came out from his sepulcher and
commanded resplendent angels to summon the eleven dis- 520
ciples and especially commanded them to tell Simon Peter
that he might see God, eternal and steadfast, in Galilee, as
he had done before.

I have learned that all his disciples then went together to 525
Galilee; they were inspired by the Spirit and they recognized
the holy Son of God, as soon as they saw where the Son of
the creator, the eternal Lord, stood on high, God in Galilee.
The disciples all ran to that place where the eternal one was. 530
They fell on the ground and bowed down at his feet; they
thanked the prince that it had come to pass that they had
seen the creator of angels.

Þa sona spræc   Simon Petrus:

535 "Eart þu þis, Drihten,   dome gewurðad?
We ðe gesawon   æt sumum cyrre:
þec gelegdon   on laðne bend
hæþene mid hondum.   Him þæt gehreowan mæg
þonne heo ende-stæf   eft gesceawiað."

540 Sume hie ne mihton   mode oncnawan
þæt wæs se deora   —Didimus wæs haten—
ær he mid hondum   hælend genom
sylfne be sidan   þær he his swat forlet;
feollon to foldan   fulwihtes bæðe.

545 Fæger wæs þæt ongin   þæt Freo-Drihten
geþrowode,   þeoden ure.
He on beame astah   and his blod ageat,
God on galgan,   þurh his gastes mægen.
Forþon men sceolon   mæla gehwylce

550 secgan Drihtne þanc   dædum and weorcum,
þæs ðe he us of hæftum   ham gelædde
up to eðle,   þær we agan sceolon
Drihtnes domas,
and we in wynnum   wunian moton.

555 Us is wuldres leoht
torht ontyned,   þam ðe teala þenceð.

[XI] Þa wæs on eorðan   ece Drihten
feowertig daga   folgad folcum,
gecyðed man-cynne   ær he in þa mæran gesceaft,

560 burh-leoda fruma,   bringan wolde
haligne gast   to heofon-rice.
Astah up on heofonum   engla scyppend,
weoroda waldend.   Þa com wolcna sweg

Then Simon Peter spoke at once: "Is this you, Lord, hon- 535
ored in glory? We saw you once: heathens had put a hateful
crown on you with their hands. They can regret that later
when they face the end of their lives."

Some of them—he was called Didymus—could not ac- 540
knowledge in their hearts that it was the beloved one until,
with his own hands, he took hold of the side of the savior
himself, where he had shed his blood; the waters of baptism
had fallen to the ground.

The passion of the noble Lord, our prince, was a splendid 545
deed. He mounted onto the tree and shed his blood, God on
the gallows, through the power of his spirit. Therefore peo-
ple must say thanks to the Lord at all times, in their deeds 550
and in their actions, because he led us home out of captivity
up to our true home, where we shall obtain the glory of the
Lord and where we may live in delights. To us, those who 555
think rightly, the radiant light of heaven will be revealed.

[XI]

Then the eternal Lord was attended by people on earth
for forty days, revealed to mankind before he, the prince of 560
citizens, desired to bring his holy spirit into that splendid
creation, the heavenly kingdom. The creator of angels, the
ruler of hosts, ascended up to the heavens. Then holy ce-
lestial music came from the clouds. In the middle of them

halig of heofonum. Mid wæs hond Godes,
565   onfeng Freo-Drihten   and hine forð lædde
to þam halgan ham,   heofna ealdor.
Him ymb flugon   engla þreatas
þusend-mælum.   Þa hit þus gelomp,
þa gyt nergende Crist   gecwæð þæt he þæs
570   ymb tene niht   twelf apostolas
mid his Gastes gife,   gingran geswiðde.
Hæfde þa gesette   sawla unrim
God lifigende.   Þa wæs Iudas of,
se ðe ær on tifre   torhtne gesalde,
575   Drihten hælend;   him seo dæd ne geþeah,
þæs he bebohte   Bearn wealdendes
on seolfres sinc;   him þæt swearte forgeald
earm æglæca   innon helle.
    Siteð nu on þa swiðran hond   Sunu his Fæderes;
580   dæleð dogra gehwæm   Drihten weoroda
help and hælo   hæleþa bearnum
geond middan-geard.   Þæt is monegum cuð
þæt he ana is   ealra gescefta
wyrhta and waldend   þurh his wuldres cræft.
585   Siteð him on heofnum   halig encgel,
waldend mid witegum.   Hafað wuldres Bearn
his seolfes seld   swegl betolden.
Leaðað us þider to leohte   þurh his læcedom,
þær we moton seolfe   sittan mid Drihtne,
590   uppe mid englum,   habban þæt ilce leoht,
þær his hired nu   halig eardað,
wunað in wynnum,   þær is wuldres bled
torht ontyned.   Uton teala hycgan

was the hand of God, which received the noble Lord and   565
took him, the prince of the heavens, away to his holy home.
Throngs of angels flew around him in their thousands.
When this happened, then Christ the savior also said that   570
he would strengthen the twelve apostles, his disciples, with
the gift of his Spirit ten days after that. The living God had
then added countless souls. Then Judas, who had previously
sold the radiant Lord, the savior, as a sacrifice, was absent;   575
that deed, by which he sold the Son of the ruler for silver
treasure, did not profit him; the miserable enemy evilly paid
him back for that in hell.

Now the Son sits on his Father's right hand; every day   580
the Lord of hosts distributes help and salvation to people
throughout the world. It is widely known that he alone is
the maker and ruler of all created beings through his glori-
ous skill. The holy angel sits in heaven, the ruler with his   585
prophets. The Son of glory has surrounded his own throne
with the sky. Through his healing remedy he summons us
there, into the light, where we ourselves may sit with the
Lord, with the angels on high, and enjoy that same light,   590
where his holy court now lives and dwells in delights, where
the radiant glory of heaven is revealed. Let us take good

þæt we hælende   heran georne,

595 Criste cweman.   Þær is cuðre lif
þonne we on eorðan mægen   æfre gestreonan.

[XII]
    Hafað nu geþingod to us   þeoden mæra,
ælmihtig God,
on dom-dæge   Drihten seolfa.

600 Hateð heh-englas   hluddre stefne
beman blawan   ofer burga geseotu
geond foldan sceatas.
Þonne of þisse moldan   men onwecnað;
deade of duste arisað   þurh Drihtnes miht.

605 Þæt bið daga lengust,   and dinna mæst
hlud gehered,   þonne hælend cymeð,
waldend mid wolcnum   in þas woruld færeð.
Wile þonne gesceadan   wlitige and unclæne
on twa healfe,   tile and yfle.

610 Him þa soð-fæstan   on þa swiðran hond
mid rodera weard   reste gestigað.
Þonne beoð bliðe   þa in burh moton
gongan in Godes rice,
and heo gesenað   mid his swiðran hond

615 cynincg alwihta,   cleopað ofer ealle:
    "Ge sind wil-cuman!   Gað in wuldres leoht
to heofona rice,   þær ge habbað
a to aldre   ece reste."
    Þonne stondað þa forworhtan,   þa ðe firnedon;

620 beoð beofigende   hwonne him bearn Godes
deman wille   þurh his dæda sped.
Wenað þæt heo moten   to þære mæran byrig

heed to obey the savior eagerly, to please Christ. Life there 595
is more excellent than we may ever obtain on earth.

[XII]
Now the glorious prince, almighty God, the Lord him-
self, has determined to come to us on the Day of Judgment.
He will command the archangels to blow the trumpets 600
loudly above the city dwellings over all the expanse of the
earth. Then people will awake from this earth; the dead will
arise from the dust through the power of the Lord. That will 605
be the longest of days and the greatest of dins, heard loudly
when the savior comes and the ruler makes his way into this
world in the clouds. Then he will divide the radiant and the
impure into two parts, the good and the evil. On his right 610
hand, the righteous will ascend to their rest with the guard-
ian of the heavens. Then those who may go into the city,
enter into God's kingdom, will be happy and the king of all
created things will bless them with his right hand, will de- 615
clare above them all:

"You are welcome guests! Enter into the glorious light,
into the kingdom of heaven, where you will have eternal
rest, forever and ever."

Then the guilty, those who have sinned, will stand there;
they will be trembling with fear of the time when the son 620
of God will judge them by the power of his deeds. They will
be hoping to be allowed to go into that celebrated city, up

up to englum   swa oðre dydon,
ac him bið reordende
625   ece Drihten,   ofer ealle gecwæð:
"Astigað nu, awyrgde,   in þæt wite-hus
ofostum miclum.   Nu ic eow ne con."
    Sona æfter þæm wordum   werige gastas,
helle hæftas,   hwyrftum scriþað
630   þusend-mælum,   and þider leaðað
in þæt sceaðena scræf,   scufað to grunde,
in þæt nearwe nið,   and no seoððan
þæt hie up þonan   æfre moton,
ah þær geþolian sceolon   earmlic wite,
635   clom and carcern,   and þone caldan grund
deopne adreogan   and deofles spellunge,
hu hie him on edwit   oft asettað
swarte susl-bonan.   Stæleð feondas
fæhðe and firne,   þær ðe hie Freo-Drihten,
640   ecne anwaldan,   oft forgeaton,
þone þe hie him to hihte   habban sceoldon.
    Uton, la, geþencan   geond þas worulde,
þæt we hælende   heran onginnen!
Georne þurh Godes gife   gemunan gastes bled,
645   hu eadige þær   uppe sittað
selfe mid swegle,   sunu hælendes!
Þær is geat gylden   gimmum gefrætewod,
wynnum bewunden,   þæm þe in wuldres leoht
gongan moten   to Godes rice,
650   and ymb þa weallas   wlitige scinað
engla gastas   and eadige sawla,
þa ðe heonon ferað.
    Þær martiras   meotode cwemað

to the angels, as the others did, but the eternal Lord will 625
speak to them and will say above them all: "Descend now
with all speed, you accursed ones, into the house of punish-
ment. I do not know you now."

Immediately after these words the evil spirits, hell's cap-
tives, will come speedily in their thousands and will sum- 630
mon them there into that devils' pit, will shove them to the
depths, into that oppressive abyss, and never afterward will
they be allowed to return up from it but they will have to
suffer harsh punishment there, fetters and imprisonment, 635
and endure the cold deep abyss and the devil's talk, how
dark tormenting devils will continually make them an object
of scorn. The devils will accuse them of feuds and violent
deeds, of continually forgetting the noble Lord, the eternal 640
ruler in whom they ought to have hoped.

O, throughout this world let us resolve to obey the sav-
ior! Let us eagerly be mindful, through the grace of God, of
the soul's glory, how the sons of the savior, the blessed them- 645
selves, sit there on high in heaven! There is a golden gate
there, adorned and delightfully encircled with gems, for
those who are allowed to enter into the light of glory, God's
kingdom, and around the walls shine the beautiful spirits of 650
angels and the blessed souls who depart from here. There
the martyrs are pleasing to the creator and, with their holy

and herigað heh-fæder   halgum stefnum,
655 cyning in cestre.   Cweþað ealle þus:
"Þu eart hæleða helm   and heofen-dema,
engla ord-fruma,   and eorðan tudor
up gelæddest   to þissum eadigan ham."
Swa wuldres weard   wordum herigað
660 þegnas ymb þeoden,   þær is þrym micel,
sang æt selde;   is sylf cyning,
ealra aldor,   in ðære ecan gesceft.
      Þæt is se Drihten,   seðe dead for us
geþrowode,   þeoden engla.
665 Swylce he fæste   feowertig daga,
Metod man-cynnes,   þurh his mildsa sped.
Þa gewearð þone weregan,   þe ær aworpen wæs
of heofonum   þæt he in helle gedeaf,
þæt he costode   cyning alwihta.
670 Brohte him to bearme   brade stanas,
bæd him for hungre   hlafas wyrcan:
"gif þu swa micle   mihte hæbbe."
      Þa him andswarode   ece Drihten:
"Wendest þu, awyrgda,   þæt awriten nære,
675 nymþe me ænne . . .
Ac geseted hafast,   sigores Agend,
lifigendum liht,   lean butan ende
on heofen-rice,   halige dreamas."
      Þa he mid hondum genom
680 atol þurh edwit   and on esle ahof,
herm bealowes gast,   and on beorh astah,
asette on dune   Drihten hælend:
"Loca nu ful wide   ofer lond-buende.
Ic þe geselle   on þines seolfes dom

voices, they praise the Father on high, the king in his city.   655
They all say: "You are the protector of men and the heavenly
judge, the source of angels, and you have led the children
of earth up to this blessed home." So the attendants about
their prince praise the guardian of heaven in these words,   660
there where there is great majesty and singing beside his
throne; he is the king himself, the ruler of all, in that eternal
creation.

That is the Lord, the prince of angels, who suffered death
for us. He who was the creator of mankind also fasted for   665
forty days out of the abundance of his mercy. Then it oc-
curred to the accursed being, who had previously been cast
out of heaven so that he plunged down into hell, that he
should tempt the king of creation. He brought large stones   670
to his lap, directing him to make loaves for himself for his
hunger: "if you have such great power."

Then the eternal Lord answered him: "Did you think,
cursed one, that it was not written except for me alone . . .   675
But you, victorious Lord, have decreed light for the living,
reward without end in the kingdom of heaven, holy joys."

Then that terrible being scornfully laid hold of him with   680
his hands and lifted him onto his shoulder, that malignant
spirit of evil, and went up a mountain and set the saving
Lord down on the mountain: "Now look far and wide over
the inhabitants of earth. I will give you people and land,

685 folc and foldan.   Foh hider to me
burh and breotone   bold to gewealde,
rodora rices,   gif þu seo riht cyning
engla and monna,   swa ðu ær myntest."
     Þa him andswarode   ece Drihten:
690 "Gewit þu, awyrgda,   in þæt wite-scræf,
Satanus seolf;   þe is susl weotod
gearo togegnes,   nalles Godes rice.
Ah ic þe hate   þurh þa hehstan miht
þæt ðu hell-warum   hyht ne abeode,
695 ah þu him secgan miht   sorga mæste,
þæt ðu gemettes   meotod alwihta,
cyning mon-cynnes.   Cer ðe onbæcling!
Wite þu eac, awyrgda,   hu wid and sid
hel-heoðo dreorig,   and mid hondum amet.
700 Grip wið þæs grundes;   gang þonne swa
oð ðæt þu þone ymbhwyrft   alne cunne,
and ærest amet   ufan to grunde,
and hu sid seo   se swarta eðm.
Wast þu þonne þe geornor   þæt þu wið God wunne,
705 seoððan þu þonne hafast   handum ametene
hu heh and deop   hell inneweard seo,
grim græf-hus.   Gong ricene to,
ær twa seondon   tida agongene,
þæt ðu merced hus   ameten hæbbe."
710   Þa þam werigan wearð   wracu getenge.
Satan seolua ran   and on susle gefeol,
earm æglece.   Hwilum mid folmum mæt
wean and witu.   Hwilum se wonna læg
læhte wið þes laþan.   Hwilum he licgan geseah
715 hæftas in hylle.   Hwilum hream astag,

348

as much as you want. Receive from me here power over the 685
city and the spacious hall of the kingdom of heaven, if you
are the true king of angels and of men, as you have thought
up to now."

Then the eternal Lord answered him: "Depart, you 690
cursed being, Satan himself, into that pit of punishment; it
is torment which is ordained and prepared for you, not the
kingdom of heaven. But I command you, by the highest
power, that you offer no hope to the inhabitants of hell but 695
instead you can tell them the worst of sorrows, that you met
the creator of all creatures, the king of mankind. Turn back!
Know too, you cursed being, how wide and spacious the
horrible hell-hall is, and measure it out with your hands. Try 700
to get to the bottom of it; then go on like that until you
know the full extent of it, and measure it first from top to
bottom, and how broad the dark blast of fire is. Then you
will know more thoroughly that you have fought against
God, after you have measured with your hands how high 705
and how deep hell, that grim grave-house, is within. Go
quickly, so that you may have measured, before two hours
have gone by, the house appointed for you."

Then vengeance pressed hard on that cursed being. Satan 710
himself, that miserable enemy, ran and fell into the torment.
At times he measured with his hands its woes and its tor-
ments. At other times the dark flame seized that loathsome
being. Sometimes he saw the captives lying in hell. At other 715

ðonne he on þone atolan   eagum gesawun.

Hæfdon gewunnon   Godes andsacan . . .

blac bealowes gast,   þæt he on botme stod.

Þa him þuhte   þæt þanon wære

720   to helle-duru   hund þusenda

mila gemearcodes,   swa hine se mihtiga het

þæt þurh sinne cræft   susle amæte.

Ða he gemunde   þæt he on grunde stod.

Locade leas wiht   geond þæt laðe scræf,

725   atol mid egum,   oð ðæt egsan gryre

deofla mænego   þonne up astag.

Wordum in witum   ongunnon þa werigan gastas

reordian and cweðan:

"Laþ us beo nu on yfele!   Noldæs ær teala!"

FINIT LIBER II. AMEN.

times there was an uproar when they turned their eyes on that horrible being. God's opponents had gained by their struggle . . . the black spirit of evil so that he stood in the abyss. Then it seemed to him that from there to the door of hell was a hundred thousand miles in extent, according as the mighty one had powerfully ordered him to measure his torment. Then he was mindful that he was standing on the bottom of hell. The false creature, that terrible being, looked all over that loathsome pit with his eyes, until fear of that terrifying place rose up in the throngs of devils. In their torments, the cursed spirits proceeded to speak and to say these words: "Be loathsome to us now in your evil! You did not wish for good before!"

FINIT LIBER II. AMEN.

In Clench Qu-Becche, under ane þorne,
liet Kenelm kine-bern, heued bereued.

In Clench Cow-Valley under a thornbush,
lies Kenelm the king's son, robbed of his head.

Note on the Texts

The texts in this volume have been newly edited, but I have also consulted the editions listed in the bibliography. Punctuation and word division have been modernized; hyphens have been added to compound nouns and adjectives and their derivatives. Manuscript abbreviations have been expanded without comment, and the Tironian note has been expanded as *ond* except in *Christ and Satan,* where it has been expanded as *and.* The apparatus lists only emendations made in this edition or conjectured restorations of damaged texts; it does not list emendations made by previous editors nor does it include scribal corrections which are made in the manuscripts themselves and which have been adopted, or not adopted, in the texts. Erasures in the manuscripts are not noted unless the erased letters or words are included in the edited text. An ellipsis (. . .) indicates illegible or lost letters in the manuscript.

All of the longer texts edited here are divided into sections, *fitte,* in the manuscripts, unnumbered in the Exeter Book and the Vercelli Book and sporadically numbered in the Junius manuscript; these sections are separated by a space between one block of text and the next, with roman numerals added where appropriate.

Notes to the Texts

The reading adopted in the text is followed by the manuscript reading.

4 heafod: heafoð   7 eorð-byrg: eorðb..g   10 forlæt: forlęt
12 cræftga: cræstga   18a þu: þa   20 eadgum: eadgu   23 myndgiað:
m.ndgiað   24 to lose: ....ose *MS damaged*   31 we: þe   49 horscne:
hosc ne   69 genedde: geneðde   91 Solimæ: Solimę   133 eft: est
153 for: *MS damaged and this reading is conjectural*   154 geseces: *MS damaged; the letters* es ne læt *visible under ultraviolet light according to the facsimile edition*   166 na: nu   169 worda: worde   206 tir-fruman: tirfruma
244 miltse: milstse   277 þe: e *with previous letter erased*   285 world-cundra: worlcundra   300 a gehealdan: age healden   304 þær:
þæt   306 wis-fæst: wis fæft   311 ne: *not in MS*   313 inhebban: in
hebba   322 stondað: stondeð   339 motan: motam   361 nied-þiowa:
med þio wa   364 genyrwad: genyrwað   371 we: þe   396 wreað:
wearð   419 wiht: niht

19 ealle: healle   61 gehwone: gehwore   86 fere: feore   112 þa:
þu   113 sceldun: scehdun   176 lif-fruma: liffruman   181 weras: wera
213 motun: motum   224 geteod: *not in MS*   226 wihte: wita   234 ge-monian: genomian   265 þa: þa þe   302 frean: fream   310 ma-gun: magum   347 wihte: wita   379 hlutre: hlutru   380 motun: mo-tum   463 innan: mnan   471 mæðleð: mædleð   481 leofstum:
leoftum   484 onfengun: onfengum   509 ywan: yðan   546 hingonge:

ingonge   564 þe gelic: we gelic   582 guton: gotun   594 gesælig
moste: moste gesælig   630 wurde: worde   664 swiðran: swiran
712 onettan: onnettan   716 wær: þær   729 læteð: lætað   731 bid-
fæstne: bið fæstne   734 fremmað: *not in MS*   740 to wrace:
wracu   745 morþor-lean: moþor lean   762 ower: oþer   767 forhog-
dun: hogdun   784 þær: þæs   786 deaðe: endedeaðe   796 giefe: gief
with letter erased after f

GUTHLAC A

13 motun: motum   18 no: nu   35 no: nu   46 mætræ: mætrę
67 eðel: eleð   71 bimutad: bimutað   105 weard: wearð   136 siþþan:
siþþam   153 gecostad: gecostað   162 ærendu: ærendo *with superscript* v
over o   178 ond wædum: *not in MS*   181 wurdun: wurdum   209 hy:
he   210 mostun: mostum   245 geðringan: gedrin gan   269 we: þe
271 us: hus   296 wid: wið   299 abonne: abunne   363 ræste: ręste
370 wægan: węgan   374 flæsc-homan: flæs homan   384 duge: buge
391 onwylled: onwyl leð   woð: soð   404 sceðþendra: sceðþenra
430 þæt: þæ   454 hean: heam   517 weolde: wolde   542 gemunde:
not in MS   mod: mond   631 wiðhogdun: wið hogdum   661 in: in
mod   663 woldun: woldum   696 þrea-niedlum: þrea medlum
712 æfstum: æftum   814 motun: motum   817 ealne: ealdne

THE DESCENT INTO HELL

There are burn holes in the manuscript on the folios with this
poem, so some of the text has disappeared.

6 reonge: reone   8 bliðe: bliðne   25 sið: *not in MS, which is damaged
here*   28 gesohte ymb siex: gesoht . . . ex *MS damaged*   29 nu is se fyrst
sceacen: nu . . . sceacen *MS damaged*   30–31 witodlice þæt us to: witod
. . . to   32 sylfa: *not in MS, which is damaged here*   42 weoruda:
weorud   60 sarige: . . . ige   61 sceoldon: *not in MS, which is damaged
here*   63 *A word follows* wræccan, *now largely lost, with only some descenders
visible*   64 nið-locan: niðloc.. *the two uncertain letters, whose lower edges are
preserved, look like* -an   65 oððe: *not in MS, which is damaged here*   79 ge-
cyðdest: ge cyddest   87 dorum: doru   90 hreowende: hreowen.. *MS*

damaged 91 mændon: . . . on *MS damaged* 92 þu us sohtest: *not in MS,*
which is damaged here 93 bimengdest: bimengdes modigast: . . . gast
MS damaged 105 meahtest: *not in MS, but no gap or damage* 108 gedyrf-
tum: gedyrstum 119 þinum: inum 120–21 Dryhten ond for: dr....
MS damaged 122 meder þære is Marian: me . . . rian *MS damaged* 123–
24 lofiað ond fore þam englum: lof . . . lum *MS damaged* 125 on þa
swiþran hond: . . . hond *MS damaged* 128 ond fore: ond *with no gap or
damage* 129 swa þeah: swaþean

The Vision of the Cross

2 þæt: hæt 17 wealdendes: wealdes 20 sorgum: surgum 47 æni-
gum: nænigum 59 sorgum: *not in MS, supplied from the Ruthwell
text* 70 greotende: reotende 71 stefn: *not in MS* 142 me: he

The Ruthwell Cross Crucifixion Poem

This text is transliterated from runes. The notes below do not in-
clude letters that are partly visible on the cross. Three dots in
square brackets signify a gap in the runes due to damage; other
dots signify missing letters.

1 ondgeredæ: ...geredæ 3 modig: .odig fore: f[. . .] 4 buga:
.ug[. . .] 7 bismæradu: ismæræ.u ætgadre: æt.ad.. miþ: .iþ
bistemid: .ist.mi. 8 bigoten: bi[. . .] 11 biheald: bi[. . .] 12 saræ:
s... wæs: w.s miþ: mi. sorgum: so.gu. gidrœfid: gidrœ..d hnag:
h.a. 14 gistoddun: gistoddu. licæs: ...æs heafdum: ...f..m 15 bi-
healdun: ...ea..u. hiæ: .i. þer: .e.

The Brussels Cross Inscription

broþor: beroþo broþor: beroþor

Andreas

4 camp-rædenne: cam rædenne 6 hlyt: lyt 31 hettend: hetted
heafod-gimmas: heafod gimme 32 agetton: ageton 33 geblendan: ge-
blondan 36 on: *not in MS* 50 sigel: segl 64 seowað: seoðað

89 sigel: sęgl   99 ne murn: ne ne murn   118 gewat him: ge him
136 hwænne: hwæne   145 hwæs: wæs   164 oft: of   171 cine-baldum:
cire baldū   195 halig: *not in MS*   196 sæ-streamas: sæ stearmas
219 wyrðeð: wyrdeð   245 mette: *not in MS*   255 fægn: frægn
267 sunde: snude   268 þissa: þiss   288 ðu us: ðus   309 bedæled:
bedæleð   323 his: is   342 duguðum: dugudum   343 ece: ęce
367 feasceafte: fea sceaftne   393 geofon: heofon   394 duguð: dugud
413 forgrunden: fore grunden   424 sund: sand   442 brun: brim
479 þinne: þine   483 este: est   489 gifene: gifeðe   þa: *not in MS*
494 hæleða: hæleð   496 beateþ: beataþ   499 yð-lade: yðlafe
501 land-sceare: lan sceare   507 þeh: þe   535 bewunden: be-
wunde   592 reonig-mode: reomig mode   630 gehwæs: gehwære
633 *2nd* ne: nu   648 nu ic þe sylfum: n. . . . þe sylfum *MS damaged by re-*
agent   651 sylfes muð: sylf . . . .uð *MS*   667 atimbred: atrim-
bred   710 he: hie   718 þe: *not in MS*   746 ge mon cigað: ge moneti-
gað   770 wæs: *not in MS*   774 on: *not in MS*   799 hwæt: hwær
826 slæp-werige sæ ofereoden: sæ werige slæp ofer eode   829 gewiton:
not in MS eft: *not in MS*   843 wisa: wis   846 þa: þā   852 gystran-
dæge: gyrstran dæge   855 wer-ðeode: weorðode   864 faran: *not in MS*
890 gefeana: *not in MS*   910 wearð: werð   942 hrinen: hrinan
heafod-magan: heafod magū   943 searo-nettum: searo mettū
952 dæled: dælan   986 hine: him   988 betolden: betolde
996 heoro-dreorige: heoro deorig   998 þrym: *not in MS*   999 Godes:
god   1000 hand-hrine: han hrine   1030 grette: grete   1035 tu hund-
teontig: tu 7 hundteontig   1037 nænigne: nænige   1039 ond: on
1074 geleah: gelah   1082 ne gemetten: gemette   1089 belidenan: be
hlidenan   1092 hilde-bedd: hildbedd   1094 burg-wara: burgwaru
1110 geongne: geone   1116 reow: hreow   1139 þrist ond: *not in MS*
1147 sceððan: sceaðan   1154 freod: freond   1180 gewyrhtum: gwyrh-
tum   wæpnes: *not in MS*   1181 ealdor-geard: eador geard   1186 wast:
wæst   1191 on: *not in MS*   1193 Satan: sata   1225 secg: sec   1241 ha-
ton: hat of   1242 untweonde: untweodne   1253 Þa: a *with preceding S*
partly erased but no other letter supplied MS   1282 wast: wæst   1291 gescyl-
dend: gescylded   1317 hwær: hwæt   1337 rode: rade   1345 him þa
earm-sceapen: hearmsceapen   1377 niedum: medū   1404 leoðu: leoð
1430 hleoðrode: hloðrode   1443 lices: lic   1456 sigel: sægl

1457 wadu: waðu   1468 sar: sas   1472 alysed: alysde   1474 lice:
lic   1478 hwæt: hæt   1492 fæste: fæstne   1493 sæl-wage: sæl wange
1496 mod-rof: mod rofe   1508 geofon: heofon   1516 Iosua: iosau
1528 searu-hæbbende: searu hæbende   1532 sealtne weg: scealtes sweg
1545 wadu: wudu   1562 her: *not in MS*   1571 mægen: *not in MS*
1579 wearð: *not in MS*   1585 geofon: heofon   1597 wifa: *not in
MS*   1604 ær: *not in MS*   1619 ne: *not in MS*   1622 ræswan: ræswum
1647 se: sio   1653 hie: he   1658 faroðe: foroðe   1659 weorc: weor
1664 is: his   1667 me: *not in MS*   1704 syððan: syð

Christ and Satan

7 cleowne ymb lyfte: deopne ybmlyt   17 holm: holme   24 wirse: wise
with ora *added above last three letters*   31 under: undẹr   33 hefde:
hẹfde   34 cleopað: cleopad   37 þe: ða þe   42 wergu: wergum   wul-
dres: wulres   48 wordum: wordun   49 bættran: ættran *with* b *erased*
52 begnornende: begrorenne   57 earm sceaða: earm. sceaðana sum *with*
na sum *erased*   66 on: un   72 hwearfedon: hwearfdon   78 spearcade:
swearcade *with* c *corrected to* t   80 wordum: word   85 wuldres: wulres
89 þa ic aseald wes on wærgðu: ⁊ wærgðu þa ic of aseald wes   106 iu:
nu   107 ær: þær   143 eadige: eadigne   146 agan: to agan   151 sweg:
not in MS   159 cwiðde: cwide   herde: herede   179 nið-synnum: mid
synnum   181 ecan: ẹcan   183 morðer: morðre   188 siðas: sidas
198 uppe: upne   202 ecne: ecne in wuldre mid   211 fægere: fægre
219 eadigra: eadigre   223 feond: feonda   261 swið: swilc   267 sceale:
sceal   273 niðæs: in ðæs   278 eðel: eðle   308 þær: þær heo
309 heo: *transferred here from line 308*   315 eala: ala *with space left for
capital and* e *in outer margin*   318 hreopan: hreowan   319 wean: wea
320 seo: ðær   330 ad: *not in MS*   331 ne: *not in MS*   351 scima:
sunnu   354 seolfa: seolfa for   360 lædeð: lædæð *probably changed
from* lædað   364 wyrcan: *not in MS*   373 ord-fruma: ordfruman
375 hynðo: to   377 seon: *not in MS*   428 segde: segdest   433 heora
freo-drihten: heora drihten   437 minre: mire   453 dimne: dimme
454 hinsið-gryre: in sið gryre   458 hof hie mid handum: hofon hine mid
him handum   462 swa: sawla   474 on: *not in MS*   477 hie afyrde: he
afyrhte   487 gehreaw: gereaw   488 þæs: *not in MS*   495 fela and: and

fela   498 ræd-boran: boran   502 on þam: 7 þa   504 sceolon: *not in MS*   512 swa: wa *with space for* s   515 stan: satan   520 gingran: gin-gran winum   526 ongeton: *not in MS*   528 þa on: þa gingran on   ge-stod: stod   538 hæþene: hæþenne   540 mode: mod   552 sceolon: *not in MS*   557 þa: a *with space for* þ   559 man-cynne: man cynnes   569 gecwæð: *not in MS*   570 tene: ane   587 betolden: betaldan *with* t *partly erased and* he *substituted above the line by corrector*   593 teala: *not in MS*   599 on: on on   605 dinna: dimma   608 gesceadan: gesceawian   624 reordende: reodi de *with two erased letters between* i *and* d, *superscript* r *above* o, *and superscript* en *above erasure in corrector's hand; one or two letters erased after this word*   638 feondas: *not in MS*   639 firne: in firne   freo-drihten: drihten   646 sunu: torht sunu   656 heofen-dema: heofen deman   658 up gelæddest: *not in MS*   669 þæt he: þa   683 lond-buende: lond b wende *with erasure of* e *after* b, *superscript* u *over erasure, and* w *underlined for cancellation*   684 on þines seolfes dom: þines seoferdum   703 sid seo: sid   eðm: eðm seo   712 æglece: æglęce   722 sinne: synne   723 þæt: þa   727 þa: þa on þa

Notes to the Translations

1   The beginning of the poem is missing; the first folio of the manuscript has been damaged by slash marks, is worn and stained, and has holes, making it very difficult to read in parts.

1–17   The liturgical source for these lines is the antiphon: *O rex gentium et desideratus earum, lapisque angularis qui facis utraque unum: veni et salva hominem quem de limo formasti.* (O king of the nations, and their desire, the cornerstone who makes both one: come and save man, whom you fashioned from clay.) The idea of the stone rejected by the builders goes back to Psalm 117:22 ("The stone which the builders rejected; the same is become the head of the corner") and was applied to Christ in the New Testament (see, for example, Matthew 21:42, Ephesians 2:20–21, and 1 Peter 2:7).

18–49   The liturgical source for these lines is the antiphon: *O clavis David, et sceptrum domus Israel, qui aperis et nemo claudit; claudis et nemo aperit: veni et educ vinctum de domo carceris, sedentem in tenebris et umbra mortis.* (O key of David and scepter of the House of Israel, who you opens and no one closes; who closes and no one opens: come and lead the prisoner, who sits in darkness and the shadow of death, out from the prison house.) My reading of ll.18–32 is much influenced by J. C. Pope, "The Text of a Damaged Passage in the Exeter Book: *Advent (Christ I)* 18–32," *Anglo-Saxon England* 9 (1981): 137–56.

50–70   The liturgical source for these lines is the antiphon: *O Hierusalem, civitas Dei summi: leva in circuitu oculos tuos, et vide Dominum tuum, quia jam veniet solvere te a vinculis.* (O Jerusalem, city of the great God: lift up your eyes round about, and see your Lord, for he is coming now to release you from your chains.) The name Jerusalem was explained as *visio pacis,* "vision of peace," throughout the Middle Ages.

71–103 The liturgical source for these lines is the antiphon: *O virgo virginum, quomodo fiet istud, quia nec primam similem visa es nec habere sequentem? Filiae Jerusalem, quid me admiramini? Divinum est mysterium hoc quod cernitis.* (O virgin of virgins, how will this be, for one like you has never been seen before nor will there ever be a successor? Daughters of Jerusalem, why do you marvel at me? What you perceive is a divine mystery.)

77 *æfter mon-wisan mod ne cuðes.* This is a difficult line and no suggestion of how to read it is wholly satisfactory; I take *mon-wisan* as an adjective.

93 *mund.* On this meaning of *mund,* see E. Stanley, "Words for the *Dictionary of Old English,*" in *The Dictionary of Old English: Retrospects and Prospects,* ed. M. J. Toswell, Old English Newsletter Subsidia 26 (Kalamazoo, Mich., 1998), 33–56, at 39–41.

104–29 The liturgical source for these lines is the antiphon: *O Oriens, splendour lucis aeternae et sol justitiae: veni et illumina sedentes in tenebris et umbra mortis.* (O rising sun, splendor of eternal light and sun of justice; come and enlighten those that sit in darkness and in the shadow of death.)

109a–11 Compare the Nicene Creed: *Et in unum Dominum Iesum Christum, Filium Dei unigenitum, et ex Patre natum ante omnia sæcula. Deum de Deo, lumen de lumine, Deum verum de Deo vero, genitum, non factum, consubstantialem Patri: per quem omnia facta sunt.* (And in one Lord Jesus Christ, the only begotten Son of God, born of the Father before all ages. God from God, Light from Light, true God from true God, begotten, not made, one in being with the Father; through whom all things were made.)

128 *symle bi gewyrhtum.* See Peter Baker, "Toller at School: Joseph Bosworth, T. Northcote Toller, and the Progress of Old English Lexicography in the Nineteenth Century," in *Textual and Material Culture in Anglo-Saxon England: Thomas Northcote Toller and*

the *Toller Memorial Lectures,* ed. D. G. Scragg (Cambridge, 2003), 283–300, at 298.

130–63 The liturgical source for these lines is the antiphon: *O Emmanuel, rex et legifer noster, exspectatio gentium et salvator earum: veni ad salvandum nos, Dominus Deus noster.* (O Emmanuel, our king and lawgiver, the desire of nations and their savior: come and save us, Lord our God.)

154 *geseces.* Only the last two letters are visible under ultraviolet light but, as Campbell, *Advent Lyrics,* 91, points out, *geseces* "produces an awkward shift of mood in the verb." Gollancz, *Exeter Book: Anthology of Anglo-Saxon Poetry,* and Cook, *Christ of Cynewulf,* both have *gesece,* the imperative fitting in much better with the context.

164–213 The liturgical source for these lines is the antiphon: *O Joseph, quomodo credidisti quod antea expavisti? Quid enim? In ea natum est de Spiritu Sancto quem Gabrihel annuncians Christum esse venturum.* (O Joseph, how did you believe that which before you feared? Well? He whom Gabriel announced would be the Christ to come is born of her by the Holy Spirit.) See Hill, "A Liturgical Source for Christ I 164–213," 12–15; this antiphon survives only in a collection compiled by Alcuin in York ca. 790. There has been much debate about who says what in this section of the poem, with opinions ranging from the three-speech arrangement adopted here to a quicker, unsignaled exchange between Mary and Joseph. The poet probably drew on a Pseudo-Augustinian homily, *Sermo* 195, for this part of the text; see the excerpt in Allen and Calder, *Sources and Analogues,* 74–76.

175 *fea-sceaftne.* In this arrangement of the text, Mary speaks this line, so the masculine *fea-sceaftne* poses a difficulty. One could read it as an instance of zeugma, where *heortan minre* refers to Mary's heart, and *fea-sceaftne* to Joseph, or one could emend to a feminine form. I have chosen the former course of action here.

214–74 The liturgical source for these lines is the antiphon: *O rex pacifice, tu ante saecula nate, per auream egredere portam: redemptos tuos visita et eos illuc revoca unde ruerunt per culpam.* (O king of peace, you who were born before the ages, come by the golden gate;

visit those whom you have redeemed, and call them back to the place from which they fell by sin.)

257   *dæd-scua.* This is a unique word, explained by *DOE* as "shadow or darkness of deeds," hence perhaps "agent of darkness." Some editors emend to *deap-scua,* "shadow of death," used of Grendel in *Beowulf,* l. 160.

275–347   The liturgical source for these lines is the antiphon: *O mundi Domina, regio ex semine orta, ex tuo jam Christus processit alvo, tanquam sponsus de thalamo; hic jacet in praesepio qui et sidera regit.* (O lady of the world, born from a royal seed, Christ has now come forth from your womb, like a bridegroom from his chamber: he who rules the stars lies in a manger.)

303b   *Esaias.* It was, rather, Ezekiel who had this vision (Ezekiel 44:1–2); Cook, *Christ of Cynewulf,* 104–5, explains the error by pointing out that the Ezekiel passage was part of the service for Wednesday in the first week of Advent and that the immediately preceding lesson was from Isaiah.

320   *gefælsian.* In l. 144 *gefælsian* has its expected meaning of "to cleanse, purify," but the context in l. 320 seems to demand a meaning like *to pass through.* *DOE* (*s.v. gefǣlsian*) comments, "? to pass through, traverse; the validity of this interpretation is based on the assumption that *gefǣlsian,* like *fǣlsian,* has the senses of Latin *lustrare,* here specifically the sense 'to traverse'; *gefǣlsian* has here otherwise been taken as 'to purify' and 'to glorify,' and also emended to a form of *gefæstnian* 'to secure.'"

348–77   The liturgical source for these lines is the antiphon: *O cælorum Domine, qui cum Patre sempiternus es una cum Sancto Spiritu, audi nos famulos: veni ad salvandum nos; jam noli tardare.* (O Lord of the heavens, you who are eternal with the Father and one with the Holy Spirit, hear your servants: come to save us; do not delay now.)

378–415   The liturgical source for these lines is not as clear as for the others but may be the antiphon: *O beata et benedicta et gloriosa Trinitas, Pater et Filius et Spiritus Sanctus.* (O happy and blessed and glorious Trinity, Father and Son and Holy Spirit.) Along with this the poet also drew on the *Sanctus* and *Benedictus* of the Mass;

see Rankin, "Liturgical Background of the Old English Advent Lyrics," 326–27, and Campbell, *Advent Lyrics,* 99.

416–39   The liturgical source for these lines is an antiphon for the octave of Christmas: *O admirabile commercium, creator generis humani animatum corpus sumens, de virgine nasci dignatus est, et procedens homo sine semine, largitus est nobis suam deitatem.* (O wonderful exchange, the creator of human kind, assuming a living body, deigned to be born from a virgin, and, coming forth as a man without seed, he bestowed on us his divinity.)

396   *wreað.* See Isaiah 6:1–3.

Christ in Judgment

15   *on brehtme.* I take *brehtme* as a form of *breahtm,* "loud noise," but *DOE* has this instance under *bearhtm,* "moment, instant," citing 1 Corinthians 15:52. See also l. 278 and Matthew 24:31 and 1 Thessalonians 4:15.

39–59   An analogue and possible source for this dual appearance of Christ is a passage in Gregory the Great's *Moralia in Iob;* see Allen and Calder, *Sources and Analogues,* 96–97.

82   Compare Apocalypse of St. John the Apostle 8:2.

86   *fyllað mid fere.* See *DOE (s.v. fær),* which suggests "fell with sudden danger" or "fill with fear." As *DOE* points out, this "has also been taken, retaining MS reading, as form of *feorh,* and transl. 'overthrow with [their] breath,' or emend[ed] to form of *fȳr* and transl. 'fill with fire')."

171b–73   The triad of thought, word, and deed is a common devotional one.

317   *forht-afongen.* Editors have differed on whether this is a compound, as here, or two adjectives. *DOE (s.v. āfōn)* prefers the latter, saying that it is "probably to be taken as two adjectival forms in asyndetic parataxis: *forht, afongen* 'fearful, caught,' a reading which fits well the context of *Juliana,* but not as readily that of *ChristC,* 'afraid, seized by fear'; *forht afongen* has also been explained as scribal error for *fyrhto (a)fongen* 'seized by fear'; a compound *forht-afongen* has also been suggested." Because *afongen*

on its own makes little sense in *Christ in Judgment*, the compound is adopted here.

435–45 That it would be better to be ashamed of one's sins before one man in life than to be shamed before all at the Last Judgment is a common motif in Old English homilies. The Latin sources on which the poem draws have no reference to confession, and it appears that the poet took this motif from vernacular homilies.

557 *mid wonnum claþum.* This refers, according to *DOE (s.v. bewindan)*, to the shrouding of the dead.

713b *leoht.* One might expect *lic,* "body," here, to give body and soul. Muir, *Exeter Anthology,* 424, suggests that this use of light "may stem from a theological concept, with God as *Lux,* the source of light (and consequently of life) in this world." See Bosworth and Toller, *Anglo-Saxon Dictionary, s.v. leoht.*

786 *deaðe.* The manuscript reads *endedeaðe* here; as *DOE (s.v. endedeað)* notes, this is "a tautological compound which is metrically irregular and where the likelihood of scribal error is strong."

GUTHLAC A

1–29 At the beginning of the text's editorial history, there was dispute about whether these lines belonged to *Guthlac A* or to the preceding poem, *Christ in Judgment*; it is now generally agreed that they are a prologue to, and a very important part of, *Guthlac A,* and they have been so treated in editions since that of Gollancz, *Exeter Book: Anthology of Anglo-Saxon Poetry,* in 1895. However, thematically, with their description of the blessed soul and heaven, they are similar to the end of *Christ in Judgment.*

4 *yldran had.* Compare Psalms 8:6.

6 The angel's speech clearly begins here but what is not so clear is where it ends. I have followed Krapp and Dobbie, *Exeter Book,* and Muir, *Exeter Anthology,* in ending it at line 10a, but editions and translations vary; Roberts, *Guthlac Poems,* continues the speech to l. 25, arguing on p. 31 that "both the excursus and the speech end neatly with line 25, if lines 26–9 are read as a rhetori-

cal question, though line 17 must also be read as a good breaking
point."

9   *tid-fara.* A nonce word for which a variety of meanings has been
suggested. These include "a traveler the time of whose journey
is come," "one who journeys for a short time," "a traveler under
summons," "a time traveler."

11   *eder-gong.* A crux which has been interpreted in a wide variety of
ways. The two principal ones are summarized by *DOE* (*s.v. eder-
gong*): "the form has been read as a compound of *eodor* 'bound-
ary; enclosure; dwelling' and *gang* 'going,' and interpreted as 'a
going into an enclosed place, a taking refuge,' or more simply
'shelter, refuge'; the compound has alternatively been read as
'departure from an enclosure.'" I have opted for "departure,"
with the sense then being that no one will want to leave heaven
because of any misery there, as there will be none.

35   As it stands in the manuscript, there is a problem with the senti-
ment of this line, which goes against the central teaching of the
poem. Emending *nu* to *no,* as in l. 18, solves this problem.

59   Compare Matthew 20:16.

72–73   Compare Isaiah 11:2–3.

84b–88a   Hill, "The Middle Way," 184, points out that the "two major as-
saults" on Guthlac correspond to the two methods of attack on
hermits mentioned here. When Guthlac is lifted up and shown
the sinful life in monasteries, he is "tempted to yield to vain
glory, *idel wuldor,* i.e. to exult in his own austere virtue, and to
judge others." When he is brought down to the gates of hell, he
is presented with something terrifying, *egesa,* to tempt him to
despair (compare ll. 574–76).

93   *neah.* Bosworth and Toller, *Anglo-Saxon Dictionary,* give "lately"
for *neah* here, but I have translated *us neah* as "near to us," as
there seems to be no other evidence for the meaning "lately."

95   *Guðlac.* The name means "battle-play" or "reward of battle." Fe-
lix's *Life of Guthlac,* written in the first half of the eighth century,
explains: *Anglorum lingua hoc nomen ex duobus integris constare vi-
detur, hoc est "Guth" et "lac," quod Romani sermonis nitore personat
"belli munus," quia ille cum vitiis bellando munera aeternae beatitudi-*

nis cum triumphali infula perennis vitae percepisset. (The name in the tongue of the English is shown to consist of two individual words, namely "Guth" and "lac," which in the elegant Latin tongue is *"belli munus"* [the reward of war], because by warring against vices he was to receive the reward of eternal bliss.) (Colgrave, *Felix's Life,* 78–79.) The poem has a number of references to Guthlac's being granted the reward of eternal salvation for his battles against evil. See Robinson, *Significance of Names,* 43–49. Lines 302b–7a also play on his name.

102   *beorg-sepel.* There has been debate about the nature of Guthlac's dwelling place, a *beorg-setl.* In Felix's life, Guthlac lives in a *tumulus,* a burial mound, but *beorg* is ambiguous; it can mean "mountain, hill" or "barrow, tumulus, burial mound." Some critics have seen Guthlac's dwelling in this poem as a burial mound; others, including Roberts, *Guthlac Poems,* argue for its being a hill. I have translated it as "hill." For Reichardt, the hill has symbolic importance and is "as much a symbol of interior spiritual achievement as a geographical location" ("*Guthlac A* and the Landscape of Spiritual Perfection," 331).

155b–58a Compare Isaiah 11:2.

160b–69 These lines allude to the three temptations of 1 John 2:16, lust of the flesh, lust of the eyes, and the pride of life.

173   *feara sum.* Presumably litotes for *alone.*

178   *ond wædum.* An addition suggested by Roberts, *Guthlac Poems;* though there is no gap in the manuscript, something is clearly missing.

182b–83 A difficult passage, which I have not emended. *DOE, s.v. cennan,* suggests as a translation: "We declare for that [*þæs*] a share precious to the Lord in [the name] Guth-lac"; the poet is playing here on the second element of Guthlac's name, meaning "reward." See Robinson, *Significance of Names,* 46–48.

205   The respite from torment which the devils enjoy for short periods does not appear to be associated with any particular period of the year in *Guthlac A.* The respite for the damned is a feature of the *Visio Pauli,* in which it is a weekly respite from the ninth hour on Saturday to the first hour of Monday (see *The Old English Vision of St. Paul,* ed. A. diPaolo Healey, Speculum Anniver-

sary Monographs 2 [Cambridge, Mass., 1978], 48–50); the re-
spite can be annual, weekly on Sunday, weekly on an unspecified
day or for uncertain periods in other Old English texts. *Guthlac
A* is unusual in that the devils, rather than the sinners in hell,
receive a respite; in the *Navigatio Sancti Brendani Abbatis* one
of the islands on which Saint Brendan lands has birds who are
fallen angels, not as guilty as Lucifer, who wander through "vari-
ous regions of the air and the firmament and the earth" but who
are given the bodies of white birds on Sundays and holy days,
on which occasions they are allowed to praise the Creator. See
Shook, "The Burial Mound in *Guthlac A*," 9–10, and *Navigatio
Sancti Brendani Abbatis,* ed. C. Selmer, Publications in Medieval
Studies 16 (Notre Dame, Ind., 1959), 24.

217 *bisæce. DOE* (*s.v. bigsæc*) offers a range of possible meanings:
"Of uncertain meaning and etymology: dispute (if **bigsacu*);
visit, visitation (if **bigsēc*); or possession, taking possession (if
emended to **bigsǣt*)." Roberts, *Guthlac Poems,* and Muir, *Exeter
Anthology,* both support "dispute," the basis for the translation
here as "claim."

368 A folio is missing after this line.

458 *myrcels.* Presumably the sign of the cross, as Roberts, *Guthlac Po-
ems,* 146, suggests.

460–66 Editions vary in how they treat ll. 460–66. I follow Krapp and
Dobbie, *Exeter Book,* here in treating these lines as part of the
demon's speech, but both Roberts, *Guthlac Poems,* and Muir, *Ex-
eter Anthology,* treat these lines as an aside by the author; they
close the quotation marks at 459 and reopen them at 467, put-
ting ll. 460–66 in brackets. The lines continue the address to
Guthlac, and ll. 465–66, in particular, are intimately linked to
the following sentence. When Guthlac in lines 505b–6a says to
the demons that *ge scyldigra / synne secgað,* he is referring back to
what they have said to him in these lines.

620b–22 As with ll. 460–66, editors vary in their treatment of these lines.
Both Roberts, *Guthlac Poems,* and Muir, *Exeter Anthology,* put
them in brackets outside Guthlac's speech; I have followed
Krapp and Dobbie, *Exeter Book,* in including them in the speech.

716 *socn.* Has been interpreted in very different ways here, as "sanc-

tuary, refuge," or, as in *Beowulf*, l. 1777, "persecution." I have cho-
sen the former translation.

816a   *sibbe ond gesihðe*. A reference to the etymology of Jerusalem; com-
pare *Advent*, l. 50a.

THE DESCENT INTO HELL

1–16   The first part of the poem, dealing with the visit of the two
Marys to the sepulcher, seems to depend on the Gospel of Mat-
thew, 28:1–10, as it specifically mentions the two women.

8   *beorge*. The poem twice refers to a *beorg*, a "mountain, hill" or
a "barrow, tumulus, burial mound (both Saxon and pre-Saxon
burial mounds; freq. in charters)" (*DOE s.v. beorg*). This first ref-
erence could possibly be to the hill of Golgotha, but its use in l.
14 suggests rather that it is Christ's sepulcher which is referred
to as a *beorg*. The poet appears to be alternating *eorð-ærn* and
beorg.

8   *bliðe*. The manuscript reads *bliðne*, which, if retained, would pre-
sumably refer to Christ, and the *hæleð* would then probably refer
to Nicodemus and Joseph of Arimathea. As they have no other
role in the poem and as it would mean breaking the time se-
quence and returning to a period before Christ was placed in
the sepulcher, it seems preferable to emend to *bliðe*, with Krapp
and Dobbie, *Exeter Book*, and with Muir, *Exeter Anthology*, and to
take this as a reference to the angels at the tomb. In Matthew
and Mark, there is only one angel, but Luke 24:4 refers to two
men in shining clothes, clearly two angels, who tell the women
that Christ has risen. In John 20:12 Mary Magdalene sees two
angels in the sepulcher.

17ff.   The poem is unusual in placing the harrowing of hell on Easter
Sunday, after the Resurrection; most texts place Christ's descent
into hell at the moment of his death, while his body lay in the
tomb.

25b   *sið*. I follow earlier editors in supplying *sið*.

28   The liturgical date for the commemoration of the Decollation
of John the Baptist is August 29, while the traditional date for

the Crucifixion, celebrated on the movable feast of Good Friday, was March 25. It is common in patristic writers to see John as preceding Christ to hell, and the same idea is found in Ælfric, *Catholic Homilies* I (456, ll. 148–51), but the exact time of John's death is not specified. However, John's birth was commemorated six months before Christ's in the liturgy, and this may have suggested the six-month interval between their deaths. The Old English poem seems to be unique in this.

53 John the Baptist's sadness at Christ's coming to hell appears puzzling, but T. Hill, "The Unchanging Hero: A Stoic Maxim in 'The Wanderer' and Its Contexts," *Studies in Philology* 101 (2004): 233–48, at 237, argues that the passage reflects a suspicion of happiness in Anglo-Saxon literary culture, in which it is regarded as an inappropriate emotion.

56 *burg-warena ord.* There has been some discussion of who this refers to, with the majority view being that it is John the Baptist, who also speaks ll. 26–32. The other candidate is Adam, who is called *ord mancynnes* in *Genesis* 1111; Krapp and Dobbie, *Exeter Book,* lxii, argue that the *burgwarena ord* must be Adam on the grounds that "the phrase *git Iohannis* in l. 135 indicates clearly that John is not the speaker here," as he would not refer to himself as John. It is certainly the case that John can no longer be the speaker by l. 135 but, as Shippey, *Poems of Wisdom and Learning,* 41, argues, the two personae, John's and the poet's, are "felt to be in substantial agreement" and, by the end of this speech, the speaker is "surely a man expressing general truths about the situation of men who are at any time without the operation of grace."

62 This line is problematic and has been treated differently by different editors. Krapp and Dobbie, *Exeter Book,* retain *monige bindeð,* while declaring it unsatisfactory; Muir, *Exeter Anthology,* emends to *þonne monigne bindeð,* and Shippey, *Poems of Wisdom and Learning,* 114, to *þonne mon gebindeð.* I have followed Shippey here.

70b–75 These lines have puzzled editors, and opinions have varied. The most convincing is that what is referred to here is Christ giving

John armor in his mother's womb. Blickling Homily 14, for the Nativity of John the Baptist, says that John, when he leaped in the womb at the approach of Christ, *wæpn gegrap mid to campienne, ærþon þe he to his lichoman leomum become; & he ær þone feþan sohte, ærþon þe he þæt leoht gesawe* ("seized weapons with which to fight before he was endowed with his bodily limbs, and he sought a battle-troop before he saw the light"), Morris, 167. Hall, "The Armaments of John the Baptist," demonstrates the existence of an established tradition of John being depicted as a soldier in the womb preparing for the coming of his king.

71   *end.* This is the only instance of this word in Bosworth and Toller's *Anglo-Saxon Dictionary*; the meanings "once, previously, formerly," have been suggested, as has emendation to *æne,* "once." However, Campbell, *Addenda,* states (*s.v. end*) that the adverb "is doubtful."

90–93   These lines have suffered a lot of damage, and the reconstruction can only be conjectural.

93–94   The meaning is very difficult to understand because of the missing words.

93   *bemengdest.* The word does not occur anywhere else. *DOE* (*s.v. bemengan*) points out that "various interpretations have been suggested based on senses of *mengan,* e.g., 'to be incarnate,' 'to confound,' 'to plumb (the depths)' with *moldgrundas* supplied."

99–106   Much has been written on these lines, although there is no problem reading the manuscript. The lines about Jerusalem are relatively straightforward in sense, although there has been debate about whether the negative *ne* in l. 101a should be retained or not; what they allude to, however, is more difficult, as the meaning of Jerusalem is complex in the poem. The allusion to the Jordan standing still probably refers to the widespread belief that it did so at the baptism of Christ.

105   A finite verb has to be supplied as there is only an infinitive in the manuscript and nothing to agree with *þu*. Different emendations have been proposed, all supplying a similar meaning

(emending *nales* to *naldes,* emending *geondflowan* to *geondflowest,* adding *mostes* or *mostan*); I have supplied *meahtest.*

107 *gedyrftum.* This word does not occur elsewhere, either in this form or in the manuscript form *gedyrstum. DOE, s.v. gedyrst,* says that "the word is doubtful," perhaps *gedyrftum,* "dative plural of a hypothesized noun *gedyrft* 'labour, effort, tribulation'" or perhaps *gedystum,* "dative plural of a hypothesized noun *gedyste,* a derivative of *dust,* 'dust.'"

THE VISION OF THE CROSS

4 *syllicre treow.* This is a comparative form, used here, probably, for the superlative. There may also be, however, a comparative sense, in that this tree is superior to all others.

8 *foldan sceatum. Sceat* can refer to the surface or the corners of the earth (see *DOE s.v. folde*). If the former is intended here, then the gems would be at the base of the cross; if, as seems more probable, the latter, then the gems would be at the end of each beam, and the cross is imagined as filling the narrator's field of vision, towering into the sky.

9a *on þam eaxle-gespanne.* A unique word, which may refer to the crossbeam or to the intersection, where both beams meet. *Eaxl* means "shoulder" and *gespann* is from the verb *spannan,* "to join." Some Anglo-Saxon stone crosses have five bosses, representing jewels, at the intersection; see Swanton, *Dream of the Rood,* 102.

9b *engel Dryhtnes.* There has been much discussion of this line, with some editors preferring to emend (to *engeldryhte* or *englas Dryhtnes* or *engeldryhta feala* or by dropping *ealle*). The *engel Dryhtnes* may be Christ, as in *Advent,* l. 104, or *Christ and Satan,* l. 585b, which would make it the first reference in the poem to Christ, or may be the cross as the messenger of the Lord (the etymology of *angelus* as *nuntius,* "messenger," is well attested in Anglo-Saxon England).

10a *forð-gesceaft. DOE* records two meanings for this word, "created being or thing; collectively: creation" and "future (state/condition/destiny)," assigning this occurrence to the latter meaning and suggesting that it refers "to the angels who were destined to maintain their original radiance." If ll. 11–12 expand on 9b–10, then *fægere þurh forð-gesceaft* refers to more than the angels—to angels, men, and creation itself honoring the cross for all time—and therefore the meaning "creation" may be more suitable.

15a *wædum geweorðode*. There has been much discussion about the garments of the cross: they possibly refer to the gold, jewels, and blood on the cross. Other suggestions are the imperial purple robes found draped across the arms of the cross in the iconographical type known as the trophy-cross or the veil that covers the cross in the Good Friday liturgy or the tassels on some processional crosses.

19a *earmra ær-gewin*. The wretched ones are either Christ and the cross or those who had suffered on the cross before Christ.

20 *swætan on þa swiðran healfe*. The Bible does not specify which of Christ's sides was pierced, but the right-hand side was established very early. *Swætan* means to sweat, but the noun *swat*, "sweat," is used for blood in the poetry; both blood and water came from Christ's side in John 19:34, and *swætan* can refer to either or both.

34b *wolde*. The sense of *wolde* here (and in l. 41) is much stronger than the normal "wished, intended," and is more like "willed, resolved." The emphasis on Christ willing the crucifixion is important theologically and thematically.

40b *on gealgan heanne*. *Heanne* is ambiguous and can mean "high" (from *hēah*) or "despised" (*hēan*).

57a *fuse*. Those who come hastening are presumably Joseph and Nicodemus (see John 19:38–39).

66 *on banan gesyhðe*. A *bana* is a "slayer, a killer"; in Old English poetry it is used of the instrument of death, such as a sword or (as here) the cross, as well as of a person who kills.

69 *mæte weorode*. Literally, "with a small company," either litotes for "all alone" or perhaps intended to refer to the women who visited the tomb or the soldiers who guarded it.

76 A half-line, at least, appears to be missing, although there is no

gap in the manuscript; it presumably mentioned the digging up of the crosses.

117   *unforht.* The manuscript here reads *unforht,* "unafraid," as at l. 110, but one would expect a very different meaning here, as the sense seems to be that those who have honored the cross will not need to be afraid. Most editors emend to *anforht,* taking *an-* as an intensive prefix, but this form does not occur anywhere in Old English. Others, such as Swanton, *Dream of the Rood,* leave the manuscript reading stand, on the grounds that the prefix *un-* can be an intensive and that the poet is very interested in wordplay and so could be using the same word, seven lines apart, in diametrically opposed meanings. Neither *unforht* or *anforht* seems very satisfactory here, but I have left the manuscript reading stand.

130   *mund-byrd.* This is a legal term denoting the protection afforded by a superior. Here the cross functions as protector.

Andreas

1–3a   The first three lines of *Andreas* appear to be modeled on the opening of *Beowulf:*

> Hwæt, we Gar-Dena   in gear-dagum,
> þeod-cyninga   þrym gefrunon,
> hu ða æþelingas   ellen fremedon.

"Yes, we have heard of the greatness of the Spear-Danes' high kings in days long past, how those nobles practiced bravery"; *The 'Beowulf' Manuscript,* ed. and trans. R. D. Fulk, Dumbarton Oaks Medieval Library 3 (Cambridge, Mass., 2010).

6   The apostles cast lots to decide where each would preach, according to a very early tradition.

15   *ig-land.* There has been discussion on whether the obvious meaning, "island," applies in this context, as Mermedonia is not an island in any other version of the legend. Following Krapp, *Andreas and the Fates of the Apostles,* 78, Brooks, *Andreas and the Fates,* suggests "land beyond the water," 78. Most recent com-

mentators, however, have taken *ig-land* as island, and it has been read in ways that stress the resonances of this setting for an English audience.

31   *heafod-gimmas.* A kenning for eyes.

38–39   In the Latin source, translated in Allen and Calder, *Sources and Analogues,* it is clearer that the drink makes the prisoners consume hay and grass; they are being fattened like cattle.

50   *heafdes sigel.* Another kenning for eyes.

90b–91 The Latin *Casanatensis* and the Old English prose life make it clear that Matthew's sight is restored at this point.

163   The reference is to Matthew.

198–200 Both the *wegas ofer wid-land* and the *here-stræta,* "the paths over wide land" and the "army roads" or "main roads," seem to be part of the description of the sea. As Olsen, *Land and Sea,* puts it: "No poet . . . is as preoccupied with these metaphorical uses of land terms in a maritime context as the author of *Andreas*" (385), and she points out that the "strongly metaphorical meaning of *widland* as 'sea' . . . allows additional ambiguity in *wegas* which can mean 'ways' and 'waves' in this case" (391).

308–10 *sæ-beorgas* and *cald cleofu.* The "sea mountains" have either been taken literally as sea cliffs or, as seems more probable, as huge waves. The latter is preferred by J. R. Hall, "Old English *sæbeorg: Exodus* 442a, *Andreas* 308a," *Papers on Language and Literature* 25 (1989): 127–34, who suggests that the poet is drawing on classical and other Latin sources; by Olsen, *Land and Sea,* who sees it as a feature of the Old English poetic tradition; and by Frank, "North-Sea Soundings," who points out the similarity to skaldic kennings for waves: "Having God speak in kennings, casually referring to his ship as a 'sea-horse' and to waves as 'sea-hills' and 'cold cliffs,' rounds off his masquerade as an old salt, an habitué of northern seas" (5).

321b   *ellor-fusne.* That is, ready to die.

421   *fealuwne flod.* As the *DOE* says (*s.v. fealu*), *fealu* is "a colour-term of varied meaning; the corpus yields the most evidence for a colour basically yellow but variously tinted with shades of red, brown or grey, often pale but always unsaturated, i.e. not vivid;

hence, 'tawny,' 'yellow(ed),' 'yellowish-red,' 'yellowish-brown,' 'yellowish-grey' all appear as translations; the ModE reflex, 'fallow,' is now obsolete except of the coat of an animal." *Fealu* is difficult to translate when it is used, as here, of the sea.

442   *bord-stæðu.* This is a much-debated compound. *Bord* in the context of seafaring means side of a ship or the ship itself; *stæþ* usually means shore. "Ship's shore" seems to be a kenning for the sides of a ship. It has also been interpreted as "rigging" or as "shores."

556   *fruma ond ende.* Alpha and omega, the first and the last; see Apocalypse of St. John the Apostle 1:8, 21:6, and 22:13.

589–94   See Matthew 14:17–21; Mark 6:38–44; Luke 9:12–17; John 6:8–13 (in John it is Andrew himself who indicates the boy with the loaves and fishes, but the *Andreas* poet does not advert to this.)

668a   *heah ond horn-geap.* Identical to *Beowulf,* l. 82, where it describes the hall Heorot.

717–20   The city alluded to is presumably heaven. In the Greek and Latin texts, the temple of the Jews has been made to look like heaven, and the images are of sphinxes made to resemble cherubim and seraphim; the sphinxes do not appear in the Old English.

788   See Genesis 49:29–33.

828   A short passage appears to be missing after this line, but there is no gap in the manuscript.

998–99a   There has been much emendation of these lines; 998b–99a read *heofon-cyninges god dryhtendom. God* has an accent in the manuscript, which usually indicates a short vowel ("God" as opposed to "goodness"), but *heofon-cyninges God* does not make sense. *Dryhtendom* does not occur elsewhere in the corpus, but analogous forms do. Krapp, *Vercelli Book,* adds *þrym* and emends *god* to give *heofon-cyninges þrym, godes dryhtendom.* Brooks, *Andreas and the Fates,* retains *heofon-cyninges god* but emends 999a to *dryhten demde.* I have followed Krapp here; *heofon-cyninges þrym* parallels l. 723b.

1000   *haliges gastes.* It seems possible that there is confusion (or deliberate wordplay) here (and in l. 1621 and in the compound *beod-*

gastes in l. 1088) between *gast*, "spirit, soul" and *gyst*, "guest, visitor, stranger." Such confusion has also been suggested in *Beowulf.* I have translated as "visitor" or "guest" in each of the three instances in *Andreas.*

1024a A leaf has been excised from the manuscript here. The source and the Old English prose version suggest that in the missing section the apostles restore sight and reason to the other prisoners; Andrew then instructs them to go to the lower part of the city and wait under a fig tree.

1035–40 There are problems with the number of released prisoners, connected to two missing half-lines. The Latin versions and Old English prose version have a total of 248 men and 49 women released. *Andreas* specifies 49 women and should, therefore, probably have 248 men. Instead, in the manuscript it has only 142, *tu ⁊ hundteontig, geteled rime / swylce feowertig*, emended here, as in most editions, to *tu hundteontig,* to give 240. A genitive noun specifying the gender of these prisoners is missing. Brooks, *Andreas and the Fates,* 98, suggests in his notes that the missing second half of l. 1036 should read *fira and eahta* and suggests *forþgerimed* to supply the second half of l. 1040.

1044–48 Matthew and the others are not mentioned again. In the Old English prose version and the Latin, Matthew and Andrew's disciples are brought by clouds to a mountain where Saint Peter remains with them.

1090 There is a break in alliteration here, but there is no gap in the manuscript and the sense is complete. Something brief is probably missing; Krapp, *Andreas and the Fates of the Apostles,* and earlier editions supply *deade* to complete the line *deade gefeormedon. Duruþegnum wearð.* Brooks, *Andreas and the Fates,* characterizes all attempts to remedy the line as "unfortunate" and prefers to postulate a lacuna of two half-lines.

1090–92 *Andreas* omits an episode in the Latin where the Mermedonians are about to eat the seven dead doorkeepers but are prevented when God directs Andrew to stop them; he prays and their swords fall from their hands, which wither. They then, as in the poem, hold a council and decide to cast lots to determine who should be killed for food. The Old English prose version also omits this entire episode, including the attempt to eat the door-keepers, the drawing lots, the choice of the old man, and Andreas's rescue of his children (only one child is mentioned in *Andreas* but, in the Latin, the old man also offers his daughter, to supply the difference in weight between his son and himself).

1171   *helle hinca.* Literally, a "hell-limper"; the word occurs only here in Old English, and the devil is not so described in the Latin. Old High German *hinkan* means "to limp." The devils are termed *adloman* in *Guthlac B,* l. 912, "fire-maimed cripples."

1181   *ealdor-geard.* The manuscript reads *eadorgeard,* which, it has been suggested, could mean "dwelling enclosure" (of the spirit). See *DOE s.v.* **ealdorgeard.*

1189   Oddly, Andrew appears to be calling the devil a devil's arrow here; Brooks, *Andreas and the Fates,* suggests it "may perhaps signify one who serves, armed with darts, in Satan's host" but does not advert to the fact that Andrew, four lines later, says that the same devil is called Satan.

1201ff.   The *Andreas* poet is not as clear as the Old English prose version or the Latin at this point. In them the devil tells the Mermedonians to search for Andrew, and God then tells Andrew to reveal himself, i.e., to give up his invisibility.

1255b–62a There is nothing like this vivid description of winter weather in the sources.

1278   *wopes hring.* This kenning, "ring of weeping," meaning "shedding of tears," occurs also in *Elene, Christ II,* and *Guthlac B.*

1296–1387 The Old English departs considerably from the Latin here. In the Latin, the devil appears in the likeness of an old man to the Mermedonians, tells them that Andrew is to blame for their hunger, and suggests that they find and eat him. The Mermedonians find Andrew but see the sign of the cross on his forehead and fall back. Satan, calling them his children, urges them on, asking why they are afraid, and they in turn tell him to kill Andrew himself if he can; the devil instead suggests that they lock Andrew up and mock him. When Andrew does not react to the taunts, the devil transforms himself and pretends to be God speaking to Andrew. Andrew sees through the deception, and the devil and his minions depart.

In the Old English, however, the devil appears when Andrew is being beaten and is appealing to God not to abandon him; the devil urges the Mermedonians to hit Andrew on the mouth to stop him talking. After more beating, Andrew is returned to his prison cell, where the devil again appears to him, this time accompanied by seven other devils; the devil taunts him, and then the group rushes at him but is repulsed by the sign of the cross. When the devil, lamenting, asks his companions about their failure, one of them suggests that he attempt to fight Andrew himself but goes on to say that they can offer better advice, which turns out to be that they go on insulting and taunting Andrew. The devil then berates Andrew and tells him that he will be killed shortly; when Andrew reasserts his faith in God, the devil flees. The Old English, then, has added a group of devils, perhaps understanding the children of the devil as more devils rather than as Mermedonians; it also has a much more extended flyting scene between Andrew and his opponents.

1311   *seofona sum.* This means that the devil was accompanied by seven others, as Brooks, *Andreas and the Fates,* points out. See also Bosworth and Toller, *Anglo-Saxon Dictionary, s.v. sum.*

1324   *Herodes.* According to the biblical accounts, this should read Pilate or Caiphas, but one Latin version also has Herod. The Greek versions vary, with Herod and Pilate mentioned and John the Baptist also appearing as the one killed by Herod. See Krapp, *Andreas and the Fates of the Apostles,* lviii.

1434   A half-line appears to have been lost here.

1478–91a Biggs argues that the *Andreas* poet explicitly developed the idea that Andrew's passion is an imitation of Christ's and the climactic moment in the saint's life; he suggests that the poet introduced this break in the narrative in order to "force his audience to reflect on his understanding of the scene's significance"; see Frederick M. Biggs, "The Passion of Andreas: *Andreas* 1398–1491," *Studies in Philology* 85 (1988): 413–27, at 426–27.

1516 Joshua and Tobias do not appear in any other versions of the story, as far as we know.

1526 *meodu-scerwan*. The closest parallel to this unique word is *ealu-scerwen* in *Beowulf* l. 769, a crux about which much has been written; it is probable that the *Andreas* poet modeled *meodu-scerwan* on it. *DOE, s. v. ealuscerwen,* takes *ealuscerwen* as probably meaning "serving, dispensing of ale," "either an ironic metaphor for the din of Beowulf's fight with Grendel as the noise of a drunken carousal or a metaphor for the coming of death and destruction as the serving of (bitter) drink (cf. *meodu-scerwen* in *Andreas,* l. 1526)." The *Andreas* poet continues the metaphor over the following passage, where "drink," salt water in which many drown, is imagined as being dispensed in enormous quantities by unstinting servingmen.

1663 Something is missing here, but probably little.

1667b I have adopted here Brooks's reading in *Andreas and the Fates,* which involves only the insertion of *me*. Krapp, *Andreas and the Fates of the Apostles,* and earlier editors, assumed that two half-lines are missing here, and the traditional numeration, which I have retained, allows for this.

Christ and Satan

1–17a This opening account of the creation of the universe has caused much difficulty for editors and critics; its dependence on patristic cosmology has recently become clearer. It seems probable that the scribe did not understand what he was copying. See the notes on the following lines, and Finnegan, *Christ and Satan,* 91.

7 The manuscript reading of the first half of the line, *deopne ybm-lyt,* does not make sense. In "Christ and Satan: 'Healing' Line 7," 508, Thornbury suggests the reading adopted here, *cleowne ymb lyfte* from *clywen* "ball, globe, sphere," and argues that the allusion is "to the theory common in Classical and patristic literature, that the heavens were structured in a series of concentric spheres surrounding the earth, the lowest of which was the air breathed by living creatures."

9   *sæ* here is the celestial sea above the firmament. See Genesis
1:6–7.

10   *grundas in heofene.* Many early editors emended *heofene* to *geofene*
"ocean." Finnegan, *Christ and Satan,* 91, was the first to recognize
the validity of the manuscript reading, and Wilcox, "Celestial
Cosmography in *Christ and Satan,*" 19, builds on his note, argu-
ing that *grundas* alludes to the firmament: "The firmament or
grundas was imagined as a solid spherical boundary that sepa-
rated the celestial waters or *sæ* from the earth's atmosphere and
prevented the earth from being flooded by the celestial waters
except when Christ permitted rain to fall as described in lines
eleven and twelve." From his vantage point in heaven, Christ
can survey the celestial sea, the firmament, and the rain falling
on earth below. As Wilcox demonstrates on p. 25, patristic cos-
mology was well known in England in the Anglo-Saxon period
through works by Ambrose, Augustine, and Isidore, through
Bede's treatments of the topic in his commentary on Genesis
and his *De natura rerum,* and through the liturgy.

19–20   This is another difficult passage, about which there has been
much disagreement; the phrase *duguðe and geþeode* in 19b is one
difficulty, and the other is that the passage appears to suggest
the creation of Adam before the fallen angels. Part of the prob-
lem is that *duguð* has an extensive range of meanings: "virtue,
strength, benefit, blessing, wealth, a troop of tried retainers,
army, host, people." *Geþeode* generally means "language, tongue,
speech." Those who retain the manuscript reading have differed
as to whether *duguðe and geþeode* is part of the direct object (then
translated "He distributed joys, blessings and tongues") or is the
indirect object of the verb ("He distributed joys to the host and
to the people"); on this hinges their interpretations of the pas-
sage. Other editors emend *geþeode* to *geoguðe,* giving the colloca-
tion *duguþ and geoguþ,* "tried and untried warriors," which is at-
tested in *Beowulf* and *Andreas.* I have retained the manuscript
reading, despite its difficulties, taking *duguþ* as an allusion to the
angelic host (as in, for example, l. 505) and *geþeode,* "tongue,"

"language" as meaning "people," as suggested by Clubb, *Christ and Satan*, 50.

Traditionally, the creation of the angels was part of the creation of light on the first day, and the creation of man was on the sixth day. It is possible that l. 20 does not imply the chronological priority of Adam's creation but asserts that Adam was first among men, in the *geþeod,* and Lucifer's band first among the angels, the *duguð,* with chiasmus. Given the exclusive focus on Satan and the fallen angels until the account of the harrowing of hell begins in l. 378b, the reference to Adam seems redundant as it is so isolated.

34 *se alda* is used to refer to the devil here and in l. 32 of *Homiletic Fragment I,* ed. Krapp, *The Vercelli Book.*

40 The end here may refer to the increased torment that the devils will suffer after the harrowing of hell or the Last Judgment or it may simply be an ironic reference to the fact that they are in the midst of torments.

63–64 Finnegan, *Christ and Satan,* 94, takes the lines to mean that Satan asserted that he was the father of *meotod,* Christ (the interpretation followed here). However, others think that this may be an allusion to Antichrist, considered the son of the devil. Hill, "The Fall of Satan," tentatively suggests that John 8:44 may lie behind this passage; in it Christ describes the devil as the father of lies, so the son of this passage would be falsehood. In the Gospel of Bartholomew Satan has a son, Salpsan.

86a *Bearn helendes. DOE (s.v. bearn)* suggests that *bearn* is plural and refers here to the angels, but l. 85b, *wuldres leoman,* referring to the *bearn,* echoes Hebrews 1:3, which describes Christ as *splendor gloriae. Helend* here seems to refer to God the Father, and the *Bearn helendes* to Christ.

143a *eadige bearn* referring to the angels; see *DOE (s.v. bearn).* The angels are referred to as *bearn hælendes* in 152b. The alternative, to retain manuscript *eadigne* and take it as modifying *sunu,* gives a very unusual word order.

145 This is one of a large number of single half-lines in *Christ and*

Satan; see A. Bliss, "Single Half-Lines in Old English Poetry," *Notes and Queries* 216 (1971): 442–49.

202–3　I have omitted the manuscript's *in wuldre mid* from l. 202, as it is repeated in the next line and seems to be an error.

228–78　There is some confusion about whether the fallen angels or Satan speaks these lines. The speech begins with the fallen angels as a group speaking but appears to switch to Satan alone, probably in l. 245, without any transition other than the change from first person plural to first person singular forms. Within his speech, Satan quotes what he said to his companions when he was instigating rebellion (248–53). My layout follows Finnegan's edition. Clubb, *Christ and Satan,* thinks that the entire speech was attributed to Satan by the poet but a scribe in error changed singular to plural verbs.

236　I have understood *byrht word* as Christ as the Word; it could also be an adjective, "bright of word, clear-voiced."

242b–44　As both Clubb and Finnegan noted in their editions, there is a dramatic inconsistency in having the souls of men being greeted by God in heaven before the fall of the angels.

306–8a　See Matthew 13:43.

319　*wind-sele.* Here and in l. 384 the original scribe wrote *winsele,* "wine hall," (as in 93, where Satan says that there is no *wloncra winsele* in hell), but the corrector has inserted a superscript *d* after the *n* in each instance. Finnegan, *Christ and Satan,* retains *winsele,* arguing that "the Corrector has missed the poet's ironic intention in terming hell a *winsele*" (104). Satan terms hell *þes windiga sele,* "this windy hall," in l. 135; the word *wind-sele* does not otherwise occur.

366　This is the only instance of the name Lucifer in Old English poetry.

382　There is a break in sense here but no gap in the manuscript. The closest parallels to the scene in which Eve has to plead for release after Adam has already been freed from hell are in the Easter homily (number seven) in the *Blickling Homilies,* a collection of Old English homilies in a manuscript written toward the end of the tenth century (ed. Morris), and a Latin text in the ninth-century book of Cerne, CUL Ll.1.10, written in England.

424   *þegen Hælendes.* There has been some debate as to who this follower of Christ is intended to be, but the consensus is that it must be Judas. His arrival in hell after his suicide (see Matthew 27:3–5) informed the dwellers there of Christ's death.

428   The manuscript reading, *segdest,* implies that Eve turns to Judas to address two lines to him, but all recent editors emend to *segde,* so that Eve merely quotes what Judas said. Presumably the scribe was confused by Eve's address to Christ in the previous lines.

429   *gelihtan.* Previous translations have taken *gelihtan* to mean "to descend, to come down," but *ham* is then a problem as it would imply that hell is Christ's home. It is preferable to take it as *gelihtan,* "to give light, to illuminate," as this is what Christ has done (compare ll. 387–89).

450   *seoððan.* In the manuscript this begins, rather than ends, a sentence.

458–59   The manuscript reads: *hofon hine mid him handum halige witigan up to eðle abrahames cynn* (The holy prophets, Abraham's kin, raised him with their hands up to his homeland). Clubb pointed out in 1925 that the manuscript reading might be erroneous as, in most accounts of the harrowing, Christ leads the rescued by the hand out of hell. Old English versions of the Gospel of Nicodemus stress this leading by the hand, and it is focal point of Anglo-Saxon visual representations of the scene. Given the poem's overwhelming emphasis on the power of Christ, it would also seem odd to have him being raised to heaven by the prophets, rather than having them raised by him. I have, therefore, emended here.

463–67   The *Christ and Satan* poet places Christ's descent into hell immediately before the Resurrection, rather than straight after his death. See Izydorczyk, "The Inversion of Paschal Events," 445 n. 3.

472–78a   There seems to be an implication here that Adam and Eve had children before the fall. In Genesis 1:28 God instructs Adam and Eve, immediately after Eve's creation, to increase and multiply, but there does not seem to be any tradition that they did so before the Fall. Clubb, *Christ and Satan,* places these lines in a parenthesis, regarding them as a kind of interruption in which the poet elucidates the doctrine "that men might have lived many, many years in paradise if they had not sinned," 110. He translates, "It would have been possible for men to dwell in that homeland many, many years, until (or but) it afterwards befell etc." (110). In his edition, Finnegan accepts this suggestion, somewhat reluctantly (113). The mood of the verbs does not support this translation.

473 Forty as the number of Adam's and Eve's children does not seem to be paralleled; Genesis mentions Cain, Abel, and Seth by name, as well as more sons and daughters (Genesis 5:4). The apocrypha have different numbers: in the *Vita Adae et Evae* they have sixty-three children, and in the book of Jubilees they have fourteen.

540–44 Clubb, *Christ and Satan,* points out that this "passage is both syntactically and logically incoherent," 118. The poet has, more or less, been following Matthew 28 (with omissions) from l. 524; Matthew 28:17 includes the words *quidam autem dubitaverunt,* "but some doubted," the source for l. 540. However, he then switched to John 20:24–29, for the doubting of Thomas. Didymus is Thomas, as explained in John 20:24. As it seems that the poet was probably responsible, I have not emended, despite the plural "some" and the singular "he." Another problem is whether *se deora,* "the beloved one," is Thomas or Christ; Christ is referred to as *se deora sunu* in l. 241 and is probably the referent here, despite the placing of 541b. See John 19:34 for the water from Christ's side, which was interpreted as the waters of baptism.

572–73a These lines may render Acts of the Apostles 2:41.

585b This idea of Christ as angel is also found in *Advent,* l. 104b, *engla beorhtast.*

646 In the manuscript this line reads *selfe mid swegle torht sunu*

hælendes. Clubb, *Christ and Satan,* omits *torht,* as here, while in his edition, Finnegan gives *selfe mid swegletorhtne sunu Hælendes,* with the *sunu* referring to Christ rather than the blessed in heaven. The blessed have already been referred to as *bearn hælendes,* however, in l. 152.

675 There is no break in the manuscript at this point, but the meaning and syntax suggest that something is missing. Satan's second temptation of Christ (Matthew 4:5–7) is missing and is probably what was omitted here.

679–80 No one has discovered a source for Satan's placing of Christ on his shoulders.

695–722 No source has been discovered for Christ's command that Satan measure hell with his hands. In l. 696 Christ calls himself the *meotod alwihta,* "the creator," or "the measurer," of all creatures or all creation. *Metod* is etymologically related to *metan,* "to measure," and the poet appears to be emphasizing that Satan, in wishing to usurp Christ's place as measurer, is punished by being forced to measure the only realm that belongs to him, hell. Hill, "The Measure of Hell," has suggested that this may even be a uniquely English concept, suggested by the verbal play of *metod/metan.*

717 Something appears to be missing here, though again there is no gap in the manuscript. It is probable that not much has been omitted.

729 In all other editions, this line reads (with variations in punctuation): *La, þus beo nu on yfele! Noldæs ær teala!* The manuscript, however, reads *laþus,* and the corrector has indicated a word division of *laþ us,* not *la þus.*

DISTICH ON KENELM

1 *Clench Qu-Becche.* Clent, in Worcestershire, is where Kenelm was supposedly buried under a thorn bush. The eleventh-century life includes a story about one of the cows pastured in the hills eating the grass near where Kenelm was buried and producing twice as much milk as the entire herd together.

Bibliography

This bibliography is selective. For more detailed bibliographical guidance, readers should consult Stanley B. Greenfield and Fred C. Robinson, *A Bibliography of Publications on Old English Literature to the End of 1972* (Toronto, 1980), as well as the annual bibliographies in the journals *Anglo-Saxon England* and the *Old English Newsletter.*

DICTIONARIES

Bosworth, J. *An Anglo-Saxon Dictionary.* Edited by T. N. Toller. Oxford, 1898. Also: *Supplement* by T. N. Toller (Oxford, 1921); and *Enlarged Addenda and Corrigenda* by A. Campbell (Oxford, 1972). Both reprinted as *Supplement with Revised and Enlarged Addenda* (Oxford, 1980).

Cameron, A., A. Crandell Amos, A. diPaolo Healey *et al. Dictionary of Old English: A to G* online. Toronto: Dictionary of Old English Project, 2007. [abbreviated to DOE]

PRIMARY SOURCES

Facsimiles

Chambers, R. W., M. Förster, and R. Flower, eds. *The Exeter Book of Old English Poetry.* London, 1933.

Gollancz, I., ed. *The Caedmon Manuscript of Anglo-Saxon Biblical Poetry: Junius 11 in the Bodleian Library.* London, 1927.

Sisam, C., ed. *The Vercelli Book.* Early English Manuscripts in Facsimile 19. Copenhagen, 1976.

Editions

Ælfric's Catholic Homilies: The First Series, Text. Edited by P. Clemoes. EETS SS 17. Oxford, 1997.

Allen, M. J. B., and D. G. Calder, eds. and trans. *Sources and Analogues of Old English Poetry: The Major Latin Texts in Translation.* Cambridge, 1976.

Anderson, J. E., ed. *Two Literary Riddles in the Exeter Book: Riddle 1 and the Easter Riddle: A Critical Edition with Full Translation.* Norman, Okla., 1986.

Boenig, R., trans. *The Acts of Andrew in the Country of the Cannibals: Translations from the Greek, Latin and Old English.* London, 1991.

Brooks, K. R., ed. *Andreas and the Fates of the Apostles.* Oxford, 1961.

Campbell, J. J., ed. *The Advent Lyrics of the Exeter Book.* Princeton, 1959.

Colgrave, B., ed. *Felix's Life of St Guthlac.* Cambridge, 1956.

Cook, A. S., ed. *The Christ of Cynewulf: A Poem in Three Parts: The Advent, the Ascension, and the Last Judgement.* 2nd ed., Boston, 1909. Repr., Hamden, Conn., 1964.

Clubb, M. D., ed. *Christ and Satan.* Yale Studies in English 70. New Haven, Conn., 1925.

Finnegan, R. E., ed. *Christ and Satan: A Critical Edition.* Waterloo, Ontario, 1977.

Gollancz, I., ed. *The Exeter Book: An Anthology of Anglo-Saxon Poetry.* Pt. I. EETS OS 104. London, 1895.

Krapp, G. P., ed. *Andreas and the Fates of the Apostles.* Boston, 1906.

———. *The Junius Manuscript.* Anglo-Saxon Poetic Records I. New York, 1931.

———. *The Vercelli Book.* Anglo-Saxon Poetic Records II. New York, 1932.

Krapp, G. P., and E. Van Kirk Dobbie, eds. *The Exeter Book.* Anglo-Saxon Poetic Records III. New York, 1936.

Morris, R., ed. *The Blickling Homilies.* EETS OS 58, 63, and 73. Oxford, 1874–1880; repr. as one volume, 1967.

Muir, B., ed. *The Exeter Anthology of Old English Poetry.* 2nd ed. 2 vols. Exeter, 2000.

Roberts, J., ed. *The Guthlac Poems of the Exeter Book.* Oxford, 1979.

Shippey, T. A., ed. *Poems of Wisdom and Learning in Old English.* Cambridge, 1976.

Sleeth, C. R., ed. *Studies in Christ and Satan.* Toronto, 1982.

Swanton, M., ed. *The Dream of the Rood.* Rev. ed. Exeter, 1987.

English Translations

Bradley, S. A. J. *Anglo-Saxon Poetry.* London, 1982.

Gordon, R. K. *Anglo-Saxon Poetry.* Rev. ed. London, 1954.

Kennedy, C. W. *The Poems of Cynewulf.* London, 1910; repr. New York, 1949.

SECONDARY SOURCES

Brantley, J. "The Iconography of the Utrecht Psalter and the Old English *Descent into Hell.*" *Anglo-Saxon England* 28 (1999): 43–63.

Burlin, R. B. *The Old English Advent: A Typological Commentary.* New Haven, Conn., 1968.

Campbell, J. J. "To Hell and Back: Latin Tradition and Literary Use of the 'Descensus ad inferos' in Old English." *Viator* 13 (1982): 107–58.

Conner, P. "The Liturgy and the Old English 'Descent into Hell.'" *Journal of English and Germanic Philology* 79 (1980): 179–91.

———. "Source Studies, the Old English *Guthlac A* and the English Benedictine Reformation." *Revue Bénédictine* 103 (1993): 380–413.

Frank, R. "North-Sea Soundings in *Andreas.*" In *Early Medieval English Texts and Interpretations: Studies Presented to Donald G. Scragg,* edited by E. Treharne and S. Rosser, 1–11. Tempe, Ariz., 2002.

Garde, J. N. *Old English Poetry in Medieval Christian Perspective.* Woodbridge, 1991.

Hall, T. N., "The Armaments of John the Baptist in Blickling Homily 14 and the Exeter Book *Descent into Hell.*" In *Intertexts: Studies in Anglo-Saxon Culture Presented to Paul E. Szarmach,* edited by V. Blanton and H. Scheck, 289–306. Medieval and Renaissance Texts and Studies 334; Arizona Studies in the Middle Ages and the Renaissance 24. Tempe, Ariz., 2008.

Hill, T. D. "The Fall of Satan in the Old English *Christ and Satan.*" *Journal of English and Germanic Philology* 76 (1977): 315–25.

———. "A Liturgical Source for *Christ I* 164–213 (Advent Lyric VII)." *Medium Ævum* 46 (1977): 12–15.

———. "The Measure of Hell: *Christ and Satan* 695–722." *Philological Quarterly* 60 (1981): 409–14.

———. "The Middle Way: *idelwuldor* and *egesa* in the Old English *Guthlac A.*" *Review of English Studies* 30 (1979): 182–87.

Izydorczyk, Z. "The Inversion of Paschal Events in the Old English *Descent into Hell.*" *Neuphilologische Mitteilungen* 91 (1990): 439–47.

Jones, Christopher A. "Envisioning the *cenobium* in *Guthlac A.*" *Medieval Studies* 57 (1995): 259–91.

Lapidge, M. "Surviving Booklists from Anglo-Saxon England." In *Learning and Literature in Anglo-Saxon England,* edited by M. Lapidge and H. Gneuss, 33–89. Cambridge, 1985.

Ó Carragáin, É. *Ritual and the Rood: Liturgical Images and the Old English Poems of the Dream of the Rood Tradition.* London, 2005.

Olsen, K. "The Dichotomy of Land and Sea in the Old English *Andreas.*" *English Studies* 79 (1998): 385–94.

Rankin, S. "The Liturgical Background of the Old English Advent Lyrics: A Reappraisal." In *Learning and Literature in Anglo-Saxon England,* edited by M. Lapidge and H. Gneuss, 317–40. Cambridge, 1985.

Reichardt, P. "*Guthlac A* and the Landscape of Spiritual Perfection." *Neophilologus* 58 (1974): 331–38.

Robinson, F. C. "The Significance of Names in Old English Literature." *Anglia* 86 (1968): 14–58.

Salvador, M. "Architectural Metaphors and Christological Imagery in the Advent Lyrics: Benedictine Propaganda in the Exeter Book?" In *Conversion and Colonization in Anglo-Saxon England,* edited by C. E. Karkov and N. Howe, 169–211. Medieval and Renaissance Texts and Studies 318. Tempe, Ariz., 2006.

Shook, L. "The Burial Mound in *Guthlac A.*" *Modern Philology* 58 (1960): 1–10.

Thornbury, Emily V. "Christ and Satan: 'Healing' Line 7." *English Studies* 87 (2006): 505–10.

Index

Roman numerals refer to the page numbers of the Introduction. The Old English poems are referred to by short titles, followed by line numbers: Adv. *(Advent)*, Judg. *(Christ in Judgment)*, Guth. *(Guthlac A)*, Des. *(Descent into Hell)*, Vision *(Vision of the Cross)*, Ruth. (Ruthwell Cross Crucifixion poem), Brus. (Brussels Cross Inscription), And. *(Andreas)*, Sat. *(Christ and Satan)*, and Distich (Distich on Kenelm). Line numbers followed by *n* refer to the notes to the translations (e.g., Adv. 1–17*n*).